开放知识图谱导论

翟 军 ◎ 编著

清华大学出版社
北京

内 容 简 介

本书以知识图谱的开放共享和推广应用为导向，以开放知识图谱为关注对象，介绍相关的基础知识和技术。全书共 8 章，内容包括知识图谱概述、数据图、知识图谱的数据编码标准、基于本体的知识图谱模式设计、知识图谱的查询语言、元数据、知识图谱验证技术，最后以欧盟 OpenAIRE 图谱为案例，介绍典型学术知识图谱的构建过程、数据模型、API 和相关服务。

本书适合作为信息管理与信息系统、大数据管理与应用、计算机科学与技术和人工智能等专业高年级本科生和研究生相关课程的教材，也可作为知识图谱研究人员和开发人员的入门读物。

版权所有，侵权必究。举报：010-62782989，beiqinquan@tup.tsinghua.edu.cn。

图书在版编目（CIP）数据

开放知识图谱导论/翟军编著. -- 北京：清华大学出版社，2025.3.
ISBN 978-7-302-68621-7

Ⅰ. G302

中国国家版本馆 CIP 数据核字第 2025C1G922 号

责任编辑：刘向威　李薇濛
封面设计：何凤霞
责任校对：王勤勤
责任印制：宋　林

出版发行：清华大学出版社
网　　址：https://www.tup.com.cn，https://www.wqxuetang.com
地　　址：北京清华大学学研大厦 A 座　　邮　编：100084
社 总 机：010-83470000　　　　　　　　　邮　购：010-62786544
投稿与读者服务：010-62776969，c-service@tup.tsinghua.edu.cn
质量反馈：010-62772015，zhiliang@tup.tsinghua.edu.cn
课件下载：https://www.tup.com.cn，010-83470236

印 装 者：天津鑫丰华印务有限公司
经　　销：全国新华书店
开　　本：170mm×230mm　　印　张：14.75　　插　页：1　　字　数：281 千字
版　　次：2025 年 4 月第 1 版　　　　　　　印　次：2025 年 4 月第 1 次印刷
印　　数：1～1500
定　　价：59.00 元

产品编号：106536-01

前言 PREFACE

国务院 2017 年发布的《新一代人工智能发展规划》明确指出,要发展"知识计算引擎与知识服务技术",重点突破知识加工、深度搜索和可视交互核心技术,实现对知识持续增量的自动获取,具备概念识别、实体发现、属性预测、知识演化建模和关系挖掘能力,形成涵盖数十亿实体规模的多源、多学科和多数据类型的跨媒体知识图谱。

当前,知识图谱已成为 AI 时代的重要基础设施,大量的开放知识图谱和语义知识图谱涌现出来,知识图谱广泛应用的时代已经到来。开放知识图谱(open knowledge graphs,OKG)是遵循"开放数据"(open data)范式发布到 Web 上的知识图谱,它允许任何人以任何目的免费获取、使用、修改和共享。到 2022 年年底,著名的开放知识图谱 DBpedia 的 SPARQL 查询端点的日均访问量已超过 720 万次,成为众多智能应用的基础。

本书以知识图谱的开放共享和推广应用为导向,以开放知识图谱为关注对象,介绍相关的基础知识和技术。书中引入大量案例帮助读者理解相关内容,包括 DBpedia、Wikidata、SemOpenAlex 和 OpenAIRE 图谱等。

本书共 8 章,主要内容如下。

第 1 章知识图谱概述,首先给出知识图谱和开放知识图谱的定义,然后引入知识图谱的概念模型和构建方法,最后介绍知识图谱管护方面的研究成果,包括生命周期模型和管护框架等。其中,开放的概念、关联数据原则和 FAIR 原则起到引领全书内容的作用。

第 2 章数据图与 RDF(资源描述框架)图,通过例子介绍常用的图模型,包括有向标定图、异构图、属性图和 RDF 图。其中,源自 W3C 标准的 RDF 图是语义知识图谱的基础模型,也是本书后续章节采用的主要模型。

第 3 章知识图谱的数据编码标准,是对 RDF 图的进一步深化,介绍了 RDF 图的各种主流的序列化方法,包括 XML 语法、Turtle 语法和 JSON-LD 语法等,最后以 SN SciGraph 学术知识图谱为例,给出 JSON-LD 格式的数据实例。W3C RDF 模型及其序列化方法的应用是贯穿全书后续内容的主线。

第 4 章基于本体的知识图谱模式设计,是全书的重点,包括本体的定义、作用、FAIR 本体和本体描述语言,以及支持本体复用的本体仓储库和 Schema.org 词汇表等。其中，较为详细地介绍了 SemOpenAlex、CS-KG 和 CODO 等知识图谱的本体模型。

第 5 章知识图谱的查询语言，面向 RDF 知识图谱，介绍 W3C SPARQL 查询语言的基本语法，列举出一些常用的开放知识图谱的 SPARQL 查询端点，进而以 Scholia 学术画像服务为例，介绍基于 Wikidata 知识图谱的 SPARQL 查询服务。

第 6 章知识图谱的元数据，面向开放知识图谱的发布、出版和使用，介绍描述知识图谱数据层和模式层（即本体）的元数据模型，包括 DCAT、VoID、DataID、VOAF 和 MOD 等，并给出知识图谱元数据记录的实例。

第 7 章知识图谱验证技术，较为系统地介绍了 W3C 的 RDF 数据验证技术 SHACL，包括 SHACL 的基本概念、语法和支持工具，并给出一些知识图谱的验证模板实例。

第 8 章学术知识图谱，以欧盟 OpenAIRE 图谱为案例，介绍它的构建过程、数据模型、API 和相关服务。

本书特色包括以下 3 点。

（1）重点介绍开放知识图谱所涉及的基础性语义 Web 技术，包括 RDF 图、RDF 序列化语法、本体、SPARQL 和 W3C SHACL 等。

（2）适当介绍知识图谱数据管理方面的知识，包括元数据、数据管护框架、生命周期模型、FAIR 原则和本体仓储库等。

（3）引入大量案例，包括 DBpedia、Wikidata、SemOpenAlex 学术知识图谱和 OpenAIRE 图谱等。

适合阅读本书的读者包括信息管理、大数据管理、管理科学与工程、计算机和人工智能等专业高年级本科生和研究生，知识图谱相关领域的研究人员，以及知识图谱系统的开发人员和应用人员。

本教材的建设及出版得到了"大连海事大学研究生教材资助建设项目"的专项资助，是大连海事大学研究生系列教材之一。本教材基于"知识管理理论与应用"课程进行编写。该课程已列入管理科学与工程学科研究生的培养方案，主要面向信息管理、大数据管理专业或领域的研究生使用。

感谢出版社的所有编辑在本书编写和审核过程中提供的无私帮助和宝贵建议。

书中示例代码可在出版社网站下载。

由于笔者的水平有限，加之本书编写时间跨度较长，书中难免会出现疏漏的地方，恳请读者批评指正。

翟 军

2025 年 2 月

目录 CONTENTS

第 1 章　知识图谱概述 ·· 1

1.1　知识图谱的定义 ·· 1
1.2　开放知识图谱 ··· 4
　　1.2.1　开放的定义 ·· 4
　　1.2.2　关联数据原则 ··· 6
　　1.2.3　FAIR 原则 ·· 10
1.3　知识图谱的概念模型 ··· 12
1.4　知识图谱的开发过程和构建方法 ·· 16
　　1.4.1　知识图谱的开发过程 ·· 16
　　1.4.2　知识图谱的构建方法 ·· 19
　　1.4.3　敏捷开发方法 ··· 21
1.5　知识图谱管护 ·· 23
　　1.5.1　数据管护 ··· 23
　　1.5.2　知识图谱的生命周期 ·· 24
　　1.5.3　知识图谱的管护框架 ·· 25
参考文献 ··· 26

第 2 章　数据图与 RDF 图 ··· 28

2.1　数据图 ·· 28
　　2.1.1　有向标定图 ··· 28
　　2.1.2　图数据集 ··· 30
　　2.1.3　异构图 ·· 31
　　2.1.4　属性图 ·· 32
2.2　RDF 图 ·· 34
　　2.2.1　局部标识符的局限 ··· 34
　　2.2.2　W3C RDF 标准系列 ··· 35

            2.2.3　RDF 图 ……………………………………………………… 36
            2.2.4　RDF 词汇表 …………………………………………………… 38
     2.3　IRI 设计 ………………………………………………………………… 42
            2.3.1　IRI 的作用 ……………………………………………………… 42
            2.3.2　IRI 的分类 ……………………………………………………… 42
            2.3.3　IRI 的设计原则 …………………………………………………… 44
            2.3.4　IRI 的组成结构 …………………………………………………… 45
     参考文献 ………………………………………………………………………… 47

第 3 章　知识图谱的数据编码标准 ……………………………………………… 49

     3.1　数据编码标准 …………………………………………………………… 49
            3.1.1　语义 Web 技术 …………………………………………………… 49
            3.1.2　W3C RDF 序列化标准 …………………………………………… 50
     3.2　基于 XML 的 RDF 序列化 ……………………………………………… 51
            3.2.1　RDF/XML 基本语法 ……………………………………………… 51
            3.2.2　语法验证和格式转换服务 ………………………………………… 54
     3.3　基于文本的 RDF 序列化 ………………………………………………… 55
            3.3.1　N-Triples ………………………………………………………… 55
            3.3.2　Turtle …………………………………………………………… 55
            3.3.3　TriG ……………………………………………………………… 56
     3.4　基于 JSON-LD 的 RDF 序列化 ………………………………………… 57
            3.4.1　JSON 模型 ……………………………………………………… 57
            3.4.2　JSON-LD 语法 …………………………………………………… 58
            3.4.3　描述 RDF 数据集 ………………………………………………… 63
     3.5　SN SciGraph 学术知识图谱的数据实例 ………………………………… 64
            3.5.1　SciGraph 开放数据集 …………………………………………… 64
            3.5.2　环境定义文件 …………………………………………………… 66
            3.5.3　学术著作数据 …………………………………………………… 66
            3.5.4　学术论文数据 …………………………………………………… 69
     参考文献 ………………………………………………………………………… 70

第 4 章　基于本体的知识图谱模式设计 ………………………………………… 71

     4.1　本体及其作用 …………………………………………………………… 71

	4.1.1　本体的定义 …………………………………………………… 71
	4.1.2　本体的作用 …………………………………………………… 71
	4.1.3　FAIR 本体 …………………………………………………… 74
4.2	本体描述语言 …………………………………………………………… 75
	4.2.1　W3C RDFS、OWL 和 SKOS ……………………………… 75
	4.2.2　SemOpenAlex 本体实例 …………………………………… 78
	4.2.3　CS-KG 本体实例 …………………………………………… 84
4.3	本体仓储库 …………………………………………………………… 88
	4.3.1　常见的本体仓储库 …………………………………………… 88
	4.3.2　OntoPortal 联盟 ……………………………………………… 91
	4.3.3　本体的 FAIR 水平评价 ……………………………………… 92
4.4	Schema.org 词汇表及其扩展 …………………………………………… 94
	4.4.1　Schema.org 简介 …………………………………………… 94
	4.4.2　Schema.org 词汇表 ………………………………………… 96
	4.4.3　cnSchema 词汇表 …………………………………………… 101
4.5	CODO 本体构建实例 ………………………………………………… 104
	4.5.1　CODO 本体模型 …………………………………………… 104
	4.5.2　CODO 本体的构建过程 …………………………………… 106
	4.5.3　CODO 本体的 FAIR 化实践 ……………………………… 107
参考文献 …………………………………………………………………… 108	

第 5 章　知识图谱的查询语言 ……………………………………… 111

5.1	知识图谱的访问方式 ………………………………………………… 111
	5.1.1　4 种主要的访问方式 ………………………………………… 111
	5.1.2　SemOpenAlex 的访问方式举例 …………………………… 112
5.2	SPARQL ……………………………………………………………… 116
	5.2.1　W3C SPARQL 标准 ………………………………………… 116
	5.2.2　SPARQL 的基本语法 ……………………………………… 118
	5.2.3　SPARQL 服务和查询端点 ………………………………… 121
5.3	基于 SPARQL 查询的学术画像 ……………………………………… 124
	5.3.1　学术画像的定义和分类 ……………………………………… 124
	5.3.2　Scholia 和 Wikidata ………………………………………… 125
	5.3.3　研究主题画像 ………………………………………………… 128

  5.3.4 出版机构画像 ………………………………………………… 130
  5.3.5 作者画像 …………………………………………………… 131
参考文献 ………………………………………………………………… 133

第 6 章 知识图谱的元数据 …………………………………………… 134

6.1 元数据的作用 ……………………………………………………… 134
6.2 数据目录词汇表 DCAT ……………………………………………… 136
  6.2.1 W3C DCAT 的开发历程 …………………………………… 136
  6.2.2 DCAT 元数据模型 …………………………………………… 137
  6.2.3 元数据实例 ………………………………………………… 139
6.3 关联数据集元数据 VoID …………………………………………… 141
  6.3.1 VoID 元数据模型 …………………………………………… 141
  6.3.2 元数据实例 ………………………………………………… 142
6.4 DBpedia Databus 元数据 …………………………………………… 146
  6.4.1 DataID 本体模型 …………………………………………… 146
  6.4.2 元数据实例 ………………………………………………… 148
6.5 本体的元数据 ……………………………………………………… 150
  6.5.1 DCAT 元数据 ……………………………………………… 150
  6.5.2 VOAF 元数据 ……………………………………………… 151
  6.5.3 AgroPortal 元数据 ………………………………………… 152
  6.5.4 MOD 元数据 ……………………………………………… 154
参考文献 ………………………………………………………………… 157

第 7 章 知识图谱验证技术 …………………………………………… 159

7.1 知识图谱验证 ……………………………………………………… 159
7.2 知识图谱的验证模式 ……………………………………………… 160
7.3 W3C SHACL 的基本概念 …………………………………………… 161
7.4 W3C SHACL 的基本语法 …………………………………………… 162
  7.4.1 引例 ………………………………………………………… 162
  7.4.2 SHACL 词汇表 ……………………………………………… 164
  7.4.3 目标声明 …………………………………………………… 166
  7.4.4 约束组件 …………………………………………………… 169
  7.4.5 路径表达 …………………………………………………… 170
  7.4.6 值约束 ……………………………………………………… 172

  7.4.7 字符串约束 …………………………………………………… 174
  7.4.8 属性对约束 …………………………………………………… 175
  7.4.9 逻辑约束 ……………………………………………………… 177
  7.4.10 封闭模板 …………………………………………………… 178
 7.5 W3C SHACL 的支持工具 ……………………………………………… 179
 7.6 验证模板实例 ……………………………………………………………… 180
  7.6.1 SN SciGraph SHACL ………………………………………… 180
  7.6.2 LUBM SHACL ………………………………………………… 182
  7.6.3 DBpedia SHACL ……………………………………………… 185
  7.6.4 Science On Schema.Org SHACL …………………………… 186
 7.7 SHACL 与 OWL 的关系 ………………………………………………… 190
  7.7.1 SHACL 与 OWL 的对比分析 ………………………………… 190
  7.7.2 Schema.org SHACL …………………………………………… 192
 参考文献 …………………………………………………………………………… 195

第 8 章　学术知识图谱 …………………………………………………………… 196

 8.1 学术知识图谱概述 ………………………………………………………… 196
 8.2 OpenAIRE 图谱的构建过程 ……………………………………………… 200
  8.2.1 知识图谱的供应链 …………………………………………… 200
  8.2.2 数据源 ………………………………………………………… 200
  8.2.3 内容聚合 ……………………………………………………… 202
  8.2.4 数据消重 ……………………………………………………… 204
  8.2.5 全文本挖掘 …………………………………………………… 206
 8.3 OpenAIRE 图谱的数据模型 ……………………………………………… 207
  8.3.1 实体类别 ……………………………………………………… 207
  8.3.2 实体关系 ……………………………………………………… 210
  8.3.3 数据实例 ……………………………………………………… 212
 8.4 OpenAIRE 图谱的 API …………………………………………………… 214
 8.5 基于 OpenAIRE 图谱的 OpenAIRE 服务 ……………………………… 218
  8.5.1 主要的服务 …………………………………………………… 218
  8.5.2 开放科学观测服务 …………………………………………… 219
  8.5.3 OpenAIRE 监测器 …………………………………………… 219
  8.5.4 OpenAIRE Connect …………………………………………… 221
 参考文献 …………………………………………………………………………… 222

第1章 知识图谱概述

1.1 知识图谱的定义

知识图谱(knowledge graph,KG)最早由谷歌(Google)公司于2012年5月正式提出,随后人们从不同的角度给出了它的定义。维基百科将谷歌知识图谱(Google knowledge graph)定义为一个知识库,其使用语义检索技术从多种来源收集信息,以提高谷歌搜索的质量。DBpedia团队认为知识图谱是一种特殊的数据库,它以机器可读的形式存储知识,并为收集、组织、共享、搜索和利用信息提供了一种手段。智利学者Aidan Hogan等认为,知识图谱是一种用于收集和表达真实世界知识的数据图(data graph)——基于图的数据模型所表达的数据。中国中文信息学会语言与知识计算专委会发布的《知识图谱发展报告(2018)》将知识图谱定义为:以结构化的形式描述客观世界中概念、实体及其关系,将互联网的信息表达成更接近人类认知世界的形式,提供一种更好地组织、管理和理解互联网海量信息的能力。

一般而言,KG就是一个大规模的有向标定图(directed labeled graph),即 $G = (V,E)$,其中的结点表示实体(entities),边表示实体间的二元关系(relations),一个简单的例子见图1.1。

可以说,KG是知识的集合,即 $G=\{<h,r,t>\} \subseteq V \times E \times V$。一条知识就是一个事实(fact),通常以三元组(triple)的形式表达,即 $<h,r,t>$ 或(head,relation,tail),对应图中的一条边,见图1.2。例如,图1.1表达了蒂姆·伯纳斯-李(Tim Berners-Lee)发明了万维网(WWW或Web)、获得图灵奖、父亲是康威·伯纳斯-李及毕业于牛津大学王后学院等事实,这些事实与描述万维网的事实连接在一起,形成一个复杂的、可扩展的图。表1.1列出了图1.1所表达的全部三元组。

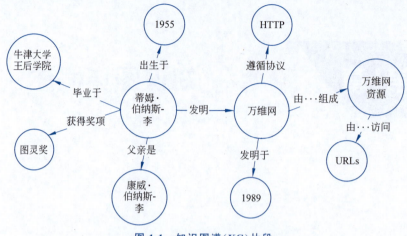

图 1.1 知识图谱(KG)片段

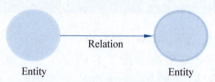

图 1.2 有向标定图中的三元组

表 1.1 图 1.1 表达的所有三元组

序 号	实体(head)	关系(relation)	实体(tail)
1	蒂姆·伯纳斯-李	出生于	1955
2	蒂姆·伯纳斯-李	毕业于	牛津大学王后学院
3	蒂姆·伯纳斯-李	获得奖项	图灵奖
4	蒂姆·伯纳斯-李	父亲是	康威·伯纳斯-李
5	蒂姆·伯纳斯-李	发明	万维网
6	万维网	遵循协议	HTTP
7	万维网	发明于	1989
8	万维网	由…组成	万维网资源
9	万维网资源	由…访问	URLs

国家标准《人工智能 知识图谱技术框架》(GB/T 42131—2022)将知识图谱定义为"以结构化形式描述的知识元素及其联系的集合"。该标准给出的其他相关概

念的定义见表1.2。

表1.2 知识图谱相关概念的定义

序号	概念	英文	定义
1	知识	knowledge	通过学习、实践或探索所获得的认识、判断或技能
2	知识元素	knowledge element	描述某一事物或概念的不必再分且独立的知识单位,如实体、概念(实体类型)、属性、关系、关系类型、事件、规则等
3	实体	entity	现实世界中独立存在的对象,如"黄山""地球"等
4	实体类型	entity type	一组具有相同属性的实体集合的抽象,如"运动员""行星"等。在知识图谱中,实体类型也是实体
5	关系	relation	实体或实体类型间的联系,如"出生地""毕业于"等
6	属性	attribute	一类对象中所有成员公共的特征,如"性别""年龄"等
7	知识单元	knowledge unit	按照一定关系组织的一组知识元素的集合
8	本体	ontology	表示实体类型以及实体类型之间关系、实体类型属性类型及其之间关联的一种模型
9	知识图谱模式	KG Schema	对知识图谱所描述的实体的类型及其关系的规范化定义和表达,通常为一个本体模型。相对于模式,知识图谱中的其他数据被称为实例(instance)数据
10	知识表示	knowledge representation	利用机器能够识别和处理的符号和方法描述人类在发现或理解客观世界时获得的知识的活动
11	知识建模	knowledge modeling	构建知识图谱的本体及其形式化表达的活动,包括实体类型定义、关系定义及属性定义
12	知识获取	knowledge acquisition	从不同来源和结构的输入数据中提取知识的活动。知识获取的数据源按数据组织结构的维度可分为结构化数据、半结构化数据、非结构化数据(如纯文本、音频和视频数据等)
13	知识融合	knowledge fusion	整合和集成知识单元(集),并形成拥有全局统一知识标识的知识图谱的活动
14	知识存储	knowledge storage	设计存储架构,并利用软硬件等基础设施对知识进行存储、查询、维护和管理的活动。常见的知识存储方式分为:基于关系数据库的存储方式、基于图数据库的存储方式、基于RDF数据库的存储方式等
15	知识演化	knowledge evolution	随本体模型、数据资源等变化产生的新知识对原有知识的补充、更新或重组的活动
16	知识溯源	knowledge provenance	在知识图谱全生存周期中追踪原始数据向知识转化的活动

续表

序号	概念	英　　文	定　　义
17	知识计算	knowledge computing	基于已构建的知识图谱和算法,发现/获得隐含知识并对外提供知识服务能力的活动。知识计算可分为统计分析、推理计算等
18	知识图谱供应方	KG supplier	使用数据、知识等构建知识图谱以满足特定需求,并提供基于知识图谱的基础工具或服务的组织
19	知识图谱集成方	KG integrator	根据知识应用需求,将知识图谱、信息系统或服务进行整合,提供知识图谱应用系统及服务的组织
20	知识图谱用户	KG user	使用知识图谱应用系统及配套服务支持以满足自身需要的组织或个人。知识图谱用户可对外输出必要数据或知识
21	知识图谱生态系统合作伙伴	KG ecosystem partner	为知识图谱供应方、集成方和用户提供知识图谱构建和应用所必需的信息基础设施、数据、工具、方法、标准和机制等的组织

相对于传统的知识库(knowledge base,KB),大数据时代,实际应用的各种KG系统的规模都很大。例如,谷歌知识图谱在发布之初(2012年5月)就含有5亿个实体、35亿个事实,半年以后(2012年12月)增长到5.7亿个实体、180亿个事实;到2016年下半年,已发展到10亿个实体、700亿个事实。微软知识图谱(Bing knowledge graph)含有20亿个实体、500亿个事实;Facebook知识图谱含有0.5亿个实体、5亿个事实;eBay知识图谱含有1亿个实体(产品)、10亿个事实。通用领域的开放知识图谱Wikidata含有超过1亿个实体、15.4亿个事实,YAGO(Yet Another Great Ontology)含有0.5亿个实体、20亿个事实。

由阿里巴巴藏经阁知识引擎团队和浙江大学知识图谱研究团队联合开发的数字商业知识图谱(AliOpenKG),致力于利用开放知识图谱激活商业数据要素和发现社会经济价值,其第一个版本已包含超过0.16亿个实体、18亿个事实,以及多达67万个核心概念、2681个类关系。

1.2　开放知识图谱

1.2.1　开放的定义

源于开源软件的开放运动在互联网时代迸发出巨大的动力,催生出一波开放政府、开放科学、开放数据、开放存取、开放创新的社会热潮,开启了开放共享的新时代。

开放知识图谱(open knowledge graphs,OKG)是指遵循"开放数据"(open data)范式发布到 Web 上的知识图谱,它允许任何人以任何目的免费获取、使用、修改和共享,唯一的限制是要注明出处(provenance)和保持开放共享性(openness)。

开放知识基金会(Open Knowledge Foundation,OKF)明确"开放"(open)必须满足四个要求:

(1) 作品在"开放许可"(open license)下发布。

(2) 整个作品可通过网络免费下载。

(3) 作品是机器可读的,即以计算机易于处理的方式提供,并且作品的各个元素也易于访问和修改。

(4) 作品必须以开放格式(open format)提供,即没有任何限制(包括费用和工具)的格式(如 Web 标准格式 XML、JSON 等),通常可以利用开源软件工具进行处理。

在开放数据环境中,知识图谱被当作一种"数据集"(dataset)。目前,存储开放科学资源的各类数据仓储库(data repositories),如 Zenodo、Figshare 和 Science Data Bank(ScienceDB)等,已收录了大量与 KG 相关的资源,包括数据集、软件、报告和出版物等。例如,Zenodo 收录的知识图谱数据集已超过 6800 个,部分实例见表 1.3。

表 1.3 开放知识图谱实例

序号	名称	开放许可	数据格式
1	Wikipedia Knowledge Graph	Creative Commons Zero v1.0 Universal	TSV (tab separated values)
2	ArCo Knowledge Graph v0.1	Creative Commons Attribution Share Alike 4.0 International	RDF N-Triples
3	Data Set Knowledge Graph (DSKG)	Creative Commons Attribution 4.0 International	RDF N-Triples
4	Software KG-PMC	Creative Commons Attribution 4.0 International	RDF N-Triples
5	The Open Event Knowledge Graph(OEKG)	Creative Commons Attribution Share Alike 4.0 International	RDF N-Triples
6	YAGO Knowledge Base	Creative Commons Attribution Share Alike 4.0 International	RDF N-Triples

(来源:https://www.zenodo.org/)

由中国中文信息学会语言与知识计算专业委员会于 2015 年发起并倡导的开

放知识图谱社区项目 OpenKG.CN，旨在促进以中文为核心的知识图谱数据的开放、互联与众包，以及知识图谱工具、算法和平台的开源开放工作。截至 2024 年 5 月初，OpenKG.CN 收录的知识图谱已有 292 个，一些例子见表 1.4。

表 1.4　中文开放知识图谱实例

序号	名称	开放许可	数据格式
1	基于 cnSchema 的浙江公共图书馆知识图谱	浙江省数据开放授权许可使用协议	JSON-LD、TTL、RDF 和 XML
2	基于 cnSchema 的浙江 A 级景区知识图谱	浙江省数据开放授权许可使用协议	JSON-LD、TTL、RDF 和 XML
3	浙江大学大规模细粒度中文概念图谱	Creative Commons Attribution	JSON-LD、TTL、JSON
4	开放的数字商业知识图谱（阿里巴巴）AliOpenKG	AliOpenKG DATASET LICENSE	JSON-LD
5	基于 COVID-19 论文集的学术知识图谱	CC-by SA 相似署名开放许可协议	JSON

（来源：http://www.openkg.cn/home）

相对于 OKG，公司内部的、应用于商业目的（搜索、推荐和广告等）的 KG 被称为企业知识图谱（enterprise knowledge graphs，EKG），如谷歌、微软和 eBay 的知识图谱。

1.2.2　关联数据原则

开放知识图谱是知识图谱与数据万维网（Web of data）相结合的产物，一方面促进了知识图谱的推广和使用，另一方面也提升了万维网的智能化水平。

数据万维网也称语义 Web（semantic Web，SW）或关联数据（linked data，LD），推动着万维网（Web）从文档互联到数据互联的转变，见图 1.3。Web 的发明者蒂姆·伯纳斯-李于 2006 年 7 月提出"关联数据"的概念，总结了发布关联数据的四条原则：

（1）使用 IRIs（internationalized resource identifiers）作为任何事物（即实体）的标识名称，不仅仅是标识文档。

（2）使用 HTTP IRIs，以便人和机器都可以在现有 Web 中查找事物、资源和实体。

（3）当访问某个实体的 IRI 时，以标准的数据格式（如 W3C RDF/XML、RDF/JSON 标准等）形式提供实体的有用信息。

（4）链接到其他实体的 IRI，使人们发现更多的资源和相关信息。

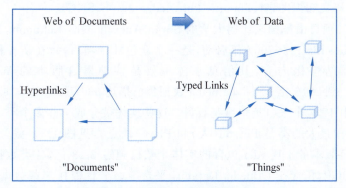

图 1.3　从文档 Web 到数据 Web

根据德国曼海姆大学发起的关联开放数据（linking open data，LOD）社区项目的统计，2007 年 5 月，发布到 Web 中的关联开放数据集（linked open datasets）仅有 12 个，而截至 2023 年 9 月，已发展到 1314 个，它们相互关联在一起，形成一个云图（cloud diagram），支撑起数据万维网的骨架。云图的中心部分见图 1.4，含有 DBpedia、Freebase 和 YAGO 等著名的关联数据集。由于采用了以 RDF（resource description framework）为代表的语义 Web 技术，这些关联数据集也被称为 RDF

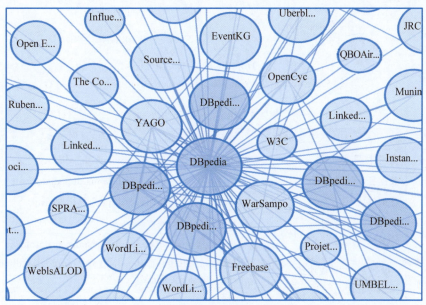

图 1.4　关联数据云图（中心部分）

（来源：https://lod-cloud.net/clouds/cross-domain-lod.svg）

知识图谱或语义知识图谱(semantic knowledge graph,SKG)。

DBpedia 项目由德国莱比锡大学的 Sören Auer 和 Jens Lehmann 及曼海姆大学的 Christian Bizer 于 2007 年启动,是一个众包社区项目,旨在从各种维基媒体信息中提取结构化内容,其信息来源主要是各种语言版本的 Wikipedia 和 Wikimedia。到 2016 年 10 月,DBpedia 数据集已描述 660 万个实体,共有 130 亿个三元组,其中 17 亿个来自英语维基百科。这些实体被分成 700 多个类(class,即实体类型),其中最大的类是 Person(人)和 Place(地点),见图 1.5。截至 2022 年年底,各种语言版本的 DBpedia 包含的实体个数已超过 2.28 亿,各类数据资源的规模达到 4150GB,托管在 DBpedia Databus 平台上。平台依托这些数据资源,利用语义 Web 技术,搭建起在线的开放知识库系统,其体系结构见图 1.6,其元数据收集在表 1.5 中。到 2022 年底,该系统 SPARQL 查询端点的日均访问量超过 720 万次,成为众多智能应用的基础。

图 1.5　DBpedia 的实体类型分布

(来源:https://www.dbpedia.org/resources/ontology/)

表 1.5　DBpedia 的元数据

序号	元数据名称		元数据的值
1	项目主页		https://www.dbpedia.org/
2	数据托管平台主页		https://databus.dbpedia.org/
3	查询端点		https://dbpedia.org/sparql
4	模式/本体	名称	DBpedia ontology
		主页	https://www.dbpedia.org/resources/ontology/
		下载地址	https://databus.dbpedia.org/ontologies/dbpedia.org/ontology--DEV/
		类的个数	768
		关系/属性个数	3000
		实例个数	4233000

续表

序号	元数据名称		元数据的值
5	外部链接	到 Freebase 的链接个数	3400000
		到 YAGO 的链接个数	18100000
		到 OpenCyc 的链接个数	20362

（来源：https://lod-cloud.net/dataset/dbpedia 和 https://www.dbpedia.org/）

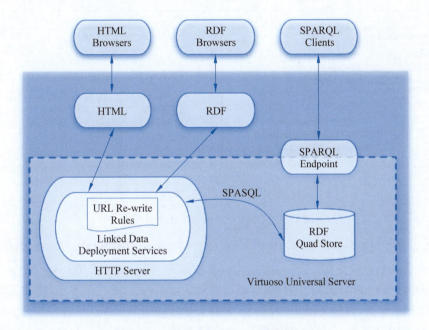

图 1.6 DBpedia 知识库系统的体系结构

（来源：https://www.dbpedia.org/about/）

　　遵循关联数据原则，DBpedia 建立了到 Freebase、YAGO、DrugBank、GeoNames 和 MusicBrainz 等数据集的链接，链接个数见表 1.5。反过来，其他关联数据集也建立了到 DBpedia 的链接，使得 DBpedia 成为关联数据云图的中心（参见图 1.4）。链接时，常用的谓词（即关系）是 owl：sameAs 等，见图 1.7。

　　Freebase 是关联数据运动早期另外一个重要的数据集，由美国 MetaWeb 公司在 2005 年启动项目，于 2007 年 3 月公开运营。2010 年 7 月，Freebase 被谷歌收

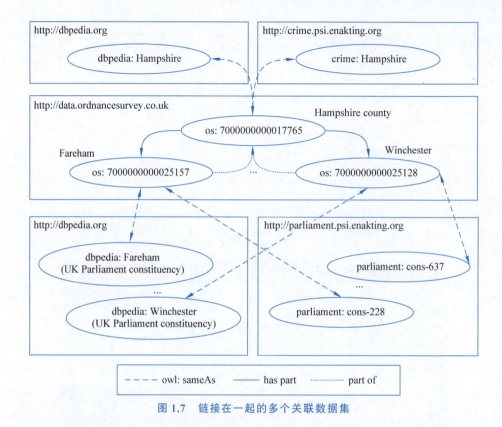

图 1.7 链接在一起的多个关联数据集

购,成为谷歌知识图谱的重要基础之一,也使得后来的知识图谱技术带有鲜明的语义 Web 和关联数据的烙印。Freebase 的内容主要源于 Wikipedia、NNDB、MusicBrainz 以及社会用户的贡献,2015 年 3 月发布的最终只读版本包含 30 亿个事实,描述了 5000 万个实体。随后,谷歌关闭了 Freebase,并将数据迁移到 Wikidata 项目。

由德国马克斯·普朗克计算机科学研究所(Max Planck Institute)研制的 YAGO,主要集成了 Wikipedia、WordNet 和 GeoNames 的数据资源,其特点是考虑了时间和空间维度的知识表示。YAGO 是 IBM Watson 的后端知识库之一。

1.2.3 FAIR 原则

开放知识图谱促进了知识和数据的共享和复用。将知识图谱发布到 Web 中,使其成为开放数据的过程,称为知识图谱的出版。KG 出版时,不仅要遵循开放数据原则和关联数据原则,还应遵循 FAIR 原则。

在数据密集型科研和开放科学环境下,跨学科、跨机构的数据共享和重用的需求日益强烈,对"科学数据管理"提出了新的挑战。应对挑战,人们认识到首要任务是确立一组共同认可的简洁、可度量的指导原则。2014 年 1 月,在荷兰莱顿的研讨会上,借鉴 2007 年的 OECD 科学数据获取原则和 2013 年的八国集团科技部长关于开放科学数据的伦敦声明,"FAIR 数据原则"(FAIR Data Principles,简称"FAIR 原则")被首次提出,经 FORCE11 工作组(www.force11.org)修改完善后,于 2016 年 3 月正式发表在 Nature Research 期刊集团旗下的 *Scientific Data* 上。

为确保能同时被人和机器所使用,FAIR 原则阐明了"数据对象"(data object,见图 1.8)应具有的基本属性,即可发现(findable)、可获取(accessible)、互操作(interoperable)和可重用(re-usable),每个属性下又有子属性,见表 1.6。

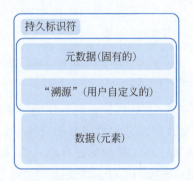

图 1.8 FAIR 数据对象——带有持久标识符(PID)的数据、元数据及溯源信息的组合体
(来源:https://www.force11.org/fairprinciples)

表 1.6 FAIR 原则的内容

序号	对象属性	子 属 性	适 用 元 素
1	可发现 (findable)	F1:对象被分配了全局唯一且持久的标识符 PID(persistent identifier)	数据和元数据
		F2:数据具有丰富的元数据	数据
		F3:元数据明确包含其描述数据的标识符	元数据
		F4:在搜索工具/服务中注册或被编入索引	数据和元数据
2	可获取 (accessible)	A1:借助标识符,可通过标准化的通信协议获取对象	数据和元数据
		A1.1:该协议是免费、开放和通用的	数据和元数据
		A1.2:必要时,该协议允许进行身份验证和授权过程	数据和元数据
		A2:即使数据不再可获取,其元数据仍然可获取	元数据

续表

序号	对象属性	子属性	适用元素
3	互操作 (interoperable)	I1：使用通用的可共享的语言进行对象的知识表示（knowledge representation），通常是本体语言	数据和元数据
		I2：使用遵循 FAIR 原则的词汇表（vocabularies）	数据和元数据
		I3：含有到其他对象的限定引用（qualified references）	数据和元数据
4	可重用 (re-usable)	R1：以多种准确且相关的属性描述对象	数据和元数据
		R1.1：发布时伴有使用许可（usage license）	数据和元数据
		R1.2：发布时伴有溯源信息（provenance）	数据和元数据
		R1.3：符合相关标准	数据和元数据

注：FAIR 是 findable、accessible、interoperable 和 re-usable 四个单词首字母的组合，也带有对数据生态系统的各方都"公平"的含义。

FAIR 原则的主要贡献者们指出，该原则不仅适用于数据及其元数据，也适用于其他科研产出和资源，对数据服务和科研基础设施（如云设施等）的建设也具有指导意义。在补充实现细节后，FAIR 原则已日趋完善，如选择 DOI（digital object identifier）作为对象的 PID，采用 HTTP 通信协议、OWL（web ontology language）和 CC0 数据许可等。目前，FAIR 原则已在美国、澳大利亚、欧洲、亚洲、拉丁美洲和非洲得到关注和应用，涉及生命科学、医疗卫生、核能、气候变化、海洋研究和人文科学等领域。

DBpedia 项目在提升 KG 的 FAIR 化水平（FAIRness）上进行了探索，包括开发 DataID 元数据和建设 Databus 平台等。

1.3 知识图谱的概念模型

实体可以分成两类：有形的具体实体（如蒂姆·伯纳斯-李）和抽象概念（如科学家）。除了对具体实体关系的描述，知识图谱中也含有对抽象概念关系的描述。例如，在图 1.9 所示的 YAGO 知识图谱片段中，除了描述马克斯·普朗克（Max Planck）出生于德国基尔（Kiel），是物理学家及获诺贝尔物理学奖外，还描述了概念"物理学家"是"科学家"的子概念（即子类），而"科学家"又是"人"的子概念。对这些概念及其关系的描述形成了知识图谱的模式（schema），也称本体（ontology）。因此，可以从逻辑上将知识图谱知识库分成两部分，即模式层（即本体层）和实例层

（即数据层），而形成 KG 的概念模型。

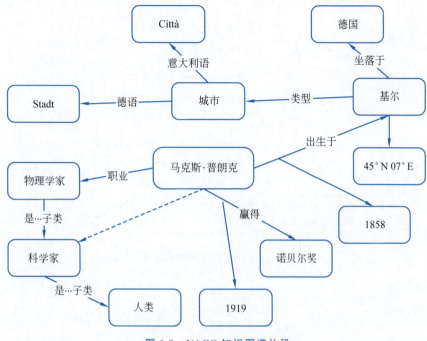

图 1.9 YAGO 知识图谱片段

国家标准《人工智能 知识图谱技术框架》(GB/T 42131—2022)给出的知识图谱概念模型将 KG 划分为本体层和实例层，见图 1.10。其中，本体层由实体类型、实体属性、实体类型间关系类型和规则等本体相关知识元素构成；实例层是对本体层的实例化，由实体类型对应的实体及其属性以及实体间关系等实体相关知识元素构成。

图 1.11 是电影知识图谱的概念模型示例，其本体中含有电影、奖项、人、演员和导演等概念及其关系。图 1.12 是 AliOpenKG 的概念模型，它将图 1.10 的两层模型拓展到四层。

DBpedia 本体是 DBpedia 知识库的模式部分，其 768 个类和 3000 个关系形成复杂的概念层次结构，见图 1.13。DBpedia 本体本身就是一个独立的知识库，可以被其他的 KG 所复用。很多实际的 KG 系统都有自己的本体层，其统计数字见表 1.7。在开放的 Web 环境中，许多 OKG 的模式都采用开放的 Schema.org 词汇表，如 YAGO(yago-knowledge.org)、KBpedia(www.kbpedia.org) 和 Datacommons.org 等。

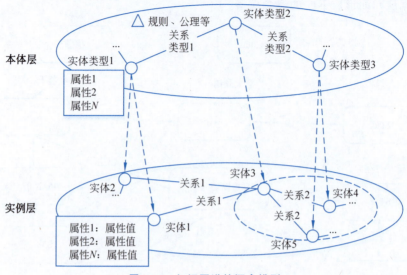

图 1.10 知识图谱的概念模型

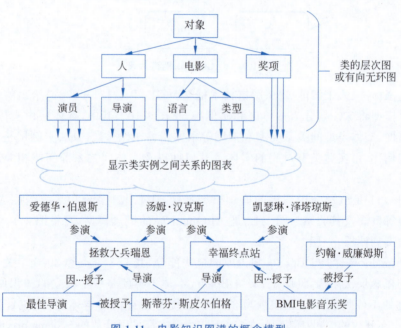

图 1.11 电影知识图谱的概念模型

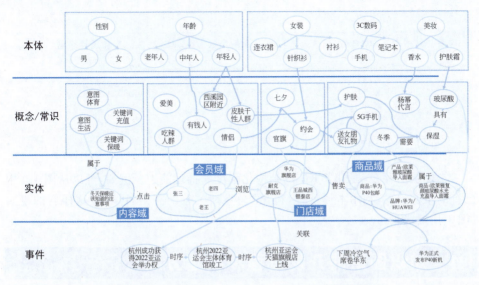

图 1.12 开放数字商业知识图谱 AliOpenKG 的概念模型

（来源：https://kg.alibaba.com/overview/index.html）

- owl:Thing
  - Activity (edit)
    - Game (edit)
      - BoardGame (edit)
      - CardGame (edit)
    - Sales (edit)
    - Sport (edit)
      - Athletics (edit)
      - TeamSport (edit)
  - Agent (edit)
    - Deity (edit)
    - Employer (edit)
    - Family (edit)
- Organisation (edit)
  - Broadcaster (edit)
    - BroadcastNetwork (edit)
    - RadioStation (edit)
    - TelevisionStation (edit)
  - Company (edit)
    - Bank (edit)
    - Brewery (edit)
    - Caterer (edit)
    - LawFirm (edit)
  - PublicTransitSystem (edit)
    - Airline (edit)
    - BusCompany (edit)

图 1.13 DBpedia 本体中类的层次结构（部分）

（来源：http://mappings.dbpedia.org/server/ontology/classes/）

表 1.7 典型知识图谱本体层的统计数字

序号	KG 名称	类/概念的个数	关系和属性个数
1	DBpedia	768	3000
2	YAGO	819292	77

续表

序号	KG 名称	类/概念的个数	关系和属性个数
3	Freebase	26507	37781
4	Wikidata	2356259	6236
5	谷歌知识图谱	1500	35000
6	AliOpenKG	≥670000	2681

本体层的存在,提升了 KG 的结构化程度和推理能力。例如,可以从图 1.9 中已有的事实出发,利用本体推理,得出"马克斯·普朗克是科学家"这样新的事实(图中用虚线表示)。

1.4 知识图谱的开发过程和构建方法

1.4.1 知识图谱的开发过程

知识图谱构建(knowledge graph construction)就是将数据先提升为信息,再提升为知识的过程,见图 1.14。整个开发过程(development process)要经历数据源辨识、本体构建、知识抽取、知识处理、知识库构建和知识维护 6 个阶段,见图 1.15。

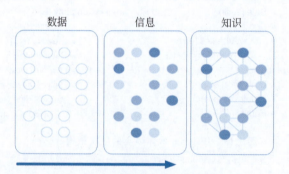

图 1.14 从数据到信息,再到知识

第一阶段是数据源辨识,主要任务是根据知识图谱的应用领域,识别可利用的数据资源,明确获取数据的途径和方法。数据资源分为结构化数据(structured data)、半结构化数据(semi-structured data)和非结构化数据(unstructured data)。结构化数据是一种具有明确结构的数据,如表格数据或关系数据库;半结构化数据

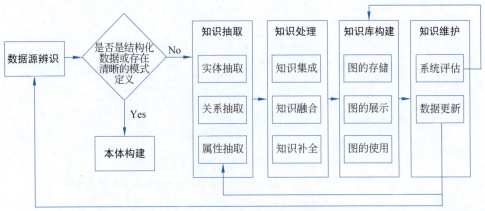

图 1.15 知识图谱的开发过程

具有一定的结构,但不严格,如 XML 数据;非结构化数据不具有预定义结构,如文本等。Web 资源可通过网络爬虫、文件下载或 API 等方式获取。

第二阶段是本体构建,为知识图谱提供模式层(见图 1.10)。本体可以手动或自动构建,通常要复用已有的本体或数据模式。可以先有本体,后有数据,称为"自顶向下"(top-down)的构建方法。也可以先有数据,后有本体,称为"自下而上"(bottom-up)的构建方法,这时本体的构建工作延后到第四阶段。

第三阶段是知识抽取,包括实体抽取(entity extraction)、关系抽取(relation extraction)和属性抽取(attribute extraction)。实体抽取主要通过"命名实体识别"(named-entity recognition,NER)技术实现,要采用各种机器学习方法。实体抽取的质量(准确率和召回率)对后续工作影响很大,因此是最基础的工作。接下来是实体间的关系抽取,结构化数据中的关系明晰、易于识别,对于半结构化数据可以使用基于模式(pattern-based)和基于规则(rule-based)的方法,非结构化数据则要使用"自然语言处理"(natural language processing,NLP)等技术。属性抽取类似于关系抽取,方法基本一致,其目标是进一步丰富实体的描述信息。

知识抽取在 DBpedia 知识图谱的构建中处于核心位置,见图 1.16。DBpedia 知识抽取框架保障系统连续、自动地从 Wikipedia 页面中抽取实体、关系和属性。基于映射的信息框抽取(mapping-based infobox extraction)是采用的方法之一,其过程见图 1.17。图中,将信息框中英文和希腊文的"作者"映射到本体概念 dbo: author。

第四阶段是知识处理,解决知识模糊、冗余或不完整等问题,以提高知识库的质量水平。核心工作是知识集成(knowledge integration)和知识融合(knowledge

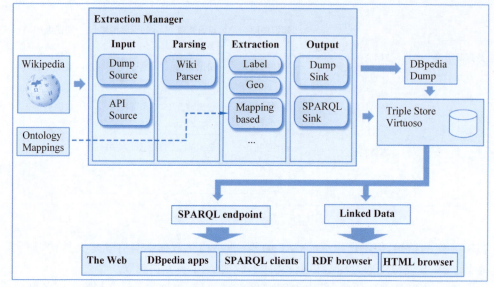

图 1.16　DBpedia 的知识抽取框架

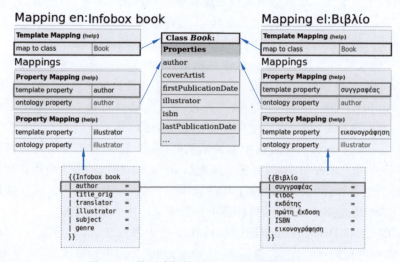

图 1.17　基于映射的 DBpedia 知识抽取示例

(来源：http://mappings.dbpedia.org/index.php/Mapping_en:Infobox_book)

fusion)，整合来自不同数据源的知识，并消除冗余和矛盾。需要将抽取出的实体指称(mention)对应到知识库中的目标实体对象，称为"实体链接"(entity linking)。在这一阶段会碰到实体指称"同名不同义、同义不同名"的问题，实体消歧(entity disambiguation)和共指消解(coreference resolution)技术应运而生。实体消歧是专门用于解决同名实体产生歧义问题的技术。在实际语言环境中,经常会遇到某个实体指称项对应多个命名实体对象的问题,例如"李娜"这个名词(指称项)可以对应作为歌手的李娜,也可以对应作为网球运动员的李娜,通过实体消歧,就可以根据当前的语境,准确建立实体链接。实体消歧主要采用无监督聚类法、基于监督学习的方法和基于图的方法等。共指消解技术主要用于解决多个指称项对应同一实体对象的问题。例如,Tim Berners-Lee、TimBL 和 Timothy John Berners-Lee 等指称项都指向蒂姆·伯纳斯-李。比较经典的实体共指消解技术有基于规则的方法、基于统计的方法和基于神经网络的方法。

在这个阶段,还要通过知识图谱推理(knowledge graph reasoning,KGR)来补全和丰富知识。基于逻辑规则的推理实例见图 1.18。

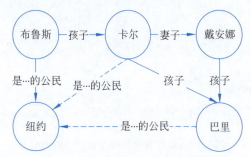

图 1.18 基于逻辑规则的推理实例

第五阶段是知识库构建,将数据存储到数据库中,搭建起知识图谱数据库管理系统(knowledge graph database management system,KGDMS)。由东京工业大学 AI 团队开发的知识图谱统一管理平台(unified workbench for knowledge graph management,UWKGM)的结构见图 1.19,具有数据存储、查询、可视化和安全管理等功能。

第六阶段是知识维护,包括系统评估(system evaluation)和数据更新(data updating)等工作。当数据源中出现新数据时,需要同步更新知识图谱中的数据。为此,DBpedia 改造了工作流程,周期性(通常是每月)地启动知识抽取和数据发布程序,保证了知识图谱数据对 Wikipedia 内容的最小延迟。

1.4.2 知识图谱的构建方法

知识库的构建经历了从个人经验到群体智能、从手工到自动化的演化过程,见图 1.20。早期的专家系统知识库依赖少数专家手工创建,现代大规模知识图谱则

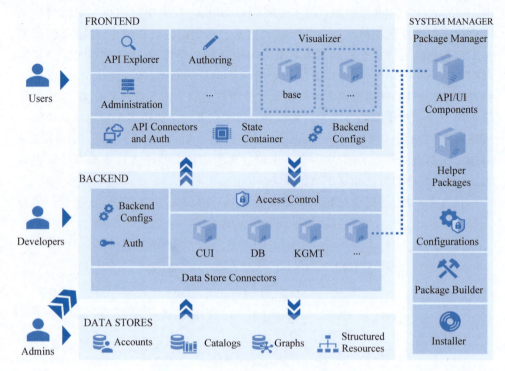

图 1.19　知识图谱管理平台：UWKGM

（来源：https://www.ai.iee.e.titech.ac.jp/UWKGM/index.html）

提升了创建过程的自动化水平，并尽可能利用群体智能（wisdom of the crowds）。

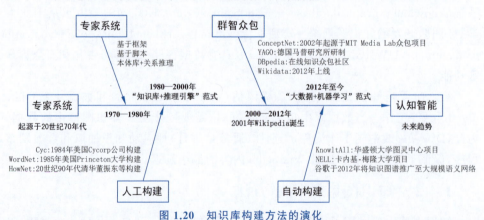

图 1.20　知识库构建方法的演化

2014年8月，继GKG(Google knowledge graph)之后，谷歌公司又推出一款知识库系统GKV(Google knowledge vault)。它通过算法自动搜集网上信息，通过机器学习把数据变成可用知识，实现知识扩充的自动化和及时性，其流程见图1.21。

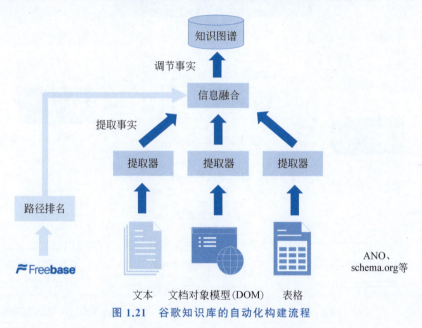

图1.21　谷歌知识库的自动化构建流程

DBpedia、Freebase和Wikidata等百科知识图谱(encyclopedia knowledge graph)都利用众包(crowdsourcing)方式收集和改进知识。众包可以在三个方面介入构建过程，分别是元知识创建、数据标注和知识精化，见图1.22。OpenBase是中文开放知识图谱的众包平台，其网址是http://openbase.openkg.cn。目前，OpenBase社区已汇聚了近百名志愿者，参与编辑的数据条数超过13.3万个。

发展至今，知识图谱的构建在各个维度上形成了一些范式(paradigm)。图1.23从三个维度进行了归纳，分别是知识抽取维度、知识库维度和机器学习方法维度。其中，在机器学习方法上，可分为基于规则的方法、无监督(un-supervised)方法、半监督(semi-supervised)方法和神经网络方法(有监督学习)等。

1.4.3　敏捷开发方法

DBpedia和GKV的持续更新能力提高了KG的"敏捷性"(agility)。

敏捷方法(agile method)来源于软件工程领域，是一种迭代、循序渐进的开发方法，能更好地应对需求和环境的快速变化。

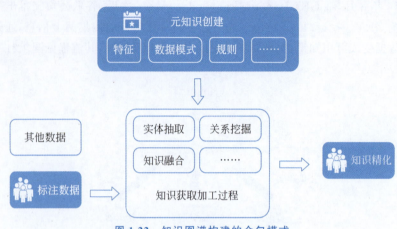

图 1.22 知识图谱构建的众包模式

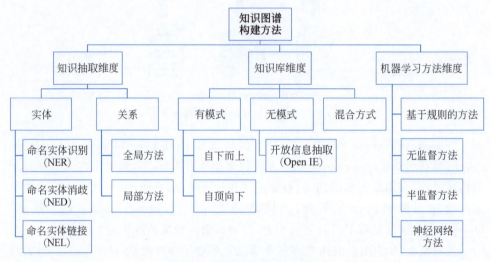

图 1.23 知识图谱构建方法分类

印度班加罗尔统计研究所文献研究中心的 D.Biswanath 等在开发基于 COVID-19 流行病学数据的 CODO(COviD-19 Ontology)知识图谱时,采用了敏捷方法,其流程见图 1.24,包括数据装载、数据转换、知识推理、KG 出版/发布和用户反馈等阶段。在数据装载阶段,输入疫情数据和 CODO 本体,产生初步的三元组存储库;数据转换阶段的任务是将三元组转换为 RDF 语义三元组,形成 RDF 图数据;知识推理阶段使用 OWL 和基于规则的推理器;然后,将知识图谱发布到 Bioportal 目录网站和 GitHub 托管平台上。这些步骤中,采用的敏捷方

法有:

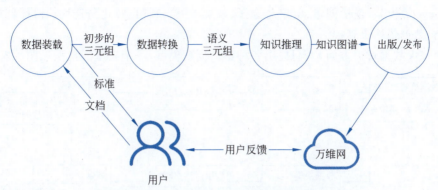

图 1.24　敏捷方法驱动的 CODO 知识图谱开发过程

① 测试驱动的本体开发;
② 快速迭代,每周迭代一次;
③ 模型重构,本体模型随着需求的变化而演进;
④ 自下而上和自上而下相结合,本体与数据共同迭代更新。

2020 年 4—9 月,随着疫情数据的积累和变化,CODO 本体从 1.0 版进化到 1.3 版。1.0 版含有 44 个类和 51 个关系,而 1.3 版含有 90 个类和 73 个关系。最后,CODO 知识图谱共描述了 71000 名患者,经推理后共产生超过 500 万个三元组。

1.5　知识图谱管护

1.5.1　数据管护

从管理的角度,目前学界主要采用数据管理、数据治理和数据管护三个概念从不同学科视角开展研究。数据管理(data management)从信息技术的角度研究如何对数据进行获取、清洗、集成、存储和检索,重点关注数据管理的系统、方法、工具和技术等。数据治理(data governance)立足于"数据是资产"的理念,通过对组织中相应职责、决策权以及角色的分配来保证数据资产的完整性、准确性、可访问性和可利用性,涉及数据原则、数据质量、元数据、数据存取和数据生命周期等研究内容。数据管护或数据监管(data curation)的重点在于数据资源的全生命周期和全过程管理,涵盖三个关键活动:全过程管护、归档(archiving)和长期保存(preservation)。

英国数字管护中心（Digital Curation Center，DCC）提出数据管护生命周期（lifecycle）模型，包括创建、鉴定与选择、采集、存储、利用、转化与迁移、社区观察与参与、数据描述等管护活动。

在大数据管护方面，人们提出各种生命周期模型，一个典型的模型见图1.25。

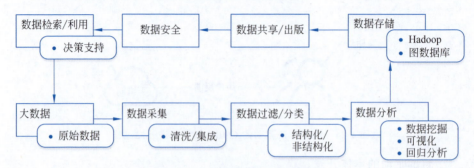

图1.25　大数据的生命周期模型

1.5.2　知识图谱的生命周期

为降低知识图谱开发的复杂程度，保障数据质量，也应对知识图谱开展生命周期管理，引入适当的数据管护活动。图1.26给出一种知识图谱生命周期模型，包括创建、托管、管护和部署四个主要阶段。管护阶段完成的工作有 RDF 数据的验证、链接和扩展。

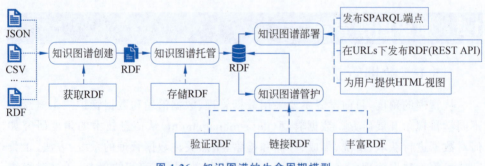

图1.26　知识图谱的生命周期模型

遵从该生命周期模型，西班牙马德里理工大学本体工程组开发了 Helio 框架，支持从异构数据源构建 KG，然后依据关联数据原则发布 KG 数据。

Helio 框架由 4 个模块组成（见图1.27），由 Java 语言开源实现，其代码已发布到 GitHub 上。目前，Helio 框架已应用到欧盟多个项目中，如 OntoCommons、

Semantic Blockchain 和 NLP 等。

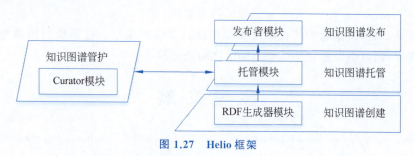

图 1.27　Helio 框架

1.5.3　知识图谱的管护框架

奥地利因斯布鲁克大学语义技术研究所 E.Huaman 等在 KG 生命周期模型的基础上，提出了知识图谱管护框架（knowledge graph curation framework，KGCF），其结构见图 1.28。

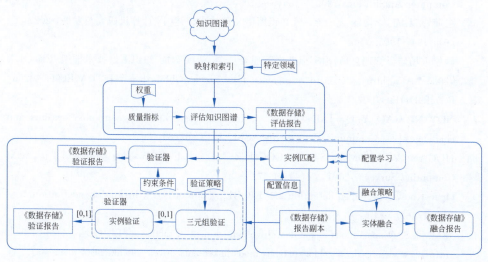

图 1.28　知识图谱的管护框架

面对一个构建完成的 KG，该管护框架的第一项工作是"质量评价"（quality assessment），总结了 20 个质量维度（quality dimension），包括可访问性（accessibility）、准确性（accuracy）、可信度（believability）、完整性（completeness）、互操作性（interoperability）、安全性（security）、时效性（timeliness）、可追溯性（traceability）和多样性（variety）等。第二项工作是"数据清洗"（data cleaning），纠

正 KG 中的语法和语义错误,提高数据的正确性(correctness)。第三项工作是"充实 KG"(enriching KG),提升知识图谱的完整性。

可见,知识图谱管护的目标是保障和提升 KG 的质量。这需要付出额外的工作和成本,同时也要在完整性和正确性之间进行权衡。

参 考 文 献

[1] Wikipedia. Google knowledge graph [EB/OL]. [2023-01-01]. https://en.wikipedia.org/wiki/Google_Knowledge_Graph.

[2] VINAY K et al. An introduction to knowledge graphs [EB/OL]. [2023-01-01]. https://ai.stanford.edu/blog/introduction-to-knowledge-graphs/.

[3] Blue Brain Nexus. Understanding knowledge graphs [EB/OL]. [2023-01-10]. https://bluebrainnexus.io/docs/getting-started/understanding-knowledge-graphs.html.

[4] ABU-SALIH B. Domain-specific knowledge graphs: A survey [J]. Journal of Network and Computer Applications, 2021, 185(5): 103076.

[5] 王萌,王昊奋,李博涵,等. 新一代知识图谱关键技术综述[J]. 计算机研究与发展,2022,59(9): 1947-1965.

[6] 国家市场监督管理总局、国家标准化管理委员会. 人工智能 知识图谱技术框架[EB/OL]. [2023-10-11]. https://openstd.samr.gov.cn/bzgk/gb/newGbInfo?hcno=B6D2A5EB6F6A5206-FC03B9D44E069D07.

[7] NOY N, GAO Y Q, JAIN A, et al. Industry-scale knowledge graphs: lessons and challenges [J]. Communications of the ACM, 2019, 62(8): 36-43.

[8] HOGAN A, BLOMQVIST E, COCHEZ M, et al. Knowledge graphs [J]. ACM Computing Surveys, 2021, 54(4): 1-37.

[9] Open Knowledge. Open definition 2.1[EB/OL]. [2023-01-02]. http://opendefinition.org/od/2.1/en/.

[10] EMMA S. Databus mods-linked data-driven enrichment of metadata [EB/OL]. [2023-01-07]. https://www.dbpedia.org/blog/databus-mods-linked-data-driven-enrichment-of-metadata/.

[11] 翟军,梁佳佳,吕梦雪,等. 欧盟开放科学数据的 FAIR 原则及启示[J]. 图书与情报,2020(6): 103-111.

[12] Institute of Data Science. Build a FAIR knowledge graph [EB/OL]. [2023-01-07]. https://maastrichtu-ids.github.io/best-practices/blog/2021/03/18/build-a-kg/.

[13] TAMAŠ AUSKAITĖ G, GROTH P. Defining a knowledge graph development process through a systematic review [J]. ACM Transactions on Software Engineering and Methodology, 2023, 32(1): 27.1-27.40.

［14］LEHMANN J，ISELE R，JAKOB M，et al. DBpedia-a large-scale，multilingual knowledge base extracted from wikipedia［J］. Semantic Web，2015(6)：167-195.

［15］刘峤,李杨,段宏,等.知识图谱构建技术综述［J］.计算机研究与发展,2016,53(3)：582-600.

［16］田玲,张谨川,张晋豪,等.知识图谱综述：表示、构建、推理与知识超图理论［J］.计算机应用，2021，41(8)：2161-2186.

［17］张吉祥,张祥森,武长旭,等.知识图谱构建技术综述［J］.计算机工程,2022,48(3)：23-37.

［18］林健,柯清超,黄正华,等.学科知识图谱的动态生成及其在资源智能组织中的应用［J］.远程教育杂志，2022，40(4)：23-34.

［19］TIWARI S，FATIMA N，GAURAV D. Recent trends in knowledge graphs：Theory and practice［J］. Soft Computing，2021(25)：8337-8355.

［20］段宗涛,李菲,陈柘.实体消歧综述［J］.控制与决策,2021,36(5)：1025-1039.

［21］DBpedia. Latest core releases［EB/OL］.［2023-02-15］. https://www.dbpedia.org/resources/latest-core/.

［22］肖仰华,等. 知识图谱：概念与技术［M］.北京：电子工业出版社,2020.

［23］DONG X，GABRILOVICH E，HEITZ G，et al. Knowledge vault：A web-scale approach to probabilistic knowledge fusion［C］. In Proceedings of the 20th ACM SIGKDD International Conference on Knowledge Discovery and Data Mining，2014：601-610.

［24］DEBELLIS M，BISWANATH D. From ontology to knowledge graph with agile methods：The case of COVID-19 CODO knowledge graph［J］. International Journal of Web Information Systems. 2022(18)：432-452.

［25］王芳,慎金花.国外数据管护(Data Curation)研究与实践进展［J］.中国图书馆学报,2014,40(4)：116-128.

［26］于明鹤,聂铁铮,李国良.数据管护技术及应用［J］.大数据,2019,5(6)：1-17.

［27］沙勇忠.迈向学科交叉的新领域：公共危机信息管理［J］.图书与情报,2020(1)：1-5.

［28］NAWSHER K，YAQOOB I，ABAKER T H I，et al. Big data：Survey，technologies，opportunities，and challenges［J］. The Scientific World Journal，2014(1)：1-18.

［29］CIMMINO A，GARCÍA-CASTRO R. Helio：A framework for implementing the life cycle of knowledge graphs［J］. Semantic Web，2024(15)：223-249.

［30］HUAMAN E，DIETER F. Knowledge graph curation：A practical framework［C］. The 10th International Joint Conference on Knowledge Graphs，2021.

第2章 数据图与RDF图

2.1 数据图

2.1.1 有向标定图

现实世界中客观存在的事物之间存在着多种联系,数据模型(data model)将不同的事物及其联系,通过筛选、归纳、总结、命名等抽象过程产生概念模型,用以表示对现实世界的抽象描述,然后转换成易被人们理解且便于计算机处理的数据表现形式,如表、树和图等。

知识图谱的实质是对数据进行"图抽象"(graph abstraction),以形成"数据图"(data graph)。因此,在知识图谱管理(knowledge graph data management,KGDM)中采用的数据模型以各种图模型(graph model)为主,其基本概念源自数学的一个分支——图论(graph theory)。

1736年,数学家欧拉在解决哥尼斯堡七桥问题时,将现实世界的岛和两岸抽象为结点(node),将桥抽象为边(edge),表示两个结点之间存在某种关系,建立了抽象的图模型,见图2.1。基本的图模型分为无向图(undirected graph)和有向图(directed graph),见图2.2。

在大数据和人工智能等新技术背景下,相对于数据库领域的经典关系模型(relational model),图模型更利于描述事物之间的"关系",有着更高的面向关系的查询效率。例如,图2.3通过两个关系表描述了6个人的名字及其父母关系(parent),当查询一个人的父母的名字时,需要两个表连接查询。图2.4则通过有向图描述同样的对象及其关系,基于parent关系的查询在一张图上即可完成,既简洁又高效。

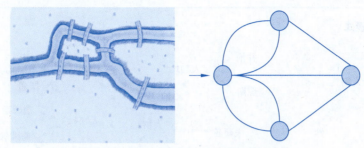

图 2.1 哥尼斯堡七桥问题的图抽象

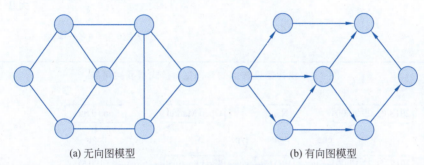

图 2.2 基本的图模型

人物			父母	
ID	名	姓	人物ID	父母ID
1	乔治	琼斯	3	1
2	安娜	斯通	3	2
3	朱莉亚	琼斯	5	4
4	詹姆斯	德维尔	5	3
5	大卫	德维尔	6	4
6	玛丽	德维尔	6	3

图 2.3 通过关系表表达家谱数据：人物及其父母关系

图 2.4 中的边不仅表示实体间的二元关系，也能表示实体的不同属性，如名（name）和姓（lastname），是通过为边赋予标识符号（labels）区分的。结点或边带有标识符的图称为标定图（labeled graph）。为表达实体间存在多个关系，需要绘制有向边标定图（directed edge-labeled graph），也称为多关系图（multi-relational graph）。例如，图 2.5 中边上不同的标识符表征着不同的二元关系，包括事件类型（type）、发生地点（venue）、所在城市（city）和通航（flight）等。

有向边标定图是描述 KG 的主要工具之一，其数学定义如下。

定义 2.1 有向边标定图是一个由三个子集组成的三元组，即 $G=(V, E, L)$，

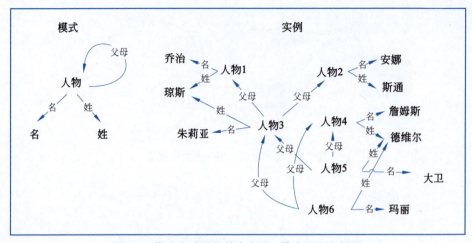

图 2.4 描述家谱数据的有向图：模式层和实例层

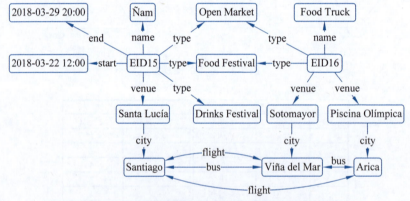

图 2.5 描述事件及其地点的有向边标定图

其中 V 是结点的集合，L 是边的标记符（即二元关系）的集合，$E \subseteq V \times L \times V$ 是边的集合。

对于图 2.5，它的数学定义中的 $V = \{\text{EID15}, \text{EID16}, \text{Arica}, \text{Santiago}, \cdots\}$，$L = \{\text{type}, \text{venue}, \text{city}, \text{flight}, \text{name}, \text{end}, \cdots\}$，$E = \{<\text{EID15}, \text{venue}, \text{Santa Lucía}>, <\text{EID15}, \text{type}, \text{Open Market}>, \cdots\}$。当 G 描述一个知识图谱时，E 就是知识的集合。

2.1.2 图数据集

图数据集（graph dataset）是由多个数据图组成的集合，其中包含一个默认图

（default graph）和多个命名图（named graphs）。每个命名图都有一个 ID（唯一标识符）用以区分，而默认图没有 ID。例如，图 2.6 含有两个命名图，分别是 Events（事件）和 Routes（路线），其数据是对图 2.5 的拆分，两个图中具有相同标识的结点（Arica 和 Santiago）表示同一个实体。默认图则给出两个命名图的元数据 updated（更新时间），这时两个命名图成为被描述的对象，其 ID 出现在结点的标识中。

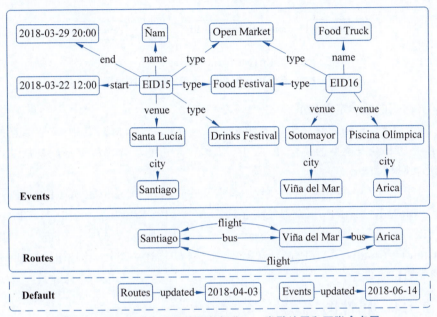

图 2.6　关于事件和路线的图数据集：一张默认图和两张命名图

虽然可以将多张图连接在一起形成一张图（如图 2.5 所示），但通过"图数据集"同时管理多张图会更有价值，例如可以对特定来源的数据进行更新，以及区分不同来源数据的可信度等。

2.1.3　异构图

异构图（heterogeneous graph），也称为异构信息网络（heterogeneous information network），是一种特殊的有向图，其中的结点和边都被分配了类型（type）。在表达边的类型时，异构图采用与有向边标定图一样的方式；在表达结点的类型时，异构图为结点增加了类型标签，而不是用 type 关系，这减少了边的条数，见图 2.7。异构图中，不同类型的结点之间的边称为异构的（如 capital），而相同类型的结点之间的边称为同构的（如 borders）。

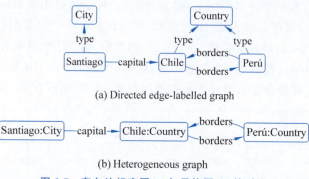

(a) Directed edge-labelled graph

(b) Heterogeneous graph

图 2.7　有向边标定图（a）与异构图（b）的对比

异构图的数学定义如下。

定义 2.2　异构图是一个四元组，即 $G=(V,E,L,M)$，其中 V 是结点的集合，L 是边和结点类型的集合，$E \subseteq V \times L \times V$ 是边的集合，$M:V \to L$ 是从结点到类型的映射。

对于图 2.7 中的异构图，它的数学定义中的 $V = \{\text{Santiago},\text{Chile},\text{Perú}\}$，$L = \{\text{capital},\text{borders},\text{City},\text{Country}\}$，$E = \{<\text{Santiago},\text{capital},\text{Chile}>$，$<\text{Chile},\text{borders},\text{Perú}>$，$<\text{Perú},\text{borders},\text{Chile}>\}$，$M(\text{Santiago}) = \text{City}$，$M(\text{Chile}) = \text{Country}$，$M(\text{Perú}) = \text{Country}$。当 G 描述一个知识图谱时，E 和 M 共同形成知识的集合。

2.1.4　属性图

许多情况下，需要对已有的有向图进行扩展，以描述更多的信息和更复杂的关系。例如，图 2.6 的 Routes（路线）子图给出 Santiago（圣地亚哥）和 Arica（阿里卡）两个城市之间具有"通航"（flight）关系，但缺乏航班的详细信息，如航空公司等。在有向图中，不能将这些信息直接添加给边，而需要增加新的结点表示航班（如 LA380），再将新边（如 company）添加给新的结点，见图 2.8。属性图（property graph，PG）则可以在不改变图结构的情况下，更加灵活地处理这种需求，见图 2.9。对比描述家谱数据的有向图 2.4，图 2.10 所示的属性图为 parent 边增加了 date 属性。

属性图中结点和边的地位是等同的，每个结点和边都有一个唯一的 ID（identifier）、一个或多个标签（label），表示基于模式的类型约束。重要的是，每个结点和边都有一组属性，每个属性是一个"名-值对"（property-value pair）。属性图的数学定义如下。

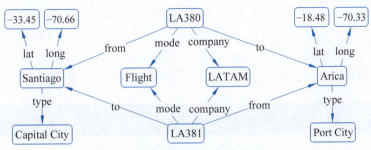

图 2.8 对图 2.6 中 Routes 子图的扩展

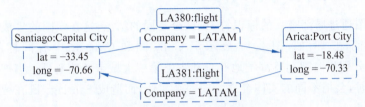

图 2.9 与图 2.8 等价的属性图

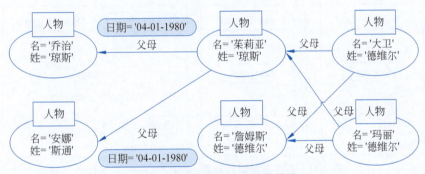

图 2.10 描述家谱数据的属性图

定义 2.3 属性图是一个九元组，即 $G = (V, E, R, T, P, U, e, m, p)$，其中 V 是结点 ID（标识符）的集合，E 是边 ID 的集合，R 是关系的集合，T 是结点类型的集合，P 是属性的集合，U 是属性值的集合，$e: E \rightarrow V \times V$ 将边映射为结点对，$m: V \cup E \rightarrow 2^{R \cup T}$ 将结点和边映射到它们所属的类型，$p: V \cup E \rightarrow 2^{P \times U}$ 将结点和边映射到它们的属性及其值的集合。

对于图 2.9 中的属性图，它的数学定义中的 $V = \{Santiago, Arica\}$，$E = \{LA380, LA381\}$，$R = \{flight\}$，$T = \{Capital City, Port City\}$，$P = \{lat, long, company\}$，$U = \{-33.45, -70.66, LATAM, -18.48, -70.33\}$，$e(LA380) = <Santiago, Arica>$，$e(LA381) = <Arica, Santiago>$，$m(Santiago) = \{Capital

City$\}$, m(Arica) = $\{$Port City$\}$, m(LA380) = m(LA381) = $\{$flight$\}$, p(Santiago) = $\{<$lat, $-33.45>, <$long, $-70.66>\}$, p(Arica) = $\{<$lat, $-18.48>, <$long, $-70.33>\}$, p(LA380) = p(LA381) = $\{<$company, LATAM$>\}$。

属性图模型被图数据库业界广泛采用，包括著名的图数据库 Neo4j 等。

2.2　RDF 图

2.2.1　局部标识符的局限

有向图通过局部唯一的标识符 ID 区分不同的结点，这在多图的集成时会带来命名冲突问题。例如，图 2.11 展示了 Chile 图和 Cuba 图中有同样的标识符 Santiago，分别指向智利首都圣地亚哥和古巴第二大城市圣地亚哥。当把两个图集成在一起时，会把不同的实体合并为同一个实体，而造成 Santiago 既在智利又在古巴的谬误。

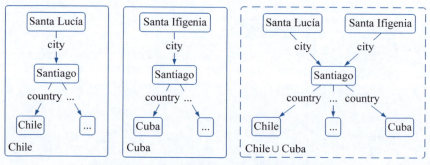

图 2.11　两个有向图的集成：命名冲突和实体消歧

为解决这一问题，需要引入全局唯一的标识符标记实体及其关系。例如，DBpedia 采用 IRI（internationalized resource identifiers，国际资源标识符）标记图 2.11 中的不同实体和关系，详见表 2.1。

表 2.1　DBpedia 标识实体和关系的 IRI 举例

序号	实体或关系	IRI
1	智利首都圣地亚哥	http://dbpedia.org/resource/Santiago
2	古巴第二大城市圣地亚哥	http://dbpedia.org/resource/Santiago_de_Cuba
3	智利	http://dbpedia.org/resource/Chile

续表

序号	实体或关系	IRI
4	古巴	http://dbpedia.org/resource/Cuba
5	所在城市	https://dbpedia.org/ontology/city
6	所属国家	https://dbpedia.org/ontology/country

DBpedia 等知识图谱采用的是面向 Web 的数据图模型——RDF(Resource Description Framework,资源描述框架)。

2.2.2　W3C RDF 标准系列

关于 RDF 的第一个标准由 W3C(万维网联盟)于 1997 年提出草案,1999 年成为正式推荐标准(W3C Recommendation)。2004 年 2 月,W3C RDFCore 工作组发布 RDF 标准 1.0 版,包含概念、语义、语法和 RDFS(RDF Schema)等 6 个标准文件。2014 年 2 月,W3C RDF 工作组发布 RDF 标准 1.1 版,主要标准见表 2.2。

表 2.2　W3C RDF 1.1 标准系列

序号	标准名称	说明
1	RDF 1.1　Concepts and Abstract Syntax	RDF 概念和抽象语法
2	RDF 1.1　Semantics	RDF 语义
3	RDF Schema 1.1	定义 RDF 词汇表,用于本体定义
4	RDF 1.1　XML Syntax	基于 XML 的 RDF 数据序列化语法
5	RDF 1.1　Turtle,RDF 1.1　TriG RDF 1.1　N-Triples,RDF 1.1　N-Quads	非 XML 的 RDF 数据序列化语法
6	JSON-LD 1.0	基于 JSON 的 RDF 和关联数据语法

(来源:https://www.w3.org/2011/rdf-wg/wiki/Main_Page)

最初,RDF 标准系列是 W3C 语义 Web 行动计划(semantic web activity)的一部分;2013 年 12 月,RDF 标准系列成为新的数据标准行动计划(data activity)的一部分,推动了开放数据环境下的"数据万维网"的发展。

其他相关标准还有查询语言标准 SPARQL 和约束语言标准 SHACL 等。RDF 的标准化保证了知识图谱的标准化,使得 RDF 成为最主要的知识图谱数据模型,其与属性图的对比见表 2.3。

表 2.3 RDF 图模型与属性图模型的比较

序号	数据模型特征	RDF 图	属 性 图
1	标准化程度	W3C 系列标准	尚未形成工业标准
2	表达能力	强于属性图	弱于 RDF 图
3	边的属性（多元关系）	通过模型扩展，如 RDF 具体化、RDF* 等	内置支持
4	本体定义	RDFS、OWL	不支持
5	查询语言	SPARQL	Cypher、PGQL、G-Core 等
6	约束语言	SHACL、ShEx	ProGS
7	序列化格式	XML、JSON、JSON-LD、N-Triples、Turtle 等	CSV
8	标识符	全局唯一的 IRI	局部 ID

2.2.3　RDF 图

在 RDF 中，任何事物（thing，即实体）都是资源（resource），包括现实世界中的物理存在、抽象概念和网络世界的文档、数字和字符等。为资源赋予"全球唯一的命名"是 RDF 的一个关键设计问题。RDF 1.1 采用 IRI 标识每一个资源。IRI 使用 Unicode 字符，是 URI（uniform resource identifier，统一资源标识符）的超集。RDF 1.0 采用 URI，包括 URL（uniform resource locators，统一资源定位符）和 URN（uniform resource name，统一资源名称）。

RDF 模型采用"三元组"（triple）形式描述两个资源间的二元关系或一个资源的属性，见图 2.12。当一个资源成为被描述的对象时，它就是"主体"（subject）；当一个资源用于表示一个二元关系或属性时，它就是"谓词"（predicate）；当一个资源是属性值时，它就是"客体"（object）。在 RDF 图中，主体和客体用"结点"（node）表示，谓词用"有向边"（directed-arc）表示。

(a) 两个资源间的二元关系　　　　(b) 一个资源的属性值

图 2.12　RDF 三元组的两种形式

RDF 三元组可以记为：

```
<subject><predicate><object>.
```

其中,主体为 IRI 或空结点;谓词只能以 IRI 出现;客体可以是 IRI、文字或空结点。"文字"(literal)作为特殊的资源,不用 IRI 标识,只能出现在属性值的位置。对于有的资源,没有必要为其分配全球唯一的 IRI,暂时用"局部名字"标识,这类资源被称为"空结点"(blank node)。IRI、文字和空结点统称为"RDF 项"(RDF term),它们是互不相交的。

RDF 三元组也称为"RDF 陈述"(RDF statement),它对应自然语言中的一句话,但有着严格的语法和明晰的语义。例如,下面是 CaLiGraph 知识图谱中描述蒂姆·伯纳斯-李(Tim_Berners-Lee)是图灵奖获得者的三元组,更多的三元组见表 2.4。

```
<http://caligraph.org/resource/Tim_Berners-Lee>
<http://www.w3.org/1999/02/22-rdf-syntax-ns# type>
<http://caligraph.org/ontology/Turing_Award_laureate>.
```

表 2.4 描述蒂姆·伯纳斯-李的一组三元组

序号	Subject(主体)	Predicate(谓词)	Object(客体)
1	http://caligraph.org/resource/Tim_Berners-Lee	http://www.w3.org/1999/02/22-rdf-syntax-ns# type	http://caligraph.org/ontology/Turing_Award_laureate
2	http://caligraph.org/resource/Tim_Berners-Lee	http://www.w3.org/2000/01/rdf-schema# label	"Tim Berners-Lee"
3	http://caligraph.org/resource/Tim_Berners-Lee	http://www.w3.org/2002/07/owl# sameAs	http://dbpedia.org/resource/Tim_Berners-Lee
4	http://caligraph.org/resource/Tim_Berners-Lee	http://www.w3.org/ns/prov# wasDerivedFrom	http://en.wikipedia.org/wiki/Category：Turing_Award_laureates
5	http://caligraph.org/resource/Tim_Berners-Lee	http://caligraph.org/ontology/birthPlace	http://caligraph.org/resource/London
6	http://caligraph.org/resource/Tim_Berners-Lee	http://caligraph.org/ontology/birthYear	"1955"
7	http://caligraph.org/resource/Tim_Berners-Lee	http://caligraph.org/ontology/nationality	http://caligraph.org/resource/United_Kingdom

(来源：http://caligraph.org/resource/Tim_Berners-Lee)

一组三元组就是 RDF 数据,称为"RDF 图"(RDF graph)。与表 2.4 等价的

RDF 图如图 2.13 所示。一个 RDF 图也是"资源",可用 IRI 标识,并有一组三元组描述它。多个 RDF 图组成"RDF 数据集"(RDF dataset),它含有一个"默认图"(default graph),零个或多个"命名图"(named graph)。RDF 图不仅可以表达实例数据,也以同样的方式(即三元组)表达模式数据,见图 2.14 给出的家谱数据的 RDF 图,它从图 2.4 演化而来。

为提高 RDF 数据的可读性,常常采用 IRI 的简化写法,即将 IRI 转换为"前缀:局部名"的形式,称为 QName(qualified name,限定名)。如图 2.15 所示,通过前缀声明(prefix declarations)将前缀(如 ex)关联到一个命名空间(namespace)的 IRI(如 http://example.org/),然后就可以在三元组中用 QName(如 ex:alice)取代 IRI(如 http://example.org/alice)。QName 也可以出现在 RDF 图中,如图 2.16 所示。

爱尔兰国立大学数字企业研究所(Digital Enterprise Research Institute,DERI)开发的 IRI 前缀查找服务 prefix.cc,可以找到常用的命名空间 IRI 及其约定俗成的前缀。例如,图 2.16 中的前缀 schema 指向的命名空间是 http://schema.org/,见图 2.17。

2.2.4　RDF 词汇表

词汇表(vocabulary),也称本体(ontology),是 Web 中的一类重要资源。词汇表本身就是知识的载体,在知识图谱的知识复用中发挥着关键作用。

表 2.4 中第一个三元组的谓词的 IRI 为:

```
http://www.w3.org/1999/02/22-rdf-syntax-ns#type
```

来自"RDF Concepts Vocabulary"(RDF 概念词汇表),用于声明一个资源是一个类(概念)的实例(instance),是被普遍采用的谓词,其 QName 是 rdf:type。这个词汇表定义的"词汇/术语"还有:

```
http://www.w3.org/1999/02/22-rdf-syntax-ns#Property
http://www.w3.org/1999/02/22-rdf-syntax-ns#Statement
http://www.w3.org/1999/02/22-rdf-syntax-ns#subject
http://www.w3.org/1999/02/22-rdf-syntax-ns#predicate
http://www.w3.org/1999/02/22-rdf-syntax-ns#object
```

它们有着相同的起始部分:

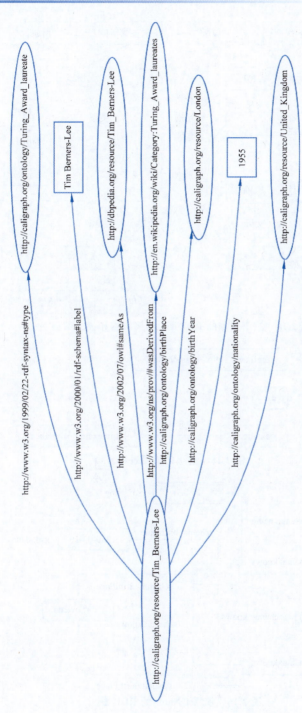

图 2.13 描述蒂姆·伯纳斯-李的 RDF 图

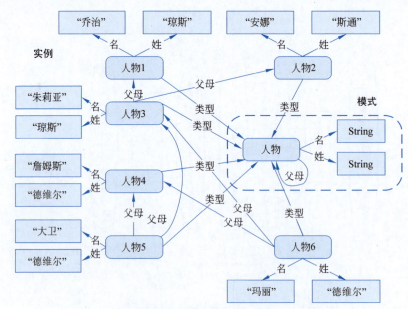

图 2.14 家谱数据的 RDF 图：实例数据和模式数据

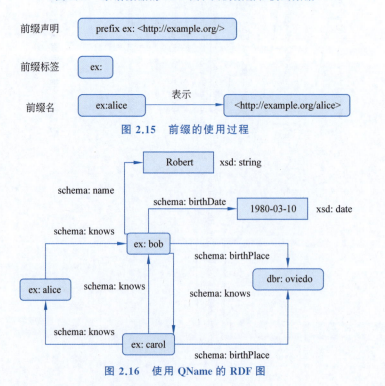

图 2.15 前缀的使用过程

图 2.16 使用 QName 的 RDF 图

图 2.17　命名空间及其前缀的查找服务

```
http://www.w3.org/1999/02/22-rdf-syntax-ns#
```

这一部分称为词汇表的"命名空间"(namespace),是标识这个词汇表的 IRI,其前缀是 rdf。

W3C RDF Schema 1.1 标准对 RDF 概念词汇表进行了补充,定义了一组新的词汇,形成 RDF 模式词汇表(RDF Schema vocabulary,RDFS),其命名空间是:

```
http://www.w3.org/2000/01/rdf-schema#
```

前缀是 rdfs,其中的词汇有 rdfs：Resource、rdfs：Class 和 rdfs：Literal 等。

这些词汇都被严格定义,有着明确的语义,为广泛应用打下了坚实的基础。这些定义也是通过三元组给出的,下面给出部分例子。

```
rdf: type a rdf: Property ;
    rdfs: label "type" ;
    rdfs: comment "The subject is an instance of a class." ;
    rdfs: range rdfs: Class ;
    rdfs: domain rdfs: Resource .
rdf: Property a rdfs: Class ;
    rdfs: label "Property" ;
    rdfs: comment "The class of RDF properties." ;
    rdfs: subClassOf rdfs: Resource .
rdfs: Resource a rdfs: Class ;
    rdfs: label "Resource" ;
    rdfs: comment "The class resource, everything." .
```

2.3 IRI 设计

2.3.1 IRI 的作用

当采用 RDF 图作为知识图谱的数据模型时,通常要经历有向图到 RDF 图的转换过程(见图 2.18),需要为此设计适当的 IRI 方案。在 Web 中,IRI 不仅起到标识和定位资源的作用,还是访问知识库的接口之一。

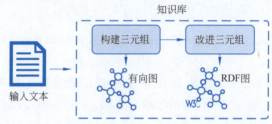

图 2.18 构建知识图谱:从有向图到 RDF 图的转换

例如,CaLiGraph 知识图谱服务器就提供了 IRI 的"解引"(dereference)服务(见图 2.19),能够通过实体的 IRI(即资源的引用)来获取它的描述文档(representation),是引用(reference)的逆过程。这时,客户端可以是普通的浏览器,还可以是专门的 RDF 浏览器(RDF Browser)。

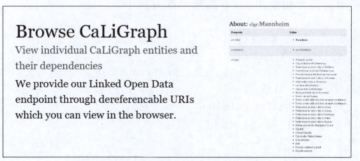

图 2.19 CaLiGraph 的 IRI 解引服务

(来源:http://caligraph.org/explore.html)

2.3.2 IRI 的分类

知识图谱描述的实体(如蒂姆·伯纳斯-李)通常存在于 Web 之外,称为"非信息资源";而 Web 中的资源称为"信息资源"(information resource)。相应地,IRI

主要分成两类：标识非信息资源的 IRI 和标识信息资源的 IRI，见表 2.5。两者的区别是，通过信息资源的 IRI（如 https://www.w3.org/TR/rdf-schema/），浏览器可以直接访问和读取信息内容；而通过非信息资源的 IRI（如 http://dbpedia.org/resource/Boston，美国波士顿市），浏览器需要经过"重定向"到一个信息资源的 IRI（如 http://dbpedia.org/page/Boston），才能访问和读取相关信息，见图 2.20。这种机制，保证了知识图谱知识库与 Web 的融合。

表 2.5 IRI 的分类

实 体 分 类	IRI 分类	说　　明
现实世界的事物 （real world things）	标识 IRI （identifier IRI）	既包括物理实体，如一个人、一所学校等；也包括抽象实体，如民族、事件等。它们不在 Web 中，但关于它们的信息在 Web 中
信息资源 （information on the web）	文档 IRI （document IRI）	Web 中的文档，用以描述"现实世界的事物"
	表现 IRI （representation IRI）	描述一个事物的文档通常有多个，这些文档的格式各不相同（如 HTML、XML、RDF 等）。这时，每个文档的 IRI 为"表现 IRI"
本体中的概念和关系 （concepts and relations）	本体 IRI （ontology IRI）	概念是个体的集合，个体是概念的实例。通过这个 IRI 找到概念及其关系的定义
词汇表/本体 （vocabulary）	本体 IRI （ontology IRI）	词汇表是一类特殊的信息资源，也需要 IRI 标识

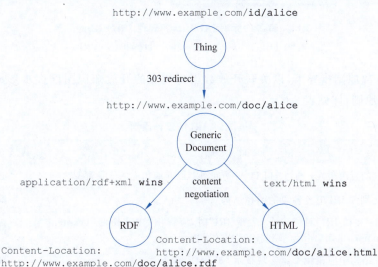

图 2.20　非信息资源重定向到信息资源

（来源：www.w3.org/TR/cooluris/）

2.3.3 IRI 的设计原则

IRI/URI 是 Web 的"心脏"。一个资源的标识 IRI/URI 和表现 IRI/URI 的分离（见图 2.21），使得 Web 有着更大的灵活性和可扩展性。

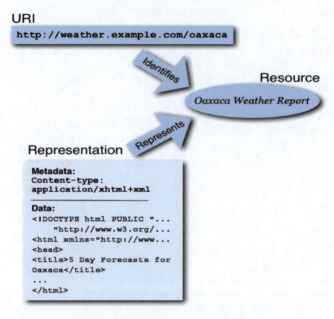

图 2.21　资源的标识 IRI/URI 和表现 IRI/URI 的分离

（来源：http://www.ltg.ed.ac.uk/～ht/WhatAreURIs/）

在分离原则指导下，以关联开放数据为代表的开放知识图谱逐步形成了一组 IRI 设计原则，详见表 2.6。

表 2.6　IRI 的设计原则

设 计 原 则	应遵守的程度
① HTTP 的可解析性：通过 HTTP 可访问 IRI，以获取相应的信息资源	必须
② 不同类别的 IRI 应有各自的路径结构	推荐
③ 当一个"文档 IRI"对应多个"表现 IRI"时，应提供"内容协商"（content negotiation）机制，向客户端响应适当的文档	推荐
④ 在 IRI 结构中应避免暴露实现技术，如 PHP、ASP 等	推荐
⑤ 至少要提供一种机器可读的格式，如 RDF/XML、JSON、TTL 等	必须

设 计 原 则	应遵守的程度
⑥ 还要提供人可读的格式,即 HTML 网页	推荐
⑦ 通过"文档 IRI"能找到所有的"表现 IRI"	推荐
⑧ IRI 路径结构中不含有任何可变部分	必须
⑨ IRI 路径结构是人可阅读和可理解的	推荐

2.3.4　IRI 的组成结构

IRI 由 4 部分组成(见图 2.22),第一部分是协议(如 http);然后是域名——对应服务器的 IP 地址;接下来的路径表示服务器上资源的位置;最后的部分(段)是可选的,用于区分一个文件内部的不同位置。

图 2.22　IRI 的组成结构

以 DBpedia 知识图谱为例,所有 IRI 的域名都是 dbpedia.org。对于每一个实体,其 IRI 的路径部分是 resource/[identifier],例如波士顿(Boston)的 IRI 是:

http://dbpedia.org/resource/Boston

重要的是,对于每一个实体的 IRI,都有一个与其对应的文档 IRI,其路径部分是 page/[identifier],例如波士顿(Boston)的文档 IRI 是:

http://dbpedia.org/page/Boston

两者的"标识符"(identifier)相同。进一步来说,对于每个文档 IRI,都有一组表现 IRI 相对应,例如波士顿(Boston)的表现 IRI 有:

http://dbpedia.org/data/Boston.rdf
http://dbpedia.org/data/Boston.json
http://dbpedia.org/data/Boston.ttl

它们的路径部分是 data/[identifier.文件扩展名]。

一个实体的这些 IRI 相互配合,充分利用 Web 平台的服务机制,实现了 Web 中对非信息资源的访问,见图 2.23。DBpedia 还提供了本体 IRI,一些实例见表 2.7。

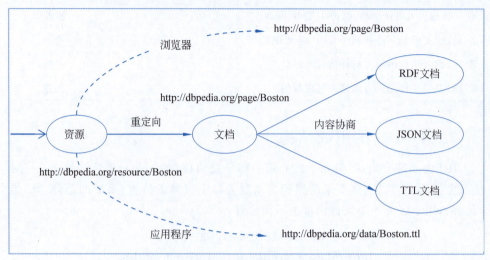

图 2.23　DBpedia 知识图谱 IRI 服务的实现机制

表 2.7　DBpedia 知识图谱的 IRI 实例

序号	IRI	类　别
1	http://dbpedia.org/resource/Tim_Berners-Lee	标识 IRI
2	http://dbpedia.org/page/Tim_Berners-Lee	文档 IRI
3	http://dbpedia.org/data/Tim_Berners-Lee.ttl	表现 IRI
4	https://dbpedia.org/ontology/Person	本体 IRI
5	http://dbpedia.org/ontology/data/definitions.ttl	文档 IRI
6	https://dbpedia.org/ontology/school	本体 IRI
7	https://dbpedia.org/data3/school.ttl	表现 IRI
8	http://dbpedia.org/ontology/	本体 IRI
9	https://dbpedia.org/data3/.json	表现 IRI
10	https://dbpedia.org/property/topics	本体 IRI

英国测绘局(Ordnance Survey)关联开放数据采用了与 DBpedia 类似的 IRI 方

案和路径结构,一些实例见表 2.8。其中,本体 IRI 的模式是:

```
http://data.ordnancesurvey.co.uk/ontology/[ontology name]/
http://data.ordnancesurvey.co.uk/ontology/[ontology name]/[Concept]
```

行政区类实例的 IRI 模式是:

```
http://data.ordnancesurvey.co.uk/id/[16 digit identifier]
```

对于"邮政区"(Postal Geography),"Postcode Unit"类的实例的 IRI 模式为:

```
http://data.ordnancesurvey.co.uk/id/postcodeunit/[postcode]
```

它对应邮编是 postcode 的递送区域。将路径中的 id 变成 doc,就成为相对应的文档 IRI。

表 2.8　英国测绘局关联数据的 IRI 实例

序号	IRI	类　　别
1	http://data.ordnancesurvey.co.uk/ontology/admingeo/	本体 IRI
2	https://data.ordnancesurvey.co.uk/ontology/admingeo/.ttl	表现 IRI
3	https://data.ordnancesurvey.co.uk/ontology/admingeo/County	本体 IRI
4	https://data.ordnancesurvey.co.uk/ontology/admingeo/County.ttl	表现 IRI
5	http://data.ordnancesurvey.co.uk/id/7000000000037256	标识 IRI
6	https://data.ordnancesurvey.co.uk/doc/7000000000037256	文档 IRI
7	https://data.ordnancesurvey.co.uk/doc/7000000000037256.ttl	表现 IRI
8	http://data.ordnancesurvey.co.uk/id/postcodeunit/SO171DP	标识 IRI
9	https://data.ordnancesurvey.co.uk/doc/postcodeunit/SO171DP	文档 IRI
10	https://data.ordnancesurvey.co.uk/doc/postcodeunit/SO171DP.ttl	表现 IRI
11	https://data.ordnancesurvey.co.uk/doc/data/os-linked-data.ttl	元数据 IRI

(来源:https://data.ordnancesurvey.co.uk/)

参 考 文 献

[1] 信俊昌,王国仁,李国徽,等.数据模型及其发展历程[J].软件学报,2019,30(1):142-163.
[2] 王鑫,邹磊,王朝坤,等.知识图谱数据管理研究综述[J].软件学报,2019,30(7):2139-2174.
[3] 　HOGAN A, BLOMQVIST E, COCHEZ M, et al. Knowledge graphs [M]. Berlin:

Springer,2021.

[4] 周贞云,邱均平.一门交叉学科的兴起：论图数据科学的构建[J].图书馆论坛,2023,43(4)：97-108.

[5] FLETCHER G. Graph data management [M]. Berlin：Springer,2018.

[6] LAN G,LIU T,WANG X,et al. A semantic web technology index [J]. Scientific Reports,2022(12)：1-11.

[7] HOGAN A. The web of data [M]. Berlin：Springer,2022.

[8] 袁满,褚冰,陈萍.知识图谱构建中的语义标准问题研究[J].情报理论与实践,2020,43(3)：131-137.

[9] 翟军.关联政府数据原理与应用[M].北京：电子工业出版社,2016.

第3章 知识图谱的数据编码标准

3.1 数据编码标准

3.1.1 语义 Web 技术

1990年,蒂姆·伯纳斯-李发明了万维网(World Wide Web),至今已形成庞大的技术体系,见图3.1。

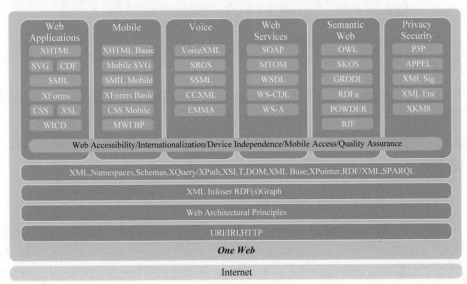

图 3.1 W3C 技术堆栈

(来源:http://www.w3.org/2004/10/RecsFigure-Smaller.png)

2001年,蒂姆·伯纳斯-李在《科学美国人》发表文章"The Semantic Web",提出了语义 Web 的愿景。随后,W3C 启动"语义 Web 行动计划"(Semantic Web Activity),开发并制定相关技术和标准,逐渐形成一套成熟的技术体系,见图 3.2。

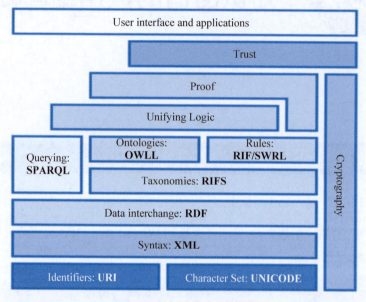

图 3.2 语义 Web 的技术堆栈

(来源:http://en.wikipedia.org/wiki/Semantic_Web_Stack)

语义 Web 技术(semantic Web technologies)是一系列 W3C 标准的集合,包括 RDF、OWL、SPARQL、RDFa、JSON-LD、SKOS、RDFS 和 RDB2RDF 等。其中,"资源描述框架"(resource description framework,RDF)的相关标准是整个技术体系的基石。

3.1.2　W3C RDF 序列化标准

知识图谱数据编码(data encoding)是数据模型的序列化(serialization),也称串行化,是将数据转换为可以存储或传输的字符串形式的过程。W3C RDF 1.1 标准提供了多种序列化语法,包括 Turtle、TriG、N-Triples、JSON-LD 和 RDF/XML 等,见图 3.3。每种语法都有各自的优势和局限,见表 3.1。

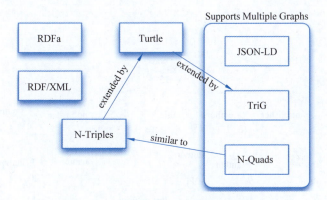

图 3.3 RDF 1.1 的各种序列化语法及其关系
(来源：http://www.w3.org/TR/2014/NOTE-rdf11-new-20140225/)

表 3.1 5 种 RDF 序列化语法的比较

序号	语　法	优　　点	缺　　点
1	RDF/XML	与 XML 兼容，有丰富的工具、社区支持	不直观，可读性差
2	N-Triples	语法简单，程序处理容易	字符串冗长
3	Turtle	可读性好，易于理解	解析和处理较复杂
4	TriG	可读性好，支持 RDF 数据集	解析和处理较复杂
5	JSON-LD	与 JSON 兼容，支持 RDF 数据集，应用广泛	支持工具不足

这些技术标准为 RDF 文档（RDF Documents）和 RDF 数据库 API 提供了标准格式，保障了各种知识图谱知识库之间的数据交换和互操作。

3.2 基于 XML 的 RDF 序列化

3.2.1 RDF/XML 基本语法

RDF 文档应是机器可解析的（machine parsable），最早被选中用于 RDF 文档的语法是 XML——可扩展标记语言（extensible markup language）。XML 是一种分层自描述模型，具有良好的语义和可扩展性，可以灵活地表示和组织数据。描述 XML 文档的数据模型有 XML 信息集（XML information set）和 XPath 模型等，都是树模型，见图 3.4。XML 信息集模型和 RDF 图模型是 W3C 技术堆栈中的基础模型，见图 3.1。

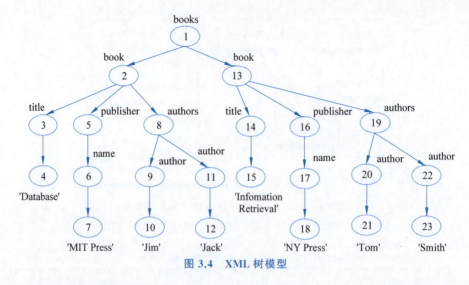

图 3.4　XML 树模型

RDF/XML 文档的根元素总是 rdf：RDF，它的子元素 rdf：Description 对应 RDF 模型中的"三元组"，基本的语法规则如下，表示图 2.12 所示的两类三元组。

```
<rdf: Description rdf: about="IRI of the statement'ssubject">
<predicateIRI rdf: resource="IRI of the statement'sobject"/>
<predicateIRI>literal </predicateIRI>
</rdf: Description>
```

对于表 2.4 给出的描述蒂姆·伯纳斯-李的 RDF 数据，其等价的 RDF/XML 文本见例 3.1。其中，在根元素 rdf：RDF 的起始标签中声明了一组前缀，用于文档中元素和属性的 QName。rdf：Description 的 rdf：about 属性的值是三元组的主体 IRI，rdf：Description 的子元素（如 rdf：type）是三元组的谓词，子元素的 rdf：resource 属性的值是客体 IRI。

例 3.1　RDF/XML 文本。

```
<?xml version="1.0" encoding="utf-8" ?>
<rdf: RDF
xmlns: rdf="http://www.w3.org/1999/02/22-rdf-syntax-ns#"
    xmlns: rdfs="http://www.w3.org/2000/01/rdf-schema#"
    xmlns: owl="http://www.w3.org/2002/07/owl#"
    xmlns: prov="http://www.w3.org/ns/prov#"
    xmlns: clgo="http://caligraph.org/ontology/" >
<rdf: Description
rdf: about="http://caligraph.org/resource/Tim_Berners-Lee">
```

```
  <rdf: type
rdf: resource="http://caligraph.org/ontology/Turing_Award_laureate"/>
  <rdfs: label>Tim Berners-Lee</rdfs: label>
  <owl: sameAs rdf: resource="http://dbpedia.org/resource/Tim_Berners
-Lee"/>
  <prov: wasDerivedFrom rdf: resource=
"http://en.wikipedia.org/wiki/Category: Turing_Award_laureates"/>
  < clgo: birthPlace rdf: resource =" http://caligraph.org/resource/
London" />
  <clgo: birthYear>1955</clgo: birthYear>
  <clgo: nationality
  rdf: resource="http://caligraph.org/resource/United_Kingdom" />
</rdf: Description>
</rdf: RDF>
```

当三元组的谓词是 rdf：type 时,可以将其省略掉,见例 3.2。

例 3.2　简化的 RDF/XML 文本。

```
<?xml version="1.0" encoding="utf-8" ?>
<rdf: RDF
xmlns: rdf="http://www.w3.org/1999/02/22-rdf-syntax-ns#"
xmlns: rdfs="http://www.w3.org/2000/01/rdf-schema#"
xmlns: clgo="http://caligraph.org/ontology/" >
<clgo: Turing_Award_laureate
  rdf: about="http://caligraph.org/resource/Tim_Berners-Lee">
<rdfs: label>Tim Berners-Lee</rdfs: label>
<clgo: birthYear>1955</clgo: birthYear>
</clgo: Turing_Award_laureate>
</rdf: RDF>
```

W3C RDF 1.1 XML 语法标准采用 RELAX NG 模式定义语言定义 RDF/XML 文档的模式,部分定义如下：

```
#RELAX NG Compact Schema for RDF/XML Syntax
namespace local =""
namespace rdf ="http://www.w3.org/1999/02/22-rdf-syntax-ns#"
start =doc
xmllang =attribute xml: lang { text }
xmlbase =attribute xml: base { text }
doc =RDF | nodeElement
RDF =element rdf: RDF { xmllang?, xmlbase?, nodeElementList }
nodeElementList =nodeElement *
```

```
nodeElement =element * -( local: * | rdf: RDF | rdf: ID | rdf: about | rdf:
parseType | rdf: resource | rdf: nodeID | rdf: datatype | rdf: li | rdf:
aboutEach | rdf: aboutEachPrefix | rdf: bagID )
{ (idAttr | nodeIdAttr | aboutAttr )?, xmllang?, xmlbase?, propertyAttr *,
propertyEltList }
aboutAttr =attribute rdf: about { URI-reference }
resourceAttr =attribute rdf: resource { URI-reference }
```

(来源：https://www.w3.org/TR/rdf-syntax-grammar/)

3.2.2 语法验证和格式转换服务

W3C 提供了 RDF 在线验证服务（validation service），其网址如下：

```
http://www.w3.org/RDF/Validator/
```

在界面输入 RDF/XML 文本或资源的 IRI，将对 RDF/XML 数据进行语法检查。如果是有效的 RDF/XML 数据，将解析出所有的三元组，并画出相应的 RDF 图。验证服务操作界面接受几种输入形式：

① 通过复制、粘贴操作输入一段 RDF/XML 文本；

② 输入 RDF/XML 文件的 URL；

③ 输入资源的 IRI/URI，该资源拥有 RDF/XML 格式的描述。

EasyRdf 网站在线提供了 RDF 数据的格式转换服务（见图 3.5），可以实现两种格式数据的转换，如从 RDF/XML 到 Turtle 等。

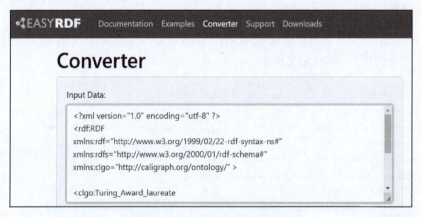

图 3.5 RDF 数据格式转换服务

（来源：https://www.easyrdf.org/converter）

3.3 基于文本的 RDF 序列化

3.3.1 N-Triples

RDF 图的 N-Triples 语法最初于 2004 年成为 W3C 标准,2014 年做了更新。N-Triples 语法是基于行的(line-based),即把每一个三元组都写在文本文件的一行内,如例 3.3 所示。其中,IRI 写在尖括号内,文字可带有类型声明,可以有空节点(如_: loc 等)。

例 3.3 N-Triples 文本。

```
<http://ex1.org/#Jen><http://xmlns.com/foaf/0.1/knows><http://ex1.org/#Ben>.
<http://ex1.org/#Jen><http://ex1.org/#location>_: loc .
_: loc <http://ex1.org/#lat>
"53.3"^^<http://www.w3.org/2001/XMLSchema#decimal>.
_: loc <http://ex1.org/#long>
"-9.0"^^<http://www.w3.org/2001/XMLSchema#decimal>.
_: alice <http://xmlns.com/foaf/0.1/knows>_: bob .
```

3.3.2 Turtle

Turtle 代表"Terse RDF Triple Language"(简洁的 RDF 三元组语言),它将 RDF 图转换为紧凑的文本形式(compact textual form),且与查询语言 SPARQL 的三元组模式(triple pattern)语法相兼容。Turtle 与 N-Triples 属于相似的语法家族,每个有效的 N-Triples 文件也是有效的 Turtle 文件,而 Turtle 允许缩写方式,使得文本更加简洁。

与 N-Triples 一样,在 Turtle 中,表示一个三元组的语法是:

```
<subject><predicate><object>.
```

其中,每个 IRI 要放到<>内,文字要放到引号内,后面可带"语言标签"(language tag)或类型说明。

其余的语法都使得表达更简洁。下面的语法用于将前缀与 IRI 联系起来:

```
@prefix pref: <iri/uri>.
```

这样，三元组中的 IRI 可以采用 QName，并且省略尖括号。

例 3.4 给出与例 3.1 的 RDF/XML 文本等价的 Turtle 文本，其中的 a 表示谓词 rdf：type。当多个谓词描述同一个主体时，分号";"用来合并主体。

例 3.4 与例 3.1 等价的 Turtle 文本。

```
@prefix rdf: <http://www.w3.org/1999/02/22-rdf-syntax-ns#>.
@prefix clgr:   <http://caligraph.org/resource/>.
@prefix clgo:   <http://caligraph.org/ontology/>.
@prefix rdfs:   <http://www.w3.org/2000/01/rdf-schema#>.
@prefix owl:    <http://www.w3.org/2002/07/owl#>.
@prefix prov:   <http://www.w3.org/ns/prov#>.
@prefix dbr:    <http://dbpedia.org/resource/>.
clgr: Tim_Berners-Lee     a    clgo: Turing_Award_laureate ;
            rdfs: label       "Tim Berners-Lee" ;
            owl: sameAs       dbr: Tim_Berners-Lee ;
            prov: wasDerivedFrom
<http://en.wikipedia.org/wiki/Category: Turing_Award_laureates>;
            clgo: birthPlace       clgr: London ;
            clgo: birthYear        "1955" ;
            clgo: nationality      clgr: United_Kingdom.
```

3.3.3　TriG

TriG 进一步扩展 Turtle 语法，以支持描述 RDF 数据集（RDF dataset），见图 3.3。RDF 数据集由一个默认图（default graph）和多个命名图（named graphs）组成，默认图没有 ID，命名图需要 IRI 标识。为此，TriG 语法增加了"图陈述"（graph statements）。对于一个命名图，"图陈述"由 IRI 和 RDF 图组成。例 3.5 给出一个 RDF 数据集的例子，有两个命名图＜http://example.org/bob＞和＜http://example.org/alice＞，它们各自的 RDF 图放在{}里，其中的[]和_: b 表示空节点，GRAPH 为关键字，可以省略。

例 3.5 TriG 文本。

```
@prefix rdf: <http://www.w3.org/1999/02/22-rdf-syntax-ns#>.
@prefix dc: <http://purl.org/dc/terms/>.
@prefix foaf: <http://xmlns.com/foaf/0.1/>.
#default graph
<http://example.org/bob>    dc: publisher   "Bob" .
<http://example.org/alice>  dc: publisher   "Alice" .
```

```
GRAPH <http://example.org/bob>
{    []      foaf: name    "Bob" ;
             foaf: mbox    <mailto: bob@oldcorp.example.org>;
             foaf: knows   _: b .  }
GRAPH <http://example.org/alice>
{    _: b  foaf: name    "Alice" ;
             foaf: mbox    <mailto: alice@work.example.org>.   }
```

3.4 基于JSON-LD的RDF序列化

3.4.1 JSON模型

JSON-LD(JSON for linking data)是轻量级的关联数据序列化语法,与JSON语法完全兼容。JSON-LD工作组(JSON-LD Working Group)于2014年1月发布JSON-LD 1.0版,2020年7月发布JSON-LD 1.1版。

JSON(JavaScript object notation)是一种易于读写的轻量级数据表示格式,可以被快速、高效地解析,广泛应用于互联网上的数据传输、数据采集和数据挖掘。

JSON模型有两种结构:

(1) 对象(object)。一个对象以"{"开始、以"}"结束,包含一系列非排序的键-值对(key-value pair),键-值对之间使用","分隔,键与值之间使用":"分隔。

(2) 数组(array)。一个数组是若干值(包括对象)的集合,以"["开始、以"]"结束,数组成员之间使用","分隔。

例3.6的代码描述了一个JSON对象,它含有四个键-值对,键和值都放在双引号内。

例3.6 JSON对象。

```
{
    "name":        "Tim Berners-Lee",
    "birthPlace":  "London",
    "birthYear":   "1955",
    "type":        "Turing_Award_laureate"
}
```

JSON数据模型与RDF数据模型有着内在的相似性,可以将JSON对象看作RDF资源(主体或客体),JSON键-值对看作RDF谓词-客体对。因此,JSON-LD的关键是将全局IRI引入JSON语法。

3.4.2 JSON-LD 语法

JSON-LD 语法的核心是定义一组关键字(keywords)和标记(tokens),以在现有 JSON 语法的基础上描述 RDF 数据。

例 3.7 使用关键词@id 和@type 作为键的名字(即谓词),用以声明一个对象的 IRI 和类型;再用 IRI 取代局部名称,便使得例 3.7 所描述的 JSON-LD 对象成为 RDF 资源,其 RDF 图如图 3.6 所示。

例 3.7 JSON-LD 对象。

```
{
  "@id": "http://caligraph.org/resource/Tim_Berners-Lee",
  "http://dbpedia.org/ontology/name": "Tim Berners-Lee",
  "http://caligraph.org/ontology/birthPlace":
  {"@id": "http://caligraph.org/resource/London"}
  "http://caligraph.org/ontology/birthYear": {"@value": "1955"},
  "@type": "http://caligraph.org/ontology/Turing_Award_laureate"
}
```

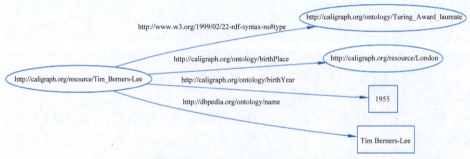

图 3.6 例 3.7 所表达的 RDF 图

例 3.7 中的 birthPlace、birthYear 和 Turing_Award_laureate 三个词汇来自同一个词汇表 http://caligraph.org/ontology/,例 3.8 使用@vocab 关键词声明默认的词汇表,这样就可以用局部名字取代 IRI,使得文档更简洁。

例 3.8 使用默认词汇表。

```
{
  "@context": { "@vocab": "http://caligraph.org/ontology/" },
  "@id":    "http://caligraph.org/resource/Tim_Berners-Lee",
  "http://dbpedia.org/ontology/name":    "Tim Berners-Lee",
```

```
    "birthPlace":    { "@id": "http://caligraph.org/resource/London" },
    "birthYear":     { "@value": "1955" },
    "@type":         "Turing_Award_laureate"
}
```

在 JSON-LD 中,还可以与 XML 和 Turtle 一样,使用前缀和 QName,见例 3.9。

例 3.9 使用前缀和 QName。

```
{
    "@context": { "@vocab": "http://caligraph.org/ontology/",
    "clgr":    "http://caligraph.org/resource/",
    "dbo":     "http://dbpedia.org/ontology/"},
    "@id":     "clgr: Tim_Berners-Lee",
    "dbo: name": "Tim Berners-Lee",
    "birthPlace":    { "@id": "clgr: London"},
    "birthYear":     { "@value": "1955"},
    "@type":         "Turing_Award_laureate"
}
```

对比例 3.9 和例 3.6,JSON-LD 对象和 JSON 对象在数据部分的表达已经基本一致,只是 JSON-LD 对象多了一个"环境"(context)定义,它通过 @context 关键词标记。"环境"(context)部分定义一组可共享的项(terms),供各方在共同的词汇表基础上交换 JSON-LD 文档。为此,"环境"部分可以单独写成一个文件,放到网上共享。例 3.10 是一个环境定义文件的例子,例 3.11 是使用这个文件的例子。在例 3.10 的定义中,xsd 是前缀;Person 是类的名字,它的 IRI 是 http://xmlns.com/foaf/0.1/Person;name 是属性的名字,也来自 FOAF 词汇表;born 是属性的名字,对应 http://schema.org/birthDate,数据类型是 xsd: date。

例 3.10 外部环境定义文件 person.jsonld。

```
{  "@context":
{  "Person": "http://xmlns.com/foaf/0.1/Person",
   "xsd": "http://www.w3.org/2001/XMLSchema#",
   "name": "http://xmlns.com/foaf/0.1/name",
   "homepage":
        { "@id": "http://xmlns.com/foaf/0.1/homepage","@type": "@id"},
   "born":
        { "@id": "http://schema.org/birthDate",
          "@type": "xsd: date" } }
}
```

(来源:https://json-ld.org/contexts/person.jsonld)

例 3.11 使用 person.jsonld 的 JSON-LD 文本。

```
{
"@context": [ "https://json-ld.org/contexts/person.jsonld",
{ "clgr": "http://caligraph.org/resource/" } ],
"@id":     "clgr: Tim_Berners-Lee",
"name":    "Tim Berners-Lee",
"homepage":    "https://www.w3.org/People/Berners-Lee/",
"born":    { "@value": "1955-06-08", "@type": "xsd: date" },
"@type":   "Person"
}
```

例 3.11 的 JSON-LD 文档所表达的三元组如表 3.2 所示,其 RDF 图见图 3.7。

表 3.2　例 3.11 所表达的三元组

序号	主　体	谓　　词	客　　体
1	clgr：Tim_Berners-Lee	rdf：type	foaf：Person
2	clgr：Tim_Berners-Lee	foaf：name	"Tim Berners-Lee"
3	clgr：Tim_Berners-Lee	foaf：homepage	https://www.w3.org/People/Berners-Lee/
4	clgr：Tim_Berners-Lee	schema：birthDate	"1955-06-08"^^xsd：date

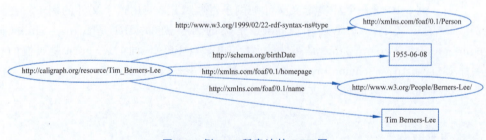

图 3.7　例 3.11 所表达的 RDF 图

进一步来说,在一个文档中,可以在多个对象间共享环境定义。例如,例 3.12 中有两个"结点对象"(node object)——Tim_Berners-Lee 和 London,见图 3.8。

例 3.12 在对象间共享环境定义。

```
{
"@context": { "@vocab": "http://caligraph.org/ontology/",
"clgr":    "http://caligraph.org/resource/",
```

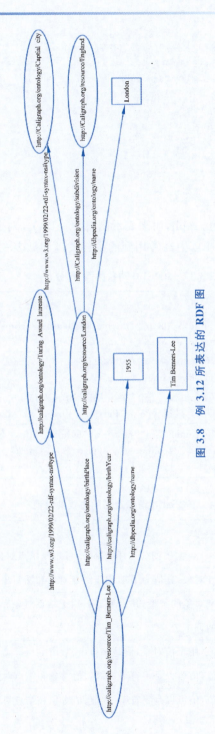

图 3.8　例 3.12 所表达的 RDF 图

```
"dbo":        "http://dbpedia.org/ontology/" },
"@graph": [ { "@id": "clgr: Tim_Berners-Lee",
"dbo: name":        "Tim Berners-Lee",
"birthPlace":     { "@id": "clgr: London" },
"birthYear":      { "@value": "1955" },
"@type":       "Turing_Award_laureate" },
{"@id":       "clgr: London",
"dbo: name":       "London",
"subdivision": { "@id": "clgr: England" },"@type": "Capital_city" } ]
}
```

例 3.12 用到了关键词@graph,用来表示图对象。JSON 对象还有结点对象和值对象等,见表 3.3。JSON-LD 中经常用到的主要关键词见表 3.4。

表 3.3 JSON-LD 对象类型(部分)

序号	对象类型	举 例
1	结点对象(node object)	{"@id": "http://me.markus-lanthaler.com/", "name": "Markus Lanthaler"}
2	值对象(value object)	{"@value": "2010-05-29T14:17:39+02:00", "@type": "xsd: dateTime"}
3	图对象(graph object)	"@graph": [{ "@id": "http://manu.sporny.org/about # manu", "@type": "Person", "name": "Manu Sporny" }]
4	列表对象(list object)	{"@context": { "nick": { "@id": "http://xmlns.com/foaf/0.1/nick", "@container": "@list" } }, "nick": ["joe", "bob", "jaybee"] }

表 3.4 JSON-LD 语法定义的主要关键词

序号	关 键 词	说 明
1	@context	声明 JSON-LD 文档的公共环境部分,可用于结点对象、值对象和图对象
2	@id	标识 JSON 对象,其值为 IRI,用于结点对象和图对象
3	@type	声明 JSON 对象的类型,其值为 IRI,用于结点对象和值对象
4	@vocab	声明默认的词汇表
5	@value	声明一个值,用于值对象,值是字符串、数值等
6	@list	声明列表值,值可以是字符串、数值、值对象和结点对象等
7	@set	声明集合值,值可以是字符串、数值、值对象和结点对象等

续表

序号	关　键　词	说　　明
8	@graph	声明 RDF 图对象,其值为结点对象或值对象的数组
9	@language	用于值对象,声明一个值的语言类型

3.4.3　描述 RDF 数据集

JSON-LD 语法支持对 RDF 数据集的描述。图 3.9 给出一个 RDF 数据集,其中含有一个默认图和两个命名图。例 3.13 是描述这个数据集的 JSON-LD 文本,例 3.14 是等价的 TriG 文本。

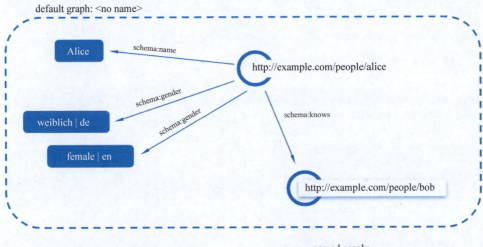

图 3.9　RDF 数据集:一个默认图,两个命名图

(来源:https://www.w3.org/TR/json-ld11/)

例 3.13 描述 RDF 数据集的 JSON-LD 文本。

```
{ "@context": {  "@vocab": "http://schema.org/",
                 "@base": "http://example.com/" },
  "@graph": [ { "@id": "people/alice",
                "gender": [{"@value": "weiblich", "@language": "de"},
                           {"@value": "female", "@language": "en"} ],
                "knows": {"@id": "people/bob" },
                "name": "Alice" },
  { "@id": "graphs/1",
    "@graph": { "@id": "people/alice", "parent": { "@id": "people/bob",
    "name": "Bob" } } },
  { "@id": "graphs/2",
    "@graph": { "@id": "people/bob", "sibling": { "name": "Mary",
    "sibling": {"@id": "people/bob" } } } ]
}
```

例 3.14 与例 3.13 等价的 TriG 文本。

```
@prefix schema: <http://schema.org/>.
<http://example.com/people/alice> schema: knows <http://example.com/people/bob>;
schema: name "Alice";
schema: gender "weiblich"@de, "female"@en .
<http://example.com/graphs/1> {
<http://example.com/people/alice> schema: parent <http://example.com/people/bob>.
<http://example.com/people/bob> schema: name "Bob" .}
<http://example.com/graphs/2> {
<http://example.com/people/bob> schema: sibling [ schema: name "Mary";
schema: sibling <http://example.com/people/bob>] .}
```

3.5 SN SciGraph 学术知识图谱的数据实例

3.5.1 SciGraph 开放数据集

SciGraph 是施普林格·自然（Springer Nature, SN）出版集团于 2015 年 5 月启动的项目，从论文、期刊、会议、著作、科学数据与科研基金等学术资源获取知识图谱，并于 2017 年上线关联数据平台，提供文献检索服务。2023 年 2 月 1 日起，

SN 不再提供 SciGraph 服务，但其数据还保留在 Figshare SN SciGraph 仓储库（见图 3.10）和 GitHub(https://github.com/springernature/scigraph)上。

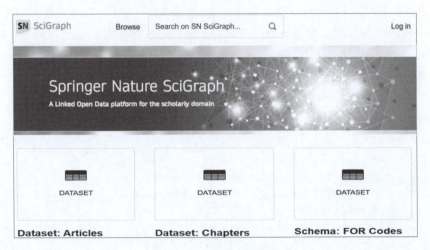

图 3.10　SciGraph 数据集

（来源：https://sn-scigraph.figshare.com/）

截至 2023 年 1 月 31 日，SciGraph 共有 15 个数据集，主要的数据集情况见表 3.5。

表 3.5　主要的 SciGraph 数据集

序号	数据集名称	实体类别	实体个数	文件规模
1	著作(books)	schema：Book	762345	177.86MB
2	论文(articles)	schema：ScholarlyArticle	22717815	8.82GB
3	章节(chapters)	schema：Chapter	11258558	4.2GB
4	基金(grants)	schema：MonetaryGrant	1984580	882.63MB
5	期刊(journals)	schema：Periodical	11747	1.7MB
6	机构(organizations)	foaf：Organization	245822	12.27MB
7	人员(persons)	schema：Person	20769183	1.42GB
8	临床试验(clinical trials)	schema：MedicalStudy	62610	45.6MB
9	专利(patents)	sgo：Patent	1090325	200.61MB

3.5.2 环境定义文件

SciGraph 采用多种数据格式描述实体，包括 RDF/XML、Turtle 和 JSON-LD。其中，JSON-LD 是最主要的一种。为此，给出了统一的环境定义文件，见例 3.15。从中可见，SciGraph 采用了 Schema.org 词汇表，并定义了自己的本体：SciGraph Core Ontology。

例 3.15　SciGraph 环境定义文件 sgcontext.json（部分）。

```
{ "@context": {
    "@vocab": "http://schema.org/",
    "sg": "http://scigraph.springernature.com/",
    "sgo": "http://scigraph.springernature.com/ontologies/core/",
    "sgo-pmc": "http://scigraph.springernature.com/ontologies/
    product-market-codes/",
    "rdf": "http://www.w3.org/1999/02/22-rdf-syntax-ns#",
    "rdfs": "http://www.w3.org/2000/01/rdf-schema#",
    "schema": "http://schema.org/",
    "owl": "http://www.w3.org/2002/07/owl#",
    "skos": "http://www.w3.org/2004/02/skos/core#",
    "xsd": "http://www.w3.org/2001/XMLSchema#",
    "id": "@id",
    "type": "@type",
    "sdDataset": { "@id": "sgo: sdDataset" },
    "isCurrent": { "@id": "sgo: isCurrent","@type": "Boolean" },
    "author": { "@id": "schema: author","@container": "@list" },
    "editor": { "@id": "schema: editor","@container": "@list" },
    "sameAs": { "@id": "schema: sameAs","@type": "@id", "@ container": "@set" },
    "isFundedItemOf": { "@reverse": "pending: fundedItem", "@type": "@id","@container": "@set" }
  }
}
```

（来源：https://springernature.github.io/scigraph/jsonld/sgcontext.json）

3.5.3 学术著作数据

著作（Book）是 SciGraph 中最重要的实体类型之一。例 3.16 给出描述著作 *Knowledge Graphs* 的 JSON-LD 文本，例 3.17 是等价的 Turtle 文本，图 3.11 是相应的 RDF 图。

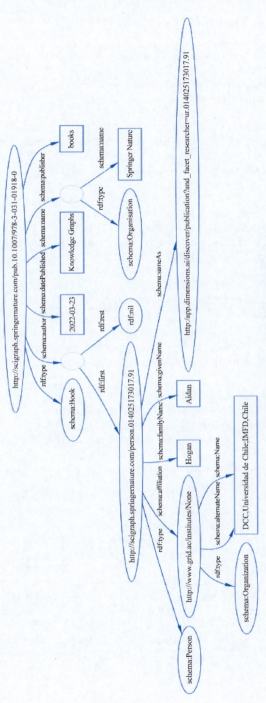

图 3.11 学术著作 *Knowledge Graphs* 的 RDF 图

例 3.16　描述著作 *Knowledge Graphs* 的 JSON-LD 文本。

```
{ "@context": "https://springernature.github.io/scigraph/jsonld/sgcontext.json",
"id": "sg:pub.10.1007/978-3-031-01918-0",
"name": "Knowledge Graphs",
"type": "Book",
"author": [ { "affiliation": {
"alternateName": "DCC, Universidad de Chile; IMFD, Chile",
"id": "http://www.grid.ac/institutes/None",
"name": [ "DCC, Universidad de Chile; IMFD, Chile" ],
"type": "Organization"    },
"familyName":   "Hogan",
"givenName":    "Aidan",
"id":           "sg:person.014025173017.91",
"sameAs": [ "https://app.dimensions.ai/discover/publication?and_facet_researcher=ur.014025173017.91" ],
"type": "Person" }],
"datePublished": "2022-03-23",
"publisher": { "name": "Springer Nature", "type": "Organisation" },
"sdDataset": "books"
}
```

例 3.17　描述著作 *Knowledge Graphs* 的 Turtle 文本。

```
@prefix schema: <http://schema.org/>.
@prefix xsd: <http://www.w3.org/2001/XMLSchema#>.
@prefix ns0: <http://scigraph.springernature.com/ontologies/core/>.
<http://scigraph.springernature.com/pub.10.1007/978-3-031-01918-0> a
schema: Book ;
schema: author (<http://scigraph.springernature.com/person.014025173017.91>);
schema: datePublished     "2022-03-23"^^xsd: string ;
schema: name              "Knowledge Graphs"^^xsd: string ;
schema: publisher [ a schema: Organisation ;
                    schema: name "Springer Nature"^^xsd: string] ;
ns0: sdDataset           "books"^^xsd: string .
<http://scigraph.springernature.com/person.014025173017.91> a schema: Person ;
schema: affiliation    <http://www.grid.ac/institutes/None>;
schema: familyName     "Hogan"^^xsd: string ;
schema: givenName      "Aidan"^^xsd: string ;
schema: sameAs < https://app.dimensions.ai/discover/publication?and_facet_researcher=ur.014025173017.91>.
```

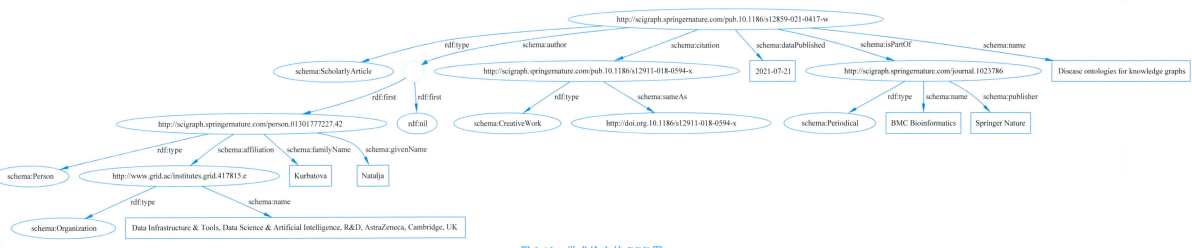

图 3.12 学术论文的 RDF 图

```
<http://www.grid.ac/institutes/None>a schema: Organization ;
schema: alternateName   "DCC, Universidad de Chile; IMFD, Chile"^^xsd:
string ;
schema: name            "DCC, Universidad de Chile; IMFD, Chile"^^xsd:
string .
```

3.5.4 学术论文数据

学术论文(Scholarly Article)是最重要的实体类型。例 3.18 给出一篇论文的 JSON-LD 文档,图 3.12 是相应的 RDF 图。其中,描述了论文间的引用关系(citation)。

例 3.18 学术论文的 JSON-LD 文档。

```
{ "@context": "https://springernature.github.io/scigraph/jsonld/
sgcontext.json",
"id":     "sg: pub.10.1186/s12859-021-04173-w",
"name":   "Disease ontologies for knowledge graphs",
"type":   "ScholarlyArticle",
"datePublished": "2021-07-21",
"author": [ {
            "affiliation": {
            "id": "http://www.grid.ac/institutes/grid.417815.e",
            "name": [ " Data Infrastructure & Tools, Data Science &
            Artificial Intelligence, R&D, AstraZeneca, Cambridge, UK" ],
            "type": "Organization" },
            "familyName":     "Kurbatova",
            "givenName":      "Natalja",
            "id":       "sg: person.01301777227.42",
            "type":     "Person"     }],
"isPartOf": [ {
            "id":     "sg: journal.1023786",
            "name":   "BMC Bioinformatics",
            "publisher":   "Springer Nature",
            "type":   "Periodical"  } ],
"citation": [ {
            "id": "sg: pub.10.1186/s12911-018-0594-x",
            "sameAs": [ "https://doi.org/10.1186/s12911-018-0594-x" ],
            "type": "CreativeWork" } ]
}
```

参 考 文 献

[1] 翟军.关联政府数据原理与应用[M].北京：电子工业出版社,2016.

[2] 袁满,褚冰,陈萍.知识图谱构建中的语义标准问题研究[J].情报理论与实践,2020,43(3)：131-137.

[3] Blue Briain Nexus. Understanding knowledge graphs [EB/OL].[2023-01-26].https://bluebrainnexus.io/docs/getting-started/understanding-knowledge-graphs.html.

[4] RDF 1.1 Concepts and Abstract Syntax [EB/OL].[2023-01-26].https://www.w3.org/TR/rdf11-concepts/.

[5] RDF 1.1 XML Syntax [EB/OL].[2023-01-26]. https://www.w3.org/TR/rdf-syntax-grammar/.

[6] 信俊昌,王国仁,李国徽,等.数据模型及其发展历程[J].软件学报,2019,30(1)：142-163.

[7] HOGAN A. The web of data [M]. Berlin：Springer, 2022.

[8] RDF 1.1 N-Triples [EB/OL].[2023-01-28]. https://www.w3.org/TR/n-triples/.

[9] RDF 1.1 Turtle [EB/OL].[2023-01-28]. https://www.w3.org/TR/turtle/.

[10] RDF 1.1 primer [EB/OL].[2023-01-28].https://www.w3.org/TR/rdf11-primer/.

[11] RDF 1.1 TriG [EB/OL].[2023-01-28]. https://www.w3.org/TR/trig/.

[12] JSON-LD 1.1 [EB/OL].[2023-01-28]. https://www.w3.org/TR/json-ld11/.

[13] JSON for linking data [EB/OL].[2023-01-28]. https://json-ld.org/.

[14] JSON-LD working group [EB/OL].[2023-01-29]. https://www.w3.org/2018/json-ld-wg/.

[15] JSON-LD best practices [EB/OL].[2023-01-29]. https://w3c.github.io/json-ld-bp/.

[16] Introducing JSON [EB/OL].[2023-01-29]. https://www.json.org/json-en.html.

[17] Ontology: SN SciGraph data model [EB/OL].[2023-01-29]. https://scigraph.springernature.com/explorer/datasets/ontology/.

[18] Datasets：At a glance [EB/OL].[2023-02-01]. https://scigraph.springernature.com/explorer/datasets/data_at_a_glance/.

[19] 宋宁远.面向智慧数据的科学知识图谱构建：以 SciGraph 为例[J].科技与出版,2017(11)：17-19.

[20] 白林林,祝忠明.Springer Nature SciGraph 关联开放数据分析[J].知识管理论坛,2018,3(1)：2-11.

[21] 周理斌,林静.SciGraph 的知识服务框架特点[J].科学技术创新,2019(21)：49-50.

第4章 基于本体的知识图谱模式设计

4.1 本体及其作用

4.1.1 本体的定义

本体(ontology)在语义 Web 中处于核心位置(参见图 3.2)。本体是一种形式化的语义数据模型和知识组织(knowledge organization)方式,并具有一定的推理(inference)功能。

W3C 将"本体"定义为"一定领域内的术语(terms)的形式化表示,术语表达一个概念(concept)、属性(property)或关系(relationship)"。W3C 不严格区分"本体"与"词汇表"(vocabulary)的内涵。通常认为,"本体"更加复杂、形式化程度更高,而对"词汇表"的约束要宽松一些。一个动物本体/词汇表的片段见图 4.1。

一个本体通常由三部分的明确定义组成:类(class,即实体类型)、属性和关系。它还可以包含若干"分类词汇表"(taxonomy),以进一步规范属性或关系的取值,见图 4.2。

Wikipedia 将本体分为领域本体(domain ontology)、顶层本体(upper ontology)和混合本体(hybrid ontology)。本体的构建方法主要有手工、自动和协作。本体的自动构建也称为"本体学习"(ontology learning,OL)。

4.1.2 本体的作用

虽然本体对于一个知识图谱系统而言不是必需的,但越来越多的知识图谱将

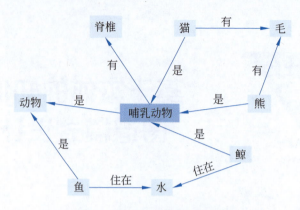

图 4.1 动物本体/词汇表片段

(来源：https://upload.wikimedia.org/wikipedia/commons/1/17/Semantic_Net-zh_cn.svg)

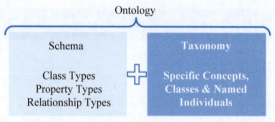

图 4.2 本体的组成

本体作为"模式层"(Schema Layer)或"基础层"(Foundation Layer)，特别是语义知识图谱和 RDF 知识图谱(参见图 1.10)。

无论是"自顶向下"(top-down)，还是"自下而上"(bottom-up)的构建方法，本体在知识图谱的构建中都发挥着关键作用(参见图 1.15)。IBM 研究院的科研团队提出了一种新的从文本构建知识图谱的方法 Text2KGBench，其过程见图 4.3。给定本体和文本语料库，该方法利用"大语言模型"(large language models, LLM)，如 GPT(generative pre-training transformer)，从文本中提取出符合本体约束的事实。该方法生成了数据集 Wikidata-TekGen 和 DBpedia-WebNLG，分别用到 10 个本体和 19 个本体。

本体还是知识图谱推理的有效手段。如图 4.4 所示，利用 Shoe Ontology 和 Color Taxonomy 的 sub-class(子类)、broader(上位词)关系的传递性，可以生成新的事实(图中用虚线表示)。

第4章 基于本体的知识图谱模式设计

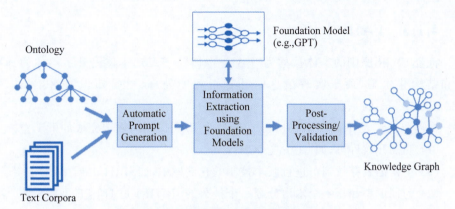

图 4.3 本体驱动的知识图谱构建方法

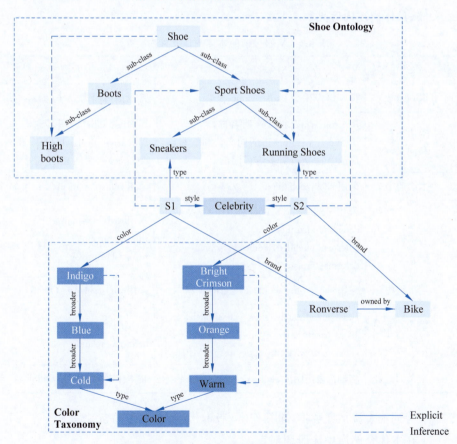

图 4.4 本体驱动的知识图谱推理示例

（来源：https://www.ontotext.com/knowledgehub/fundamentals/what-is-a-knowledge-graph/）

4.1.3　FAIR 本体

符合 FAIR 原则的本体被称为"FAIR 本体"。FAIR 本体提升了本体的标准化和结构化水平,便于实现信息的计算机智能处理,更是知识图谱 FAIR 化(FAIRification)的基础。

将遗留词汇表(legacy vocabulary)转换为 FAIR 本体,需要完成如下工作:

(1) 明确开放许可,如 CC0 或 CC-BY 等。

(2) 将词汇表存放到可进行版本控制的仓储库中,如 GitHub 或 GitLab 等。

(3) 为词汇表和每一个术语分配一个持久的 IRI,IRI 是 HTTP 可解析的。

(4) 利用 W3C OWL 或 SKOS 语言,描述词汇表和术语,产生机器可读的本体描述文件,具体描述内容见表 4.1。

表 4.1　机器可读的本体描述文件内容

序号	描述内容	SKOS 语言	OWL 语言
1	识别术语	将术语声明为 skos：Concept	将术语声明为 owl：Class
2	术语名称和同义词	用 skos：prefLabel 声明名称, 用 skos：altLabel 声明同义词和缩写词, 用语言标签声明多语言词汇	用 rdfs：label 声明名称, 用 skos：prefLabel 和 skos：altLabel 声明同义词
3	术语的定义	采用 skos：definition	采用 rdfs：comment
4	元数据	采用 dcterms：creator, dcterms：created, dcterms：identifier, dcterms：modified, dcterms：source, dcterms：replaces, rdfs：seeAlso	采用 owl：versionInfo, rdfs：comment, rdfs：isDefinedBy
5	层次结构	采用 skos：broader 和 skos：narrower	采用 rdfs：subClassOf
6	术语间的关系	skos：broadMatch, skos：closeMatch, skos：exactMatch, skos：narrowMatch, skos：relatedMatch	owl：equivalentClass dcterms：relation
7	定义词汇表	将词汇表声明为 skos：ConceptScheme	将本体声明为 owl：Ontology

(5) 为词汇表添加元数据,包括作者、版本、发布者和许可等。

(6) 在本体仓储库中注册词汇表。

4.2 本体描述语言

4.2.1 W3C RDFS、OWL 和 SKOS

为了形式化定义和描述词汇表和本体，W3C 开发了 RDFS（RDF Schema）、OWL（Web Ontology Language）、SKOS（Simple Knowledge Organization System）和 RIF（Rule Interchange Format）等技术和标准规范，统称为"本体描述语言"（Ontology Language），起到本体模型的作用（即元模型），见图 4.5。

RDFS 是一种简单的本体描述语言，其提供的构造子（construct）见表 4.2，可用来定义类和属性以及它们的层次结构。

表 4.2　RDFS 的构造子

构造子	语　法	说　明
Class	C rdf：type rdfs：Class	C (a resource) is an RDF class
Property	P rdf：type rdf：Propert	P (a resource) is an RDF property
type	I rdf：type C	I (a resource) is an instance of C (a class)
subClassOf	C1 rdfs：subClassOf C2	C1 (a class) is a subclass of C2 (a class)
subPropertyOf	P1 rdfs：subPropertyOf P2	P1 (a property) is a sub-property of P2
domain	P rdfs：domain C	domain of P (a property) is C (a class)
range	P rdfs：range C	range of P (a property) is C (a class)

（来源：https://www.w3.org/TR/rdf11-primer/）

为了提供更加丰富的语义和更强的推理能力，W3C OWL 工作组在 RDF 和 RDFS 的基础上开发了 OWL，目前已发展到版本 2。OWL 2 是庞大的语言家族，含有功能各异的子语言（见图 4.6）。OWL 的部分构造子见表 4.3，表达能力有了显著的提升。

表 4.3　OWL 的部分构造子

构造子	语　法	说　明
Class	C rdf：type owl：Class	声明一个类
Property	P rdf：type owl：DatatypeProperty	声明一个数据类型属性
Relation	P rdf：type owl：ObjectProperty	声明一个二元关系（对象属性）

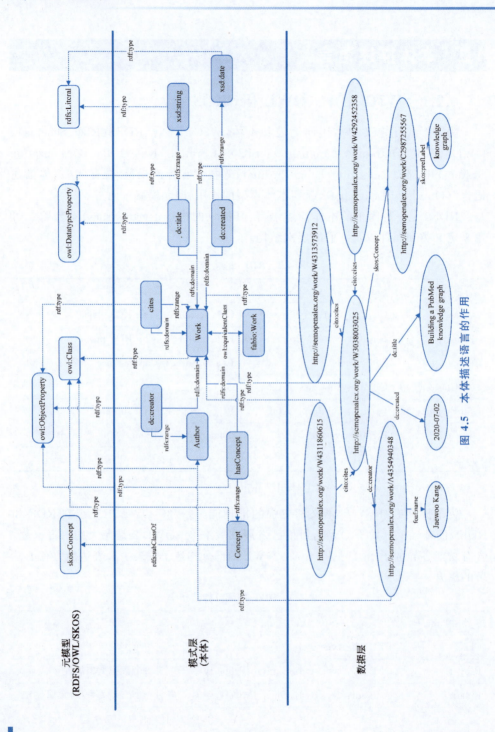

图 4.5 本体描述语言的作用

续表

构造子	语法	说明
equivalentClass	C1 owl：equivalentClass C2	声明两个类等价
equivalentProperty	P1 owl：equivalentProperty P2	声明两个属性等价
disjointWith	C1 owl：disjointWith C2	声明两个类的交集为空集
unionOf	owl：unionOf(C1 C2 C3)	类的并
SymmetricProperty	P rdf：type owl：SymmetricProperty	声明对称关系
FunctionalProperty	P rdf：type owl：FunctionalProperty	声明一个函数关系
inverseOf	P1 owl：inverseOf P2	声明逆关系
sameAs	I1 owl：sameAs I2	声明两个 IRI 指向同一个实体
differentFrom	I1 owl：differentFrom I2	声明两个 IRI 指向不同的实体
Thing	C rdfs：subClassOf owl：Thing	表示全集
Nothing	owl：Nothing rdfs：subClassOf C	表示空集

图 4.6　OWL 2 的子语言

(来源：http://www.euclid-project.eu/modules/chapter1)

SKOS 是基于 RDF、RDFS 和 OWL 的共享和链接"知识组织系统"(knowledge organization systems，KOS)的通用数据模型(common data model)。它提供同义词表、分类法(taxonomies)、叙词表(thesauri)和地名辞典等受控词汇表(controlled vocabularies)的形式化描述方法。同 RDF/RDFS 相比，SKOS 的关联描述能力更强，而与 OWL 相比，其逻辑描述能力较弱。

SKOS 的构造子有 skos：Concept、skos：ConceptScheme、skos：broader 和 skos：narrower 等，它们与 OWL 构造子的对应关系见图 4.7 中的例子。

```
ex:element-80 a skos:Concept;                          ex:element-80 a owl:Class;
    skos:prefLabel "mercury"@en;                           rdfs:label "mercury"@en;
    skos:prefLabel "mercurio"@es;                          rdfs:label "mercurio"@es;
    skos:altLabel "quicksilver"@en;                        skos:altLabel "quicksilver"@en;
    skos:notation "Hg";                                    rdfs:label "Hg";
    skos:definition "A heavy,silvery d-block element,mercury is the only   rdfs:comment "A heavy,silvery d-block element,mercury is the only
metallic element that is liquid at standard conditions for temperature and   metallic element that is liquid at standard conditions for temperature and
pressure.";                                            pressure.";
    dcterms:identifier "7439-97-6";                        dcterms:identifier "7439-97-6";
    dcterms:source <https://en.wikipedia.org/wiki/Mercury_(element)>;   dcterms:source <https://en.wikipedia.org/wiki/Mercury_(element)>;
    skos:broader ex:group-12,ex:period-6;                  rdfs:subClassOf ex:group-12,ex:period-6;
    skos:exactMatch <http://purl.obolibrary.org/obo/CHEBI_16170>;   owl:equivalentClass <http://purl.obolibrary.org/obo/CHEBI_16170>;
    skos:inScheme ex:periodicTable;                        rdfs:inDefinedBy ex:periodicTable;
```

图 4.7　SKOS 与 OWL、RDFS 的构造子比较

4.2.2　SemOpenAlex 本体实例

SemOpenAlex 知识图谱由德国卡尔斯鲁厄理工学院（Karlsruhe Institute of Technology，KIT）AIFB 研究所开发，是世界上最大的学术知识图谱之一，包含超过 300 亿个关于科学出版物（Work）及其相关实体（作者、机构和领域等）的三元组。该知识图谱的模式以 SemOpenAlex 本体的形式给出，含有 14 个类（classes）、23 个关系（relations）和 70 个属性（attributes），其模型见图 4.8。

例 4.1 给出了 SemOpenAlex 本体的形式化描述代码，包括 5 部分：命名空间和前缀声明、本体的元数据、类的定义、关系的定义和属性的定义。

例 4.1　SemOpenAlex Ontology 的 OWL 描述代码（部分）。

```
#命名空间和前缀声明
@prefix owl: <http://www.w3.org/2002/07/owl#>.
@prefix xsd: <http://www.w3.org/2001/XMLSchema#>.
@prefix skos: <http://www.w3.org/2004/02/skos/core#>.
@prefix rdfs: <http://www.w3.org/2000/01/rdf-schema#>.
@prefix rdf: <http://www.w3.org/1999/02/22-rdf-syntax-ns#>.
@prefix sh: <http://www.w3.org/ns/shacl#>.
@prefix foaf: <http://xmlns.com/foaf/0.1/>.
@prefix dcterms: <http://purl.org/dc/terms/>.
@prefix soa: <https://semopenalex.org/ontology/>.
#本体的元数据
<https://semopenalex.org/ontology/> a owl:Ontology;
rdfs: label "SemOpenAlex Ontology"@en;
rdfs: comment "The Semantic OpenAlex Ontology, described using W3C RDF
Schema and the Web Ontology Language OWL."@en ;
dcterms: created "2022-05-12"^^xsd: date ;
dcterms: modified "2023-10-24"^^xsd: date ;
```

第4章 基于本体的知识图谱模式设计

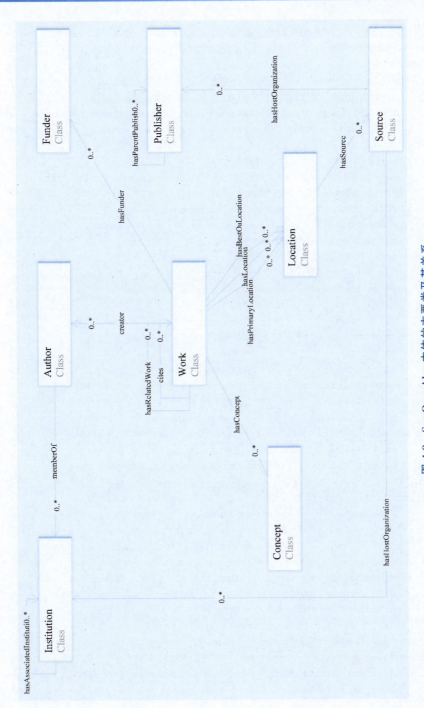

图 4.8 **SemOpenAlex 本体的主要类及其关系**

(来源：https://semopenalex.org/resource/semopenalex: UniversalSearch)

```
dcterms: issued    "2023-10-18"^^xsd: date ;
dcterms: creator   <https://orcid.org/0000-0001-5458-8645>.
#本体的作者之一
<https://orcid.org/0000-0001-5458-8645>a foaf: Person;
        rdfs: label    "Michael F?rber";
        foaf: homepage <https://www.aifb.kit.edu/web/Michael_F?rber>;
        foaf: mbox     <mailto: michael.faerber@kit.edu>.
#类的定义
<https://semopenalex.org/ontology/Work>  a  owl: Class;
        owl: equivalentClass   <http://purl.org/spar/fabio/Work>;
        rdfs: label     "Work"@en ;
        rdfs: comment   "This class represents a work."@en.
<https://semopenalex.org/ontology/Author>  a  owl: Class;
        rdfs: label     "Author"@en ;
        rdfs: comment   "This class represents an author."@en.
<https://semopenalex.org/ontology/Concept>  a  owl: Class;
        rdfs: subClassOf   skos: Concept;
        rdfs: label     "Concept"@en ;
        rdfs: comment   "This class represents a concept."@en.
<https://semopenalex.org/ontology/Publisher>  a  owl: Class;
        rdfs: label     "Publisher"@en ;
        rdfs: comment   "This class specifies a publisher."@en .
<https://semopenalex.org/ontology/Institution>  a owl: Class;
        rdfs: label     "Institution"@en ;
        rdfs: comment   "This class represents an institution."@en.
<https://semopenalex.org/ontology/Location>  a  owl: Class;
        rdfs: label     "Location"@en ;
        rdfs: comment   "This class represents a location."@en.
#关系的定义
<http://purl.org/spar/cito/cites>  a  owl: ObjectProperty;
        rdfs: domain   <https://semopenalex.org/ontology/Work>;
        rdfs: range    <https://semopenalex.org/ontology/Work>;
        rdfs: comment  "This property specifies a cited work."@en;
        rdfs: label    "cites"@en .
<https://semopenalex.org/ontology/hasConcept>a owl: ObjectProperty;
        rdfs: domain   <https://semopenalex.org/ontology/Work>;
        rdfs: range    <https://semopenalex.org/ontology/Concept>;
        rdfs: comment  "This property specifies a concept."@en;
        rdfs: label    "has concept"@en .
<http://purl.org/dc/terms/creator>  a  owl: ObjectProperty;
        rdfs: domain   <https://semopenalex.org/ontology/Work>;
        rdfs: range    <https://semopenalex.org/ontology/Author>;
```

第4章 基于本体的知识图谱模式设计

```
        rdfs: comment "This property specifies the creator of a work."@en;
        rdfs: label  "creator"@en .
#属性的定义
<http://purl.org/dc/terms/title>  a  owl: DatatypeProperty;
        rdfs: domain  <https://semopenalex.org/ontology/Work>;
        rdfs: range  xsd: string ;
        rdfs: comment "This property specifies the title of a work."@en;
        rdfs: label  "title"@en .
<http://purl.org/dc/terms/created>  a  owl: DatatypeProperty;
        rdfs: domain [ a owl: Class;
        owl: unionOf(<https://semopenalex.org/ontology/Work>
               <https://semopenalex.org/ontology/Institution>
               <https://semopenalex.org/ontology/Concept>
               <https://semopenalex.org/ontology/Author>
            <https://semopenalex.org/ontology/Publisher>)];
        rdfs: range  xsd: date ;
        rdfs: comment "This property specifies the creation date of a
        resource."@en;
        rdfs: label  "created"@en .
```

(来源：https://github.com/metaphacts/semopenalex/blob/main/ontologies/semopenalex-ontology.ttl)

SemOpenAlex 还定义了研究主题词汇表，以规范本体中二元关系 hasConcept 的取值。例如，图 4.9 展示了 Computer science（计算机科学）主题下的部分子概念，它们的形式化描述见例 4.2，对应的 RDF 图见图 4.10。

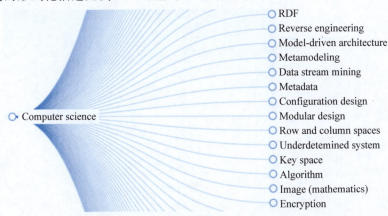

图 4.9 "计算机科学"（Computer science）研究主题词汇表（部分）

（来源：https://semopenalex.org/concept/C41008148）

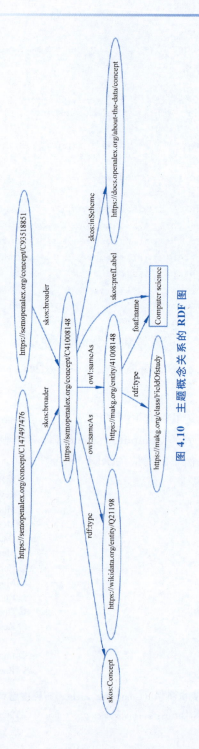

图 4.10 主题概念关系的 RDF 图

例 4.2 SemOpenAlex 的研究主题词汇表——计算机科学主题（部分）。

```
@prefix owl: <http://www.w3.org/2002/07/owl#>.
@prefix xsd: <http://www.w3.org/2001/XMLSchema#>.
@prefix skos: <http://www.w3.org/2004/02/skos/core#>.
@prefix rdfs: <http://www.w3.org/2000/01/rdf-schema#>.
@prefix rdf: <http://www.w3.org/1999/02/22-rdf-syntax-ns#>.
@prefix foaf: <http://xmlns.com/foaf/0.1/>.
<https://semopenalex.org/concept/C41008148> a skos: Concept;
owl: sameAs   <http://www.wikidata.org/entity/Q21198>,
              <https://makg.org/entity/41008148>;
skos: prefLabel   "Computer science"^^xsd: string;
skos: inScheme   <https://docs.openalex.org/about-the-data/concept>.
<https://makg.org/entity/41008148>
rdf: type   <https://makg.org/class/FieldOfStudy>;
foaf: name   "Computer science"^^xsd: string.
<https://semopenalex.org/concept/C147497476>
skos: broader   <https://semopenalex.org/concept/C41008148>.
<https://semopenalex.org/concept/C93518851>
skos: broader   <https://semopenalex.org/concept/C41008148>.
<https://semopenalex.org/concept/C2987255567>
skos: broader   <https://semopenalex.org/concept/C41008148>.
```

利用上述本体和主题词汇表，描述论文"Building a PubMed Knowledge Graph"的三元组如例 4.3 所示，论文所属的主题之一是"Knowledge graph"，是"Computer science"主题下的子主题之一。

例 4.3 描述一篇论文的 RDF 三元组。

```
@prefix xsd: <http://www.w3.org/2001/XMLSchema#>.
@prefix skos: <http://www.w3.org/2004/02/skos/core#>.
@prefix rdfs: <http://www.w3.org/2000/01/rdf-schema#>.
@prefix soa: <https://semopenalex.org/ontology/>.
@prefix dct: <http://purl.org/dc/terms/>.
@prefix rdf: <http://www.w3.org/1999/02/22-rdf-syntax-ns#>.
@prefix foaf: <http://xmlns.com/foaf/0.1/>.
<https://semopenalex.org/work/W3038003025> a soa: Work;
      dct: title      "Building a PubMed knowledge graph";
      dct: created    "2020-07-02"^^xsd: date;
      soa: hasConcept    <https://semopenalex.org/concept/C2987255567>;
      dct: creator    <https://semopenalex.org/author/A5022526821>.
```

```
<https://semopenalex.org/concept/C2987255567> a skos: Concept;
    skos: prefLabel  "Knowledge graph".
<https://semopenalex.org/author/A5022526821> a soa: Author;
foaf: name   "Xin Li".
<https://semopenalex.org/work/W4311860615><http://purl.org/spar/
cito/cites><https://semopenalex.org/work/W3038003025>.
<https://semopenalex.org/work/W4313573912><http://purl.org/spar/
cito/cites><https://semopenalex.org/work/W3038003025>.
<https://semopenalex.org/work/W4292452358><http://purl.org/spar/
cito/cites><https://semopenalex.org/work/W3038003025>.
```

（来源：https://semopenalex.org/sparql）

4.2.3 CS-KG 本体实例

CS-KG（computer science knowledge graph）是由意大利卡里亚里大学（University of Cagliari）的科研团队开发的计算机科学领域的学术知识图谱。CS-KG 含有 3.5 亿个 RDF 三元组，描述了约 1000 万个研究实体（research entity），包括"任务"（tasks）、"方法"（methods）和"材料"（materials）等。

CS-KG 的基本知识组织单元是"陈述"（cskg-ont：Statement），形式是 ＜subject，predicate，object＞，每个陈述有一个编号，如 cskg：statement_48289124。CS-KG 中的陈述共有约 4100 万个，从 670 万篇论文中抽出。CS-KG 通过自动流水线（pipeline）从文本中抽取实体和关系，用到的工具（cskg-ont：Tool）有 4 种：DyGIE＋＋、Stanford CoreNLP、CSO Classifier 和 PoS Tagger，见图 4.11。

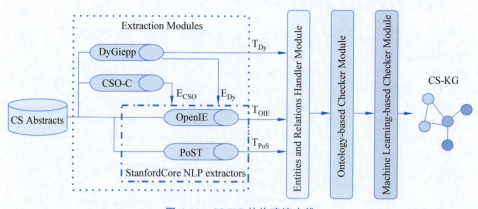

图 4.11 CS-KG 的构建流水线

CS-KG 描述"陈述"时采用了"RDF 具体化"(RDF reification)语法。图 4.12 描述了一个编号为 cskg：statement_466816 的陈述,其内容是<cskg：human_face_detection, skos：broader, cskg：computer_vision>,它从两篇论文中抽出,采用的工具是 DyGIEpp 和 OpenIE。

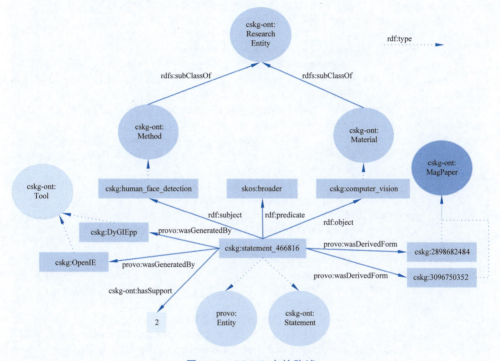

图 4.12　CS-KG 中的陈述

(来源：https://scholkg.kmi.open.ac.uk/cskg/documentation.php)

CS-KG 本体定义了 CS-KG 的模式,含有 11 个类和 179 个语义关系,部分定义见例 4.4 中的代码,其可视化见图 4.13。

例 4.4　CS-KG Ontology 的 OWL 描述代码(部分)。

```
@prefix dct: <http://purl.org/dc/terms/>.
@prefix owl: <http://www.w3.org/2002/07/owl#>.
@prefix rdf: <http://www.w3.org/1999/02/22-rdf-syntax-ns#>.
@prefix xsd: <http://www.w3.org/2001/XMLSchema#>.
@prefix rdfs: <http://www.w3.org/2000/01/rdf-schema#>.
@prefix cskg-ont: <http://scholkg.kmi.open.ac.uk/cskg/ontology#>.
@prefix cskg: <http://scholkg.kmi.open.ac.uk/cskg/resource/>.
```

```
@base <http://scholkg.kmi.open.ac.uk/cskg/ontology#>.
<http://scholkg.kmi.open.ac.uk/cskg/ontology#>
rdf: type    owl: Ontology ;
rdfs: comment   "The Computer Science Knowledge Graph Ontology models
entities and their relationships in the scholarly domain"@en ;
rdfs: label   "Computer Science Knowledge Graph Ontology" .
cskg-ont: ResearchEntity   rdf: type    owl: Class .
cskg-ont: Material          rdf: type    owl: Class ;
rdfs: subClassOf  cskg-ont: ResearchEntity ;
rdfs: comment     "An object that is processed, used, or returned by
methods in order to pursue a task. In computer science it is typically a
data set, a knowledge base, or a system. " .
cskg-ont: Method         rdf: type  owl: Class ;
rdfs: subClassOf  cskg-ont: ResearchEntity ;
rdfs: comment    "A specific approach, usually adopted to address a task.
Some examples include 'neural networks', 'support vector machine', and '
fuzzy logic'.".
cskg-ont: Task        rdf: type    owl: Class ;
rdfs: subClassOf  cskg-ont: ResearchEntity ;
rdfs: comment   "A piece of work to carry out, usually to solve a specific
challenge. Some examples include 'knowledge discovery', 'dimensionality
reduction', 'computer vision', and 'authentication'." .
cskg-ont: Statement       rdf: type       owl: Class ;
rdfs: subClassOf      rdf: Statement .
cskg-ont: hasSupport    rdf: type      owl: DatatypeProperty ;
                rdfs: domain     cskg-ont: Statement ;
                rdfs: range      rdfs: Literal ;
                rdfs: comment "This property indicates the number
of papers from where the predicate between subject and object comes
from." .
     cskg-ont: based-on      rdf: type  owl: ObjectProperty ;
              owl: inverseOf   cskg-ont: bases .
cskg-ont: based-onMethod    rdf: type   owl: ObjectProperty ;
          rdfs: subPropertyOf   cskg-ont: based-on ;
             owl: inverseOf    cskg-ont: methodBases ;
              rdf: type   owl: TransitiveProperty ;
             rdfs: domain  [ rdf: type owl: Class ;
              owl: unionOf ( cskg-ont: Material
                          cskg-ont: Method
                          cskg-ont: Task ) ] ;
             rdfs: range   cskg-ont: Method ;
              rdfs: comment    " It is designed based on the
following predicates extracted by the NLP pipeline: base, ground, found,
construe, build, establish" .
```

```
cskg-ont: MagPaper   rdf: type    owl: Class ;
                     rdfs: comment   "A paper indexed in the Microsoft
Academic Graph dataset" .
cskg-ont: hasDOI    rdf: type    owl: ObjectProperty ;
                    rdfs: domain   cskg-ont: MagPaper ;
                    rdfs: comment   "This property is used to link a paper
to its DOI"@en ;
                    rdfs: label    "hasDOI"@en .
cskg-ont: Tool      rdf: type    owl: Class ;
                    rdfs: comment "A base tool or sub-module of the CS-KG
pipeline used to extract triples from scientific text"@en .
    cskg: DyGIEpp    rdf: type    owl: NamedIndividual , cskg-ont: Tool ;
                     rdfs: comment "Entity represnting the tool DyGIEpp"@en .
cskg: OpenIE         rdf: type    owl: NamedIndividual , cskg-ont: Tool ;
rdfs: comment "The entity representin the tool Stanford Core NLP OpenIE"@en .
cskg: PoSTagger     rdf: type    owl: NamedIndividual , cskg-ont: Tool ;
rdfs: comment "The entity representing the module to build triples on top
of part-of-speech tags within the CS-KG pipeline"@en .
```

（来源：https://scholkg.kmi.open.ac.uk/cskg/ontology.html）

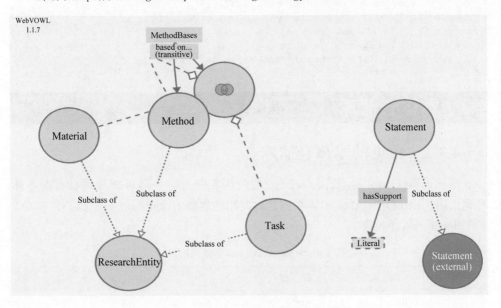

图 4.13　CS-KG 本体的可视化（部分）

（来源：https://service.tib.eu/webvowl/#file=CS-KG%20ontology.ttl）

例 4.5 给出通过 CS-KG 本体描述一个陈述的例子。这个陈述是＜cskg：robot，cskg-ont：based-onMethod，cskg：a_star_and_dijkstra_algorithm＞，从论文"A Multiple Mobile Robots Path Planning Algorithm Based on a Star and Dijkstra Algorithm"中抽出，采用的工具是 cskg：PoSTagger。

例 4.5 CS-KG 陈述的例子。

```
@prefix cskg: <http://scholkg.kmi.open.ac.uk/cskg/resource/>.
@prefix provo: <http://www.w3.org/ns/prov#>.
@prefix rdf: <http://www.w3.org/1999/02/22-rdf-syntax-ns#>.
@prefix xsd: <http://www.w3.org/2001/XMLSchema#>.
@prefix rdfs: <http://www.w3.org/2000/01/rdf-schema#>.
@prefix cskg-ont: <http://scholkg.kmi.open.ac.uk/cskg/ontology#>.
@prefix dct: <http://purl.org/dc/terms/>.
cskg: statement_48289124    rdf: type      cskg-ont: Statement, provo: Entity;
                            rdf: subject   cskg: robot;
                            rdf: predicate cskg-ont: based-onMethod;
                            rdf: object
cskg: a_star_and_dijkstra_algorithm;
cskg-ont: hasSupport   "1"^^xsd: integer;
provo: wasDerivedFrom cskg: 2182059131;
provo: wasGeneratedBy cskg: PoSTagger.
cskg: 2182059131          rdf: type cskg-ont: MagPaper;
dct: title    "a multiple mobile robots path planning algorithm based on a star and dijkstra algorithm" ;
cskg-ont: hasDOI   "https://doi.org/10.14257/ijsh.2014.8.3.07" .
```

4.3 本体仓储库

4.3.1 常见的本体仓储库

本体工程(Ontology Engineering)的最佳实践之一是尽可能复用已有的本体和词汇表。SemOpenAlex 本体在构建时复用的本体有 Dublin Core、CiTO、FOAF和 DBpedia 等，详见表 4.4。

表 4.4　SemOpenAlex 本体复用的本体

序号	本体	前缀	URI
1	Dublin Core	dcterms	http://purl.org/dc/terms/
2	CiTO	cito	http://purl.org/spar/cito/

续表

序号	本体	前缀	URI
3	FaBiO	fabio	http://purl.org/spar/fabio/
4	BiDO	bido	http://purl.org/spar/bido/
5	PRISM	prism	http://prismstandard.org/namespaces/basic/2.0/
6	DBpedia	dbo	https://dbpedia.org/ontology/
7	DBpedia	dbp	https://dbpedia.org/property/
8	FOAF	foaf	http://xmlns.com/foaf/0.1/
9	W3C ORG	org	http://www.w3.org/ns/org#
10	GeoNames	gn	https://www.geonames.org/ontology#

为促进本体的复用，西班牙马德里理工大学（Universidad Politécnica de Madrid）计算机工程学院的本体工程研究组（Ontology Engineering Group, OEG）于 2011 年 3 月启动关联开放词汇表（Linked Open Vocabularies, LOV）项目，建设了本体仓储库（ontology repositories），已收录各个领域的本体资源超过 800 个。

LOV 本体仓储库采用 VOAF（vocabulary of a friend）元数据和语义 Web 技术，主要提供本体的管护和搜索服务，其结构见图 4.14。

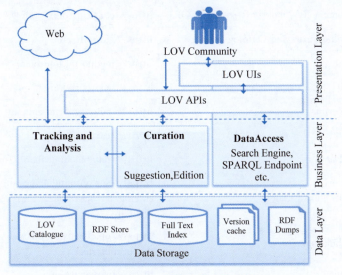

图 4.14 LOV 本体仓储库的结构

表4.5汇集了目前常见的本体仓储库和搜索服务,收集的词汇表的数量见表4.6。

表4.5 常见的本体仓储库和搜索服务

序号	名称	网址
1	Linked Open Vocabularies(LOV)	https://lov.linkeddata.es/dataset/lov/
2	Repository of Biomedical Ontologies(BioPortal)	https://bioportal.bioontology.org/
3	Open Biological and Biomedical Ontology Foundry	http://obofoundry.org/
4	SIFR BioPortal	https://bioportal.lirmm.fr/
5	AgroPortal	https://agroportal.lirmm.fr/
6	EcoPortal	https://ecoportal.lifewatch.eu/
7	Ontology Lookup Service (OLS)	https://www.ebi.ac.uk/ols4
8	Scholia	https://scholia.toolforge.org/ontology/
9	FAIRsharing	https://fairsharing.org/
10	中文开放知识图谱	http://openkg.cn/
11	Semantic Publishing and Referencing(SPAR)	http://www.sparontologies.net/
12	Gene Ontology (GO) Knowledge Base	https://geneontology.org/
13	ESIP's Community Ontology Repository(COR)	http://cor.esipfed.org/ont# /
14	FINnish Thesaurus and Ontology service	https://finto.fi/en/
15	MedPortal	http://medportal.bmicc.cn/
16	MatPortal	https://matportal.org/
17	IndustryPortal	http://industryportal.enit.fr/
18	EarthPortal	https://earthportal.eu/
19	DBpedia Databus	https://databus.dbpedia.org/ontologies
20	OntoUML/UFO Catalog	https://scs-ontouml.eemcs.utwente.nl/catalog/b663ca18-8085-44a7-bcfe-2c2b5ba1faa8
21	EU Vocabularies	https://op.europa.eu/en/web/eu-vocabularies
22	LiveSchema	http://liveschema.eu/

表 4.6　本体仓储库中词汇表的数量

序号	本体仓储库名称	词汇表数量
1	Linked Open Vocabularies(LOV)	822
2	Repository of Biomedical Ontologies(BioPortal)	1067
3	Open Biological and Biomedical Ontology Foundry	184
4	SIFR BioPortal	40
5	AgroPortal	158
6	EcoPortal	25
7	Ontology Lookup Service（OLS）	258
8	FINnish Thesaurus and Ontology service	49
9	MedPortal	60
10	MatPortal	27
11	IndustryPortal	99
12	LiveSchema	958

（调查时间：2023 年 9 月 23 日）

4.3.2　OntoPortal 联盟

OntoPortal(ontoportal.org)是用于构建本体仓储库的开源软件平台，最初由斯坦福生物医学信息学研究中心开发，目前由 OntoPortal 联盟（OntoPortal Alliance)社区维护。OntoPortal 联盟由各个领域的研究和基础设施团队组成，致力于科学领域本体仓储库的协作和推广工作。OntoPortal 联盟的成员主要来自生物医学、农学、生态学、材料科学和地球科学等领域，见图 4.15。

联盟成员之一的 BioPortal 是世界上最全面的生物医学本体仓储库，由美国斯坦福大学国家生物医学本体中心（National Center for Biomedical Ontology，NCBO)开发建设，其愿景是促进所有生物医学知识和数据以本体形式在互联网上传播，保障知识和数据的语义互操作性，促进语义技术在生物医学科学和临床上的应用。

AgroPortal 是农学及其相关领域的本体仓储库，由法国蒙彼利埃大学、美国斯

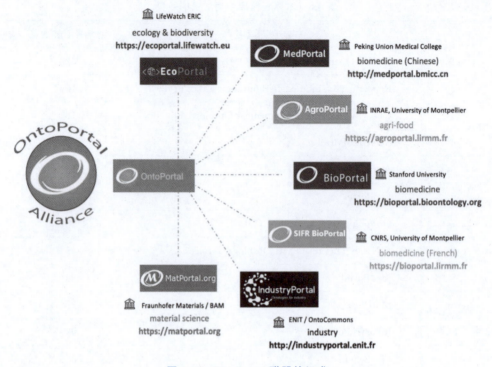

图 4.15 OntoPortal 联盟的组成

(来源：https://ontoportal.org/about/)

坦福大学和联合国粮农组织(FAO)联合建设。AgroPortal 平台利用了 BioPortal 的技术，实现本体资源的托管、搜索、版本控制、可视化、评价和推荐等服务。

EcoPortal 是欧洲生态学研究基础设施 LifeWatch ERIC(www.lifewatch.eu)的一项服务，用于访问和共享生态领域的语义资源，包括 OWL 本体、SKOS 词汇表和 RDF 数据集。

4.3.3 本体的 FAIR 水平评价

AgroPortal、SIFR BioPortal 和 IndustryPortal 等仓储库开展了本体的"FAIR 水平评价"(FAIRness assessment)工作，采用的都是 O'FAIRe(Ontology FAIRness evaluator)开源评估器。以 AgroPortal 为例，评价结果的总体情况见图 4.16。

对于植物本体(plant ontology)而言，它的 FAIR 水平分值是 354，总体符合率为 74%，具体到各个指标的得分情况见表 4.7。

第4章 基于本体的知识图谱模式设计

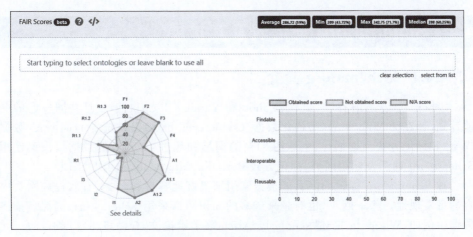

图 4.16　FAIR 水平评价结果

（来源：https://agroportal.lirmm.fr/）

表 4.7　植物本体的 FAIR 水平评价结果

FAIR	指　　标	得　分	失　分
可发现性	F1：本体及其元数据被分配了全局唯一且持久的标识符	33	8
	F2：本体具有丰富的元数据	25	2
	F3：本体元数据明确包含其描述本体的标识符	21	0
	F4：本体及其元数据在仓储库中注册或被编入索引	16	8
可获取性	A1：本体及其元数据借助标识符,可通过标准化的通信协议获取	37	6
	A1.1：该协议是免费、开放和通用的	28	0
	A1.2：必要时,该协议允许进行身份验证和授权过程	22	0
	A2：即使本体不再可获取,其元数据仍然可获取	20	0
互操作	I1：本体及其元数据使用通用的可共享的语言进行知识表示	42	2
	I2：本体及其元数据使用遵循 FAIR 原则的词汇表	10	22
	I3：本体或元数据含有对其他对象的限定引用	7	26
可重用	R1：本体及其元数据以多种准确且相关的属性被描述	7	27
	R1.1：本体及其元数据发布时伴有使用许可	37	0
	R1.2：本体及其元数据发布时伴有溯源信息	13	25
	R1.3：本体及其元数据符合相关标准	36	0

（来源：https://agroportal.lirmm.fr/ontologies/PO）

4.4 Schema.org 词汇表及其扩展

4.4.1 Schema.org 简介

Schema.org 是由谷歌、微软、Yahoo 和 Yandex 于 2011 年 6 月共同发起的一项计划,旨在为 Web 中的"结构化数据"(structured data)提供统一的词汇表(数据模型)和标记方式。据估计,全球约 31% 的网站和超过 1200 万的数据提供商使用 Schema.org 词汇表标记网页,标记方式有 RDFa、Microdata 和 JSON-LD。

被 Schema.org 标记的网页能被搜索引擎更好地解析和分类,有效提高网页内容的可发现性。除了网页,也有越来越多的知识图谱采用 Schema.org 词汇表描述数据。例如,Wikidata 描述"scholarly article"(学术论文,Q13442814)条目的三元组代码中使用了 schema:name、schema:description、schema:about、schema:version 和 schema:dateModified 等属性,详见例 4.6 和图 4.17。

例 4.6 Schema.org 词汇表在 Wikidata 知识图谱中的应用实例。

```
@prefix rdf:      <http://www.w3.org/1999/02/22-rdf-syntax-ns#>.
@prefix xsd:      <http://www.w3.org/2001/XMLSchema#>.
@prefix rdfs:     <http://www.w3.org/2000/01/rdf-schema#>.
@prefix owl:      <http://www.w3.org/2002/07/owl#>.
@prefix wikibase: <http://wikiba.se/ontology#>.
@prefix skos:     <http://www.w3.org/2004/02/skos/core#>.
@prefix schema:   <http://schema.org/>.
@prefix wd:       <http://www.wikidata.org/entity/>.
@prefix data:     <https://www.wikidata.org/wiki/Special:EntityData/>.
wd:Q13442814       a    wikibase:Item ;
rdfs:label         "scholarly article"@en ;
skos:prefLabel     "scholarly article"@en ;
schema:name        "scholarly article"@en ;
rdfs:label         "学术文章"@zh ;
skos:prefLabel     "学术文章"@zh ;
schema:name        "学术文章"@zh ;
schema:description
"article in an academic publication, usually peer reviewed"@en,
"学术出版物中的文章,通常经过同行评审"@zh-cn.
data:Q13442814     a    schema:Dataset ;
schema:about       wd:Q13442814 ;
schema:softwareVersion    "1.0.0" ;
schema:version     "1990889268"^^xsd:integer ;
schema:dateModified    "2023-10-13T15:18:27Z"^^xsd:dateTime .
```

(来源:https://www.wikidata.org/wiki/Special:EntityData/Q13442814.ttl)

第4章 基于本体的知识图谱模式设计

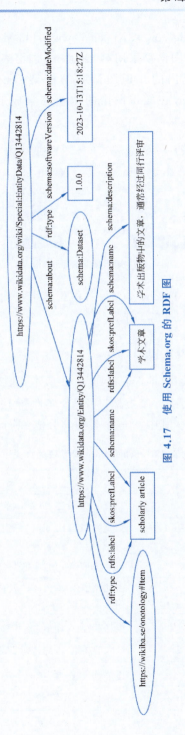

图 4.17 使用 Schema.org 的 RDF 图

YAGO(yago-knowledge.org)、KBpedia(www.kbpedia.org)和 Data Commons (datacommons.org)等知识图谱都采用 Schema.org 词汇表作为数据模型。在 IBM Research AI 研究中心提出的知识图谱归纳框架(knowledge graph induction framework)中,Schema.org 在知识图谱的构建和集成上也发挥着关键作用,见图 4.18。

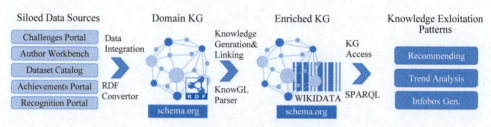

图 4.18 知识图谱的归纳框架

2015 年 4 月,W3C 成立 Schema.org 社区工作组,吸引更多的组织和人员参与 Schema.org 的扩展、协作和推广工作。

4.4.2 Schema.org 词汇表

2013 年 4 月,Schema.org 词汇表发布了 v1 版本,到 2024 年 2 月 12 日已发展到 v26.0。该最新版本含有 806 个类型、1474 个属性和 14 个数据类型,另有 90 个枚举类型和 480 个枚举值。其中,806 个类型共分成 11 个大类,见表 4.8。

表 4.8 Schema.org 词汇表的大类

序号	大 类	说 明
1	Person(人)	只有一个子类 Patient(病人)
2	Place(地点)	类别数量占比 8.48%,有"游客目的地""行政区域""市政结构"等子类
3	Product(产品)	占比 1.41%,有"车辆""药物"等 8 个子类
4	Organization(机构)	占比达到 21.3%,有"教育机构""研究机构""政府机构""图书馆"等子类
5	MedicalEntity(医疗实体)	占比超过 7%,有"医疗设备""药物类别"等子类
6	IntangibleEntity(无形实体)	最大的类别,占比达到 27.5%,有"语言""服务"等子类
7	Event(事件)	占比约 4%,有"展览""节日""编程马拉松"等子类
8	CreativeWork(作品)	占比 17.7%,有"论文""书籍""游戏""数据集"等子类

续表

序号	大 类	说 明
9	Action（活动）	占比11.6%，有"消费""评估""搜索""交易"等子类
10	BioChemEntity（生物化学实体）	有"化学物质""基因""分子实体""蛋白质"四个子类
11	Taxon（税收）	没有子类

（来源：https://www.schema.org/docs/schemas.html）

Schema.org 词汇表的所有类型形成一个概念的层次结构，最大的类是 Thing（https://schema.org/Thing），它有12个属性，具体见表4.9，它们的形式化定义见例4.7。这些属性已被其他子类广泛复用。

表 4.9 Thing 的属性

序号	属 性	类 型	说 明
1	additionalType	URL	实体的附加类型
2	alternateName	Text	实体的别名
3	description	Text	简介
4	disambiguatingDescription	Text	消除歧义说明
5	identifier	URL、Text 或其他	实体的唯一标识符
6	image	Text 或 ImageObject	实体的图像
7	mainEntityOfPage	URL 或 Creative Work	描述实体的网页或文档等
8	name	Text	名称
9	potentialAction	Action	相关活动
10	sameAs	URL	指向同一个实体的另外 URL
11	subjectOf	CreativeWork 或 Event	about 的逆属性
12	url	URL	实体的 URL

例 4.7 类 Thing 及其部分属性的定义。

```
@prefix schema: <https://schema.org/>.
@prefix rdf: <http://www.w3.org/1999/02/22-rdf-syntax-ns#>.
@prefix rdfs: <http://www.w3.org/2000/01/rdf-schema#>.
@prefix owl: <http://www.w3.org/2002/07/owl#>.
@prefix dc: <http://purl.org/dc/terms/>.
```

```
@prefix xml: <http://www.w3.org/XML/1998/namespace>.
@prefix xsd: <http://www.w3.org/2001/XMLSchema#>.
schema: Thing    a   rdfs: Class ;
        rdfs: label     "Thing" ;
        rdfs: comment    "The most generic type of item." .
schema: additionalType  a   rdf: Property ;
        rdfs: label     "additionalType" ;
        schema: domainIncludes   schema: Thing ;
        schema: rangeIncludes    schema: URL, schema: Text ;
        rdfs: subPropertyOf    rdf: type .
schema: alternateName   a   rdf: Property ;
        rdfs: label     "alternateName" ;
        schema: domainIncludes   schema: Thing ;
        schema: rangeIncludes    schema: Text ;
        rdfs: comment    "An alias for the item." .
schema: name    a   rdf: Property ;
        rdfs: label     "name" ;
        schema: domainIncludes   schema: Thing ;
        schema: rangeIncludes    schema: Text ;
        rdfs: comment    "The name of the item." ;
        rdfs: subPropertyOf    rdfs: label ;
        owl: equivalentProperty   dc: title .
schema: identifier   a   rdf: Property ;
        rdfs: label     "identifier" ;
        schema: domainIncludes   schema: Thing ;
        schema: rangeIncludes    schema: PropertyValue, schema: Text, schema: URL ;
        owl: equivalentProperty   dc: identifier .
```

(来源：https://github.com/schemaorg/schemaorg/blob/main/data/schema.ttl)

Schema.org 通过枚举类型进一步规范属性的取值。例如，枚举类 DayOfWeek 能够规范属性 dayOfWeek 的值，可以是 schema：Monday、schema：Tuesday、schema：Wednesday 等 7 个值之一，其定义见例 4.8 中的代码。

例 4.8　枚举类 DayOfWeek 的定义。

```
@prefix schema: <https://schema.org/>.
@prefix rdf: <http://www.w3.org/1999/02/22-rdf-syntax-ns#>.
@prefix rdfs: <http://www.w3.org/2000/01/rdf-schema#>.
@prefix owl: <http://www.w3.org/2002/07/owl#>.
@prefix dc: <http://purl.org/dc/terms/>.
@prefix xml: <http://www.w3.org/XML/1998/namespace>.
```

```
@prefix xsd: <http://www.w3.org/2001/XMLSchema#>.
schema: Intangible   a   rdfs: Class ;
     rdfs: label      "Intangible" ;
     rdfs: comment     "A utility class that serves as the umbrella for a number of 'intangible' things such as quantities, structured values, etc." ;
     rdfs: subClassOf    schema: Thing .
schema: Enumeration   a   rdfs: Class ;
     rdfs: label     "Enumeration" ;
     rdfs: comment     "Lists or enumerations—for example, a list of cuisines or music genres, etc." ;
     rdfs: subClassOf    schema: Intangible .
schema: DayOfWeek   a   rdfs: Class ;
     rdfs: label     "DayOfWeek" ;
     schema: contributor<https://schema.org/docs/collab/GoodRelationsClass>;
     rdfs: subClassOf    schema: Enumeration .
schema: Monday   a   schema: DayOfWeek ;
     rdfs: label    "Monday" ;
     schema: sameAs    <http://www.wikidata.org/entity/Q105>;
     rdfs: comment    "The day of the week between Sunday and Tuesday." .
schema: Tuesday   a   schema: DayOfWeek ;
     rdfs: label   "Tuesday" ;
     schema: sameAs  <http://www.wikidata.org/entity/Q127>;
     rdfs: comment   "The day of the week between Monday and Wednesday." .
schema: Wednesday   a   schema: DayOfWeek ;
     rdfs: label     "Wednesday" ;
     schema: sameAs   <http://www.wikidata.org/entity/Q128>;
     rdfs: comment   "The day of the week between Tuesday and Thursday." .
schema: Thursday   a   schema: DayOfWeek ;
     rdfs: label     "Thursday" ;
     schema: sameAs    <http://www.wikidata.org/entity/Q129>;
     rdfs: comment   "The day of the week between Wednesday and Friday." .
schema: Friday   a   schema: DayOfWeek ;
     rdfs: label    "Friday" ;
     schema: sameAs <http://www.wikidata.org/entity/Q130>;
     rdfs: comment   "The day of the week between Thursday and Saturday." .
schema: Saturday   a   schema: DayOfWeek ;
     rdfs: label    "Saturday" ;
     schema: sameAs    <http://www.wikidata.org/entity/Q131>;
     rdfs: comment     "The day of the week between Friday and Sunday." .
```

```
schema: Sunday    a    schema: DayOfWeek ;
    rdfs: label    "Sunday" ;
    schema: sameAs    <http://www.wikidata.org/entity/Q132>;
    rdfs: comment    "The day of the week between Saturday and Monday." .
schema: dayOfWeek    a    rdf: Property ;
    rdfs: label    "dayOfWeek" ;
    schema: domainIncludes    schema: OpeningHoursSpecification ;
    schema: rangeIncludes    schema: DayOfWeek ;
    rdfs: comment    "The day of the week for which these opening hours
are valid." .
```

(来源：https://github.com/schemaorg/schemaorg/blob/main/data/schema.ttl)

在 Schema.org 词汇表的基础上构建知识图谱的模式层，需要进行一定的"定制"（customization）处理。例如，YAGO 通过 W3C SHACL 技术（详见第 7 章）明确类的属性及其约束，例子见例 4.9 的代码。

例 4.9　YAGO 知识图谱的模式层：CreativeWork 和 Book（部分）。

```
@prefix ys: <http://yago-knowledge.org/schema#>.
@prefix yago: <http://yago-knowledge.org/resource/>.
@prefix rdf: <http://www.w3.org/1999/02/22-rdf-syntax-ns#>.
@prefix xsd: <http://www.w3.org/2001/XMLSchema#>.
@prefix rdfs: <http://www.w3.org/2000/01/rdf-schema#>.
@prefix owl: <http://www.w3.org/2002/07/owl#>.
@prefix schema: <http://schema.org/>.
@prefix wd: <http://www.wikidata.org/entity/>.
@prefix wdt: <http://www.wikidata.org/prop/direct/>.
@prefix sh: <http://www.w3.org/ns/shacl#>.
schema: CreativeWork rdf: type rdfs: Class, sh: NodeShape ;
    ys: fromClass    wd: Q17537576, wd: Q386724 ;
    sh: property    ys: CreativeWork_property_20,
ys: CreativeWork_property_27, ys: CreativeWork_property_21,
ys: CreativeWork_property_38, ys: CreativeWork_property_28,
ys: CreativeWork_property_19 ;
    rdfs: subClassOf    schema: Thing .
ys: CreativeWork_property_20    sh: path    schema: award ;
    sh: node    yago: Award ;
    ys: fromProperty    wdt: P166 .
ys: CreativeWork_property_21    sh: path    schema: author ;
    sh: or    ys: list_22 ;
        ys: fromProperty    wdt: P170, wdt: P50 .
```

```
ys: CreativeWork_property_27   sh: path   schema: contentLocation ;
    sh: node   schema: Place ;
    ys: fromProperty   wdt: P840 .
ys: CreativeWork_property_28   sh: path   schema: dateCreated ;
    sh: or   ys: list_29 ;
    sh: maxCount   1 ;
    ys: fromProperty   wdt: P571 .
ys: CreativeWork_property_38   sh: path   schema: inLanguage ;
    sh: node   schema: Language ;
    ys: fromProperty   wdt: P407 .
schema: Book   rdf: type   rdfs: Class, sh: NodeShape ;
    ys: fromClass   wd: Q571 ;
    sh: property   ys: Book_property_39, ys: Book_property_40,
ys: Book_property_42, ys: Book_property_41,
ys: Book_property_48 ;
    rdfs: subClassOf schema: CreativeWork .
ys: Book_property_39   sh: path   schema: isbn ;
    sh: datatype   xsd: string ;
    sh: maxCount   1 ;
    ys: fromProperty   wdt: P957, wdt: P212 ;
    sh: pattern "^(97[89]-([0-57]-(\\d-\\d{7}|\\d\\d-\\d{6}|\\d\\d\\d-\\d{5}|\\d{4}-\\d{4}|\\d{5}-\\d\\d\\d|\\d{6}-\\d\\d|\\d{7}-\\d)|[89]\\d-(\\d-\\d{6}|\\d\\d-\\d{5}|\\d\\d\\d-\\d{4}|\\d{4}-\\d\\d\\d|\\d{5}-\\d\\d|\\d{6}-\\d)|[69]\\d\\d\\d-(\\d-\\d{5}|\\d\\d-\\d{4}|\\d\\d\\d-\\d\\d\\d|\\d{4}-\\d\\d|\\d{5}-\\d)|99[0-8]\\d-\\d-\\d{4}|99[0-8]\\d-\\d\\d-\\d{3}|99[0-8]\\d-\\d\\d\\d-\\d\\d|99[0-8]\\d-\\d{4}-\\d|999\\d\\d-\\d-\\d\\d|999\\d\\d-\\d\\d-\\d|999\\d\\d-\\d\\d\\d-\\d)-\\d|\\d{9}(\\d|X))|(\\d{1,5}-\\d{1,7}-\\d{1,6}-[0-9X])$" .
```

（来源：https://yago-knowledge.org/downloads）

4.4.3　cnSchema 词汇表

cnSchema 是一个基于社区维护的开放知识图谱模式标准规范，由 OpenKG 管理和维护，为中文领域的知识图谱构建提供一个基础的、共享的和可复用的 Schema 参考标准。

cnSchema 由来自清华大学、浙江大学、北京大学、复旦大学、东南大学、南京大学、英国阿伯丁大学等十多所国内外高校的计算机科学专家，以及微软亚洲研究院、海知智能、狗尾草科技、文因互联等企业共同发起、建立与维护，并得到 Schema.org 的支持。

cnSchema 词汇表包含上千种概念分类、数据类型、属性和关系等常用概念定义，一些属性的定义见例 4.10。

例 4.10 cnSchema 中部分属性的定义（JSON-LD 格式）。

```
{ "@context": { "@vocab": "http://cnschema.org/" },
  "@graph": [
{ "@id": "http://cnschema.org/affiliation",
       "alternateName": [],
       "category": "property",
       "description": "An organization that this person is affiliated with. For example, a school/university, a club, or a team.",
       "descriptionZh": "人所属的组织(例如学校/大学,俱乐部或团队)",
       "name": "affiliation",
       "nameZh": "所属机构",
       "schemaorgUrl": "http://schema.org/affiliation",
       "supersededBy": "",
       "version": 3.2,
       "wikidataName": "affiliation",
       "wikidataUrl": "http://www.wikidata.org/entity/P1416",
       "wikipediaUrl": "" },
{ "@id": "http://cnschema.org/album",
       "alternateName": [],
       "category": "property",
       "description": "A music album.",
       "descriptionZh": "将一定数量以上的歌曲或乐曲集结在一起,并对外发行的一种媒体类型",
       "name": "album",
       "nameZh": "专辑",
       "schemaorgUrl": "http://schema.org/album",
       "supersededBy": "",
       "version": 3.2,
       "wikidataName": "",
       "wikidataUrl": "",
       "wikipediaUrl": "https://en.wikipedia.org/wiki/Album" },
  { "@id": "http://cnschema.org/author",
       "alternateName": [],
       "category": "property",
       "description": "The author of this content or rating. Please note that author is special in that HTML 5 provides a special mechanism for indicating authorship via the rel tag. That is equivalent to this and may be used interchangeably.",
       "descriptionZh": "此内容或评分的作者。",
```

```
              "name": "author",
              "nameZh": "作者",
              "schemaorgUrl": "http://schema.org/author",
              "supersededBy": "",
              "version": 3.2,
              "wikidataName": "author",
              "wikidataUrl": "http://www.wikidata.org/entity/P50",
              "wikipediaUrl": "https://en.wikipedia.org/wiki/Author"   }
]}
```

(来源：https://github.com/cnschema/cnSchema/blob/master/data/releases/3.4/cns-core.jsonld)

为支持 cnSchema 的应用，OpenKG 开发了开源工具 EasySchema，帮助用户基于 cnSchema 定制、扩展和编辑自己的模式，并生成相关联的三元组文件。

目前，在中文开放知识图谱网站 OpenKG.CN 中，已有 10 多个知识图谱采用 cnSchema，包括"浙江公共图书馆知识图谱"、"《三体》人物关系知识图谱"和"基于 CNSchema 的城市知识图谱"等。其中，基于 CNSchema 的城市知识图谱中的部分数据见例 4.11。

例 4.11　基于 CNSchema 的城市知识图谱的部分三元组。

```
@prefix ukg:  <http://urbankg.org/>.
@prefix cns:  <http://cnschema.org/>.
<http://urbankg.org/SubWayTrip/317428>
       <http://www.w3.org/2000/01/rdf-schema#subClassOf>
                                  <http://cnschema.org/event>;
       cns: attendee     <http://urbankg.org/tcardholder/2400661248>;
       cns: endDate      "2015/04/16";
       cns: endTime      "19: 46: 46";
       cns: fromLocation <http://cnschema.org/subwaystation/064>;
       cns: startDate    "2015/04/16";
       cns: startTime    "12: 32: 18";
       cns: toLocation   <http://cnschema.org/subwaystation/064>.
<http://urbankg.org/SubWayTrip/168221>
       <http://www.w3.org/2000/01/rdf-schema#subClassOf>
                                  <http://cnschema.org/event>;
       cns: attendee     <http://urbankg.org/tcardholder/2202986562>;
       cns: endDate      "2015/04/16";
       cns: endTime      "09: 02: 53";
```

```
            cns: fromLocation  <http://cnschema.org/subwaystation/137>;
            cns: startDate      "2015/04/16";
            cns: startTime      "08: 52: 17";
            cns: toLocation     <http://cnschema.org/subwaystation/162>.
<http://urbankg.org/tcardholder/2104512013>
            <http://www.w3.org/2000/01/rdf-schema#subClassOf>
                                <http://cnschema.org/person>;
            <http://www.w3.org/2001/vcard-rdf/3.0#UID>"2104512013" .
```

（来源：http://data.openkg.cn/dataset/urbankg）

4.5　CODO 本体构建实例

4.5.1　CODO 本体模型

CODO(Ontology for collection and analysis of COviD-19 data)是用于描述 COVID-19 疫情数据的本体模型，由印度班加罗尔统计研究所开发。到 2023 年 3 月，CODO 已发展到 1.5 版，含 399 个类、214 个关系、124 个属性和 732 个实例数据。

作为 CODO 知识图谱的模式层，CODO 复用了 Schema.org 和 FOAF 等本体，其模型见图 4.19，形式化描述代码见例 4.12。

例 4.12　CODO 本体中"病人"(Patient)类的定义及其实例数据。

```
@prefix : <http://w3id.org/codo#>.
@prefix owl: <http://www.w3.org/2002/07/owl#>.
@prefix rdf: <http://www.w3.org/1999/02/22-rdf-syntax-ns#>.
@prefix xml: <http://www.w3.org/XML/1998/namespace>.
@prefix xsd: <http://www.w3.org/2001/XMLSchema#>.
@prefix rdfs: <http://www.w3.org/2000/01/rdf-schema#>.
@base <http://w3id.org/codo>.
<http://w3id.org/codo#>   rdf: type   owl: Ontology ;
      owl: versionIRI   <http://w3id.org/codo/1.5>;
      <http://purl.org/dc/terms/created>   "2020-04-27T10: 00: 00"^^xsd: dateTime ;
      <http://purl.org/dc/terms/creator>
"Biswanath Dutta (Indian Statistical Institute, India)"@en ,
            "Michael DeBellis (Semantic Web Consultant, USA)"@en ;
      <http://purl.org/dc/terms/license>
"https://creativecommons.org/licenses/by/4.0/"^^xsd: anyURI ;
            <http://purl.org/dc/terms/publisher>   "Indian Statistical Institute"@en ;
```

```
        <http://purl.org/dc/terms/title>    "An Ontology for Representation
and Publication of COVID-19 Cases and Patient Information"@en ;
        <http://www.isibang.ac.in/ns/mod#browsingUI>
"http://www.isibang.ac.in/ns/codo"^^xsd: anyURI .
###https://schema.org/Patient
<https://schema.org/Patient>    rdf: type    owl: Class ;
            rdfs: subClassOf    <http://xmlns.com/foaf/0.1/Person>,
                            [ rdf: type owl: Restriction ;
                                    owl: onProperty : hasDiagnosis ;
                                    owl: someValuesFrom : Diagnosis ] ;
            rdfs: label    "Patient"@en .
###http://w3id.org/codo#Diagnosis
: Diagnosis    rdf: type    owl: Class ;
            rdfs: comment "SCTID: 439401001"@en , "identifying the
nature or cause of some phenomenon."@en .
###http://w3id.org/codo#COVID-19Diagnosis
: COVID-19Diagnosis rdf: type owl: Class ;
            rdfs: subClassOf : Diagnosis ;
            rdfs: label "COVID-19 Diagnosis"@en .
###http://w3id.org/codo#hasDiagnosis
: hasDiagnosis rdf: type owl: ObjectProperty ;
            owl: inverseOf : isDiagnosisFor ;
            rdfs: domain    <https://schema.org/Patient>;
            rdfs: range     : Diagnosis ;
            rdfs: comment  "The diagnosis details of a patient."@en ;
            rdfs: label    "has diagnosis"@en .
###http://w3id.org/codo#hadCovidTest
: hadCovidTest    rdf: type    owl: DatatypeProperty ,
                            owl: FunctionalProperty ;
        rdfs: domain   <http://xmlns.com/foaf/0.1/Person>;
        rdfs: range    xsd: boolean .
###http://w3id.org/codo#p000001
: p000001    rdf: type    owl: NamedIndividual ,    : DiagnosedWithCovid ,
                : Man , : TestData ,
                <http://xmlns.com/foaf/0.1/Agent>,
                <http://xmlns.com/foaf/0.1/Person>,
                <https://schema.org/Patient>;
        : hasDiagnosis : P000001Diagnosis ;
        : hasSymptom  : Fever , : URTI ;
        : hasTestResult  : P000001-Vitals1 ;
        : mostRecentTestResult  : P000001-Vitals1 ;
        <https://pending.schema.org/gender>  : Male ;
        : hadCovidTest    "true"^^xsd: boolean ;
        : hasID    "T1" .
```

(来源: https://www.isibang.ac.in/ns/codo/ontology.ttl)

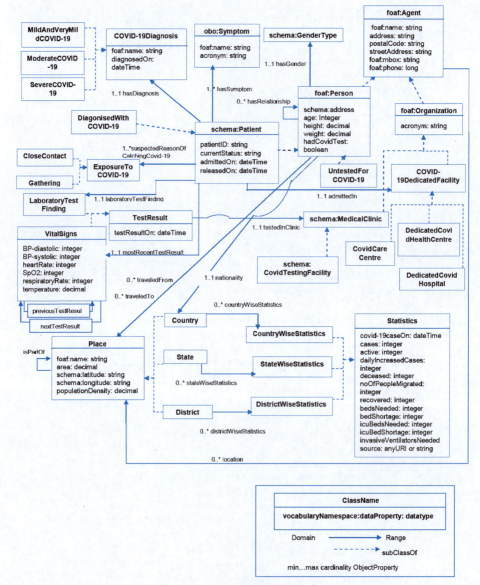

图 4.19 CODO 本体模型（1.0 版）

4.5.2 CODO 本体的构建过程

CODO 本体的构建过程如图 4.20 所示，包括的主要步骤如下：
① 明确本体构建的目的；

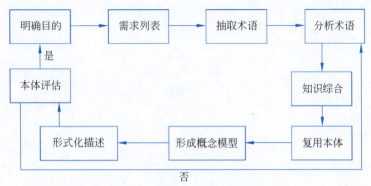

图 4.20 CODO 本体的构建过程

② 通过"问题列表"细化需求；
③ 抽取术语(如"病人""医生"等)；
④ 分析术语；
⑤ 通过知识综合形成术语的层次结构；
⑥ 复用本体(如 Schema.org 词汇表)；
⑦ 形成概念模型(如图 4.19 所示)；
⑧ 形式化描述(采用 OWL DL 和 Protégé 工具,如例 4.12 所示)；
⑨ 本体评估。

该构建过程源于本体构建的 YAMO(yet another methodology for ontology)方法框架,见图 4.21。YAMO 是由印度班加罗尔统计研究所提出的一种新型本体构建方法,具有"自顶向下"(top-down)和"自下而上"(bottom-up)的双重属性。

4.5.3　CODO 本体的 FAIR 化实践

CODO 本体是在 FAIR 原则指导下开发的,相关的 FAIR 化实践主要体现在如下几方面：

(1) 采用开放许可(license)。在 CODO 本体元数据中(见例 4.12)声明的许可是 CC BY 4.0。

(2) 将词汇表文件及相关资源存放到开源软件托管平台 GitHub 中,网址是 https://github.com/biswanathdutta/CODO,其中提供了各个版本(v1.0、v1.2 和 v1.3)的 OWL 文件。

(3) 为词汇表和术语分配持久的 IRI 标识符,IRI 是 HTTP 可解析的。采用 w3id-org(http://w3id.org)标识符解决方案,CODO 本体的 IRI 是 https://w3id.

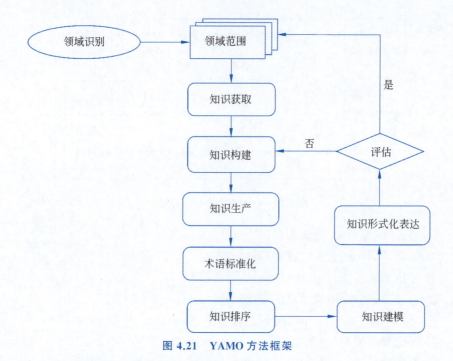

图 4.21 YAMO 方法框架

org/codo♯,解析时重定向到本体的主页,URL 为 https://www.isibang.ac.in/ns/codo/index.html。

(4) 在本体的主页提供多种格式的本体文件,包括 JSON-LD、RDF/XML、N-Triple 和 Turtle。

(5) 为词汇表添加元数据,包括作者、版本、发布者、URL 和许可等,见例 4.12。

(6) 在 BioPortal 本体仓储库中注册词汇表,CODO 本体的网页是:

https://bioportal.bioontology.org/ontologies/CODO

参 考 文 献

[1] Ontology (information science)[EB/OL].[2024-05-15]. https://en.wikipedia.org/wiki/Ontology_(information_science).

[2] FATIMA A A, CHAN H Y, HOON G K. From ontology to knowledge graph trend: Ontology as foundation layer for knowledge graph[C]. Proceedings of the Conference on Knowledge Graphs and Semantic Web,2022:330-340.

第4章 基于本体的知识图谱模式设计

[3] NANDANA M, TIWARI S M, ENGUIX C F, et al. Text2KGBench: A benchmark for ontology-driven knowledge graph generation from text[J]. ArXiv abs/2308.02357, 2023.

[4] SIMON J D C, ALEJANDRA N, MAGAGNA B, et al. Ten simple rules for making a vocabulary FAIR[J]. PLoS Computational Biology, 2021(6): 15.1-15.15.

[5] 朱妍昕,徐维,王霞,等.基于 FAIR 原则的循证医学文献本体构建——以哮喘药物治疗文献本体为例[J].情报理论与实践,2022,45(1): 187-195.

[6] MICHAEL F, LAMPRECHT D, KRAUSE J T, et al. SemOpenAlex: The scientific landscape in 26 billion RDF triples[J]. ArXiv abs/2308.03671, 2023.

[7] DANILO D, FRANCESCO O, RECUPERO R, et al. CS-KG: A large-scale knowledge graph of research entities and claims in computer science[C]. In: The Semantic Web-ISWC 2022. Lecture Notes in Computer Science, Springer, Cham, 13489: 678-696.

[8] VANDENBUSSCHE P Y, GHISLAIN A A, MARÍA P V, et al. Linked open vocabularies (LOV): A gateway to reusable semantic vocabularies on the Web[J]. Semantic Web, 2014(8): 437-452.

[9] WHETZEL P L, NOY N F, SHAH N H, et al. BioPortal: Enhanced functionality via new web services from the national center for biomedical ontology to access and use ontologies in software applications[J]. Nucleic Acids Res, 2011(6): W541-5.

[10] JONQUET C, TOULET A, ARNAUD E, et al. AgroPortal: A vocabulary and ontology repository for agronomy[J]. Computers and Electronics in Agriculture, 2018, 144: 126-143.

[11] XENI K, VAIRA L, TOMASSINO P, et al. EcoPortal: An environment for FAIR semantic resources in the ecological domain[C]. Joint Ontology Workshops, 2021.

[12] FUMAGALLI M, BOFFO M, SHI D, et al. LiveSchema: Gateway towards learning on knowledge graph schemas[J]. ArXiv, abs/2207.06112.2022,2022.

[13] AMDOUNI E, BOUAZZOUNI S, JONQUET C. O'FAIRe: ontology FAIRness evaluator in the AgroPortal semantic resource repository[C]. 19th Extended Semantic Web Conference, 2022.

[14] Schema.org[EB/OL]. [2024-05-15].https://en.wikipedia.org/wiki/Schema.org.

[15] An introduction to knowledge graphs[EB/OL]. [2024-05-15]. https://ai.stanford.edu/blog/introduction-to-knowledge-graphs/.

[16] MIHINDUKULASOORIYA N, SAVA M, ROSSIELLO G, et al. Knowledge graph induction enabling recommending and trend analysis: a corporate research community use case[C]. International Workshop on the Semantic Web, 2022.

[17] DUTTA B, DEBELLIS M. CODO: An ontology for collection and analysis of COVID-19 Data[C]. 12th International Conference. Conf. on Knowledge Engineering and Ontology Development, 2020.

[18] DEBELLIS M, DUTTA B. From ontology to knowledge graph with agile methods: The case of COVID-19 CODO knowledge graph [J]. International Journal of Web Information Systems, 2022, 18(5/6): 432-452.

[19] ABDUL S, SALWANA E, NAZIR M, et al. Comparative analysis of methodologies for domain ontology development: A systematic review [J]. International Journal of Advanced Computer Science and Applications, 2020, 11(5): 99-108.

[20] DUTTA B, CHATTERJEE U, MADALLI D. YAMO: Yet another methodology for large-scale faceted ontology construction[J]. Journal of Knowledge Management, 2015, 19 (2): 6-24.

第5章 知识图谱的查询语言

5.1 知识图谱的访问方式

5.1.1 4种主要的访问方式

知识图谱为分散、异构的各类数据源提供统一的知识视图,进而实现海量数据的一站式浏览、查询、分析、挖掘和应用,见图 5.1。RDF 数据分析包括数据立方(data cube)分析、统计分析和质量分析等,见图 5.2。任何数据分析都要获取知识图谱中的数据,这要求应用程序能高效、灵活地访问知识图谱系统。对于 RDF 知识图谱系统,主要的访问方式有 4 种,分别是语义 Web 查询语言 SPARQL、关键词搜索、交互访问(浏览、分面搜索等)和自然语言访问(如问答系统等),都要依赖于 SPARQL 查询语言,见图 5.3。

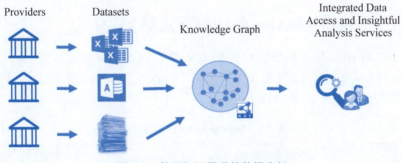

图 5.1 基于知识图谱的数据分析

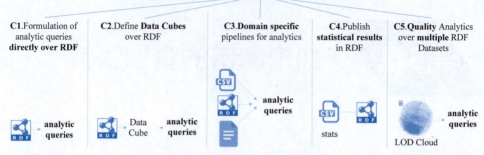

图 5.2　RDF 数据分析的种类

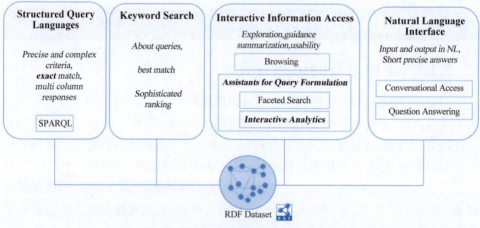

图 5.3　RDF 知识图谱的主要访问方式

5.1.2　SemOpenAlex 的访问方式举例

SemOpenAlex 学术知识图谱提供了多种访问方式。截至 2024 年 5 月初，SemOpenAlex 包含超过 300 亿个 RDF 三元组，各类实体的个数超过 3.3 亿个，见表 5.1。

表 5.1　SemOpenAlex 的实体个数

序　号	实体类型	实体个数
1	成果（work）	2.45 亿
2	作者（author）	0.93 亿

续表

序 号	实 体 类 型	实体个数
3	机构(institution)	10.7 万
4	数据源(source)	24.8 万
5	主题(topic)	6.5 万
6	出版机构(publisher)	1.0 万
7	资助机构(funder)	3.2 万

SemOpenAlex 为每个实体分配了 IRI，并提供 IRI 解析（IRI Resolution）服务。例如，论文"Building a PubMed Knowledge Graph"的 IRI 为

https://semopenalex.org/work/W3038003025

浏览器可以通过这个 IRI 直接访问到实体的全部信息，见图 5.4。在页面中，还包含相关论文的链接，体现了关联数据原则。

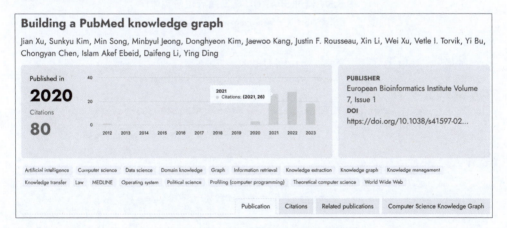

图 5.4 浏览器通过 IRI 访问实体

（来源：https://semopenalex.org/work/W3038003025）

还可以利用 IRI，构建 SPARQL 查询（见例 5.1），通过 SPARQL 查询端点获取实体的相关信息，见图 5.5。

例 5.1 关于实体的 SPARQL 查询（SELECT 查询或 DESCRIBE 查询）。

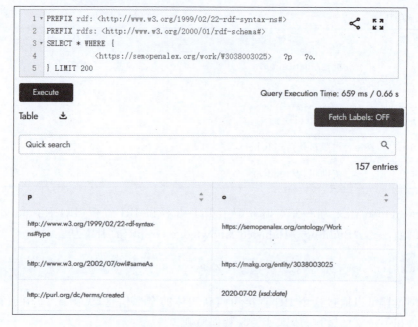

图 5.5　通过 SPARQL 查询端点访问实体

（来源：https://semopenalex.org/sparql）

```
PREFIX rdf: <http://www.w3.org/1999/02/22-rdf-syntax-ns#>
PREFIX rdfs: <http://www.w3.org/2000/01/rdf-schema#>
SELECT * WHERE {
         <https://semopenalex.org/work/W3038003025>?p ?o.
} LIMIT 200
```

或者：

```
DESCRIBE <https://semopenalex.org/work/W3038003025>
```

通过 SPARQL 查询端点能够构造复杂的查询，以获取有价值的信息。例 5.2 给出的查询是检索出 2024 年 Knowledge graph 领域发表的论文（前 100 篇）。

例 5.2　复杂的 SPARQL 查询如下所示。

```
PREFIX xsd: <http://www.w3.org/2001/XMLSchema#>
PREFIX rdf: <http://www.w3.org/1999/02/22-rdf-syntax-ns#>
PREFIX rdfs: <http://www.w3.org/2000/01/rdf-schema#>
```

```
PREFIX fabio: <http://purl.org/spar/fabio/>
PREFIX dcterms: <http://purl.org/dc/terms/>
PREFIX soa: <https://semopenalex.org/ontology/>
PREFIX skos: <http://www.w3.org/2004/02/skos/core#>
SELECT DISTINCT ?paperTitle ?paper ?oaUrl WHERE {
        ?paper fabio: hasPublicationYear "2024"^^xsd: integer .
        ?paper soa: hasConcept < https://semopenalex. org/concept/
        C2987255567> .
        <https://semopenalex.org/concept/C2987255567>
skos: prefLabel    "Knowledge graph"^^xsd: string .
        ?paper dcterms: title ?paperTitle .
        ?paper soa: hasOpenAccess ?openAccess .
        ?openAccess soa: oaUrl ?oaUrl .
} LIMIT 100
```

针对不同类别的实体，SemOpenAlex 提供了"关键词搜索"界面，见图 5.6。还可以根据主题(topic)汇聚相关的出版物，例如 Knowledge Graph 主题下已有 9629 个出版物，见图 5.7。

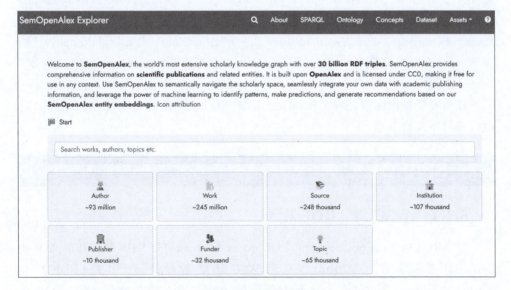

图 5.6　关键词搜索

（来源：https://semopenalex.org/resource/semopenalex：UniversalSearch)

SemOpenAlex 共设有 65073 个主题，分成 19 个领域，分别是"艺术"(art)、"生物

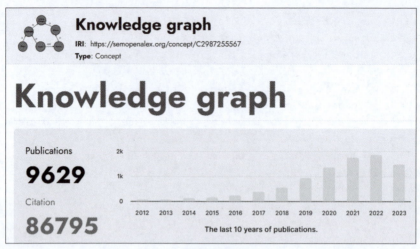

图 5.7　根据主题进行查询

(来源：https://semopenalex.org/concept/C2987255567)

学"(biology)、"商科"(business)、"化学"(chemistry)、"计算机科学"(computer science)、"经济学"(economics)、"工程"(engineering)、"环境科学"(environmental science)、"地理"(geography)、"地质学"(geology)、"历史"(history)、"材料科学"(materials science)、"数学"(mathematics)、"医学"(medicine)、"哲学"(philosophy)、"物理学"(physics)、"政治学"(political science)、"心理学"(psychology)和"社会学"(sociology)。

作为开放知识图谱，SemOpenAlex 定期更新 RDF 数据文件(RDF dump)，在 CC0 许可下免费下载。

5.2　SPARQL

5.2.1　W3C SPARQL 标准

SPARQL(sparql protocol and RDF query language)是 RDF 数据和语义 Web 的结构化查询语言。SPARQL 1.0 由 W3C RDF 数据访问工作组(RDF Data Access Working Group)于 2008 年 1 月发布，包括 3 个独立的规范：SPARQL 查询语言，查询结果 XML 格式规范，SPARQL HTTP 规范。

2013 年 3 月，W3C SPARQL 工作组发布 SPARQL 1.1 标准，含 11 个文档，见表 5.2。

表 5.2　W3C SPARQL 1.1 标准的组成

序号	标准名称	说明
1	SPARQL 1.1 Overview	总体介绍
2	SPARQL 1.1 Query Language	RDF 查询语言
3	SPARQL 1.1 Update	RDF 更新语言
4	SPARQL 1.1 Service Description	描述 SPARQL 服务(即查询端点)的词汇表
5	SPARQL 1.1 Federated Query	多个 SPARQL 端点/服务的联合查询
6	SPARQL 1.1 Query Results JSON Format	查询结果 JSON 格式规范
7	SPARQL 1.1 Query Results CSV and TSV Formats	查询结果 CSV 和 TSV 格式规范
8	SPARQL Query Results XML Format (Second Edition)	查询结果 XML 格式规范(第二版)
9	SPARQL 1.1 Entailment Regimes	在推理环境（RDFS 和 OWL）中使用 SPARQL 1.1 的规则
10	SPARQL 1.1 Protocol	向 SPARQL 服务发送查询和更新请求的规范
11	SPARQL 1.1 Graph Store HTTP Protocol	通过 HTTP 管理 RDF 图

(来源：https://www.w3.org/2009/sparql/wiki/Main_Page)

2023 年 9 月，W3C RDF Star 工作组发布了 SPARQL 1.2 规范的工作草案 (W3C Working Draft)，主要文档见表 5.3。

表 5.3　W3C SPARQL 1.2 规范的组成

序号	规范名称	说明
1	SPARQL 1.2 Query Language	RDF 查询语言
2	SPARQL 1.2 Update	RDF 更新语言
3	SPARQL 1.2 Service Description	描述 SPARQL 服务的词汇表
4	SPARQL 1.2 Federated Query	多个 SPARQL 端点/服务的联合查询
5	SPARQL 1.2 Query Results JSON Format	查询结果 JSON 格式规范
6	SPARQL 1.2 Query Results CSV and TSV Formats	查询结果 CSV 和 TSV 格式规范
7	SPARQL 1.2 Query Results XML Format	查询结果 XML 格式规范

续表

序号	规范名称	说　明
8	SPARQL 1.2 Entailment Regimes	在推理环境中使用 SPARQL 的规则
9	SPARQL 1.2 Protocol	向 SPARQL 服务发送查询和更新请求的规范
10	SPARQL 1.2 Graph Store Protocol	通过 HTTP 管理 RDF 图

(来源：https://www.w3.org/groups/wg/rdf-star/publications/)

5.2.2　SPARQL 的基本语法

SPARQL 查询涉及的基本概念如下。

定义 5.1　RDF 三元组(RDF triple)：给定一个 IRI 集合 R、空结点集合 B 和文字描述集合 L，一个 RDF 三元组是 (s,p,o)，其中 $s \in R \cup B, p \in R, o \in R \cup B \cup L$。

定义 5.2　三元组模式(triple pattern)：三元组模式 $tp=<s,p,o>$ 是一个含有变量的三元组。VAR 代表变量集合，则有 $s \in VAR \cup R \cup B, p \in VAR \cup R, o \in VAR \cup R \cup B \cup L$。

定义 5.3　基本图模式(basic graph pattern)：由一组三元组模式组成，也称为连接查询(join query)。

定义 5.4　三元组模式查询(triple pattern query)：三元组模式查询 $Q=(q_1, q_2, \cdots, q_n)$ 是由三元组组成的元组，其中每个 q_i 是一个三元组模式。

SPARQL 查询的结构如下，包括 6 部分：①前缀声明；②明确数据源；③明确查询模式和返回变量；④WHERE 子句；⑤聚合；⑥结果修饰符。

```
######(1) base and prefix declarations
[BASE i]?
[PREFIX i]*
######(2) dataset construction
[FROM i]*
[FROM NAMED i]*
######(3) query type and solution modifiers
[SELECT S：：[DISTINCT|REDUCED]?[v|(e AS v)]+
|ASK|DESCRIBE v|CONSTRUCT {B}]
######(4) where clause
WHERE { P：：[B'|{P}
[.|UNION|OPTIONAL|MINUS|FILTER EXISTS|FILTER NOT EXISTS] {P} |
```

```
P FILTER (e) |BIND (e AS v) |VALUES ([v]+) {[([x|UNDEF]+)]*} |
GRAPH [v|i] {P} |SERVICE [SILENT]? i {P} |{ SELECT S }
] : : P}
######(5) aggregation
[GROUP BY [v|e]+]?
[HAVING e]?
######(6) solution modifiers
[ORDER BY [[v|e]|ASC([v|e])|DESC([v|e])]+]?
[LIMIT n]?
[OFFSET n]?
: : S
```

SPARQL 标准规范提供了 4 种查询模式(Query Forms),分别是:

(1) SELECT。用实际数据绑定查询模式中的变量,返回变量值。

(2) ASK。返回一个布尔值,指明查询模式是否能被实际数据所匹配。

(3) DESCRIBE。返回一个描述资源 IRI 的 RDF 图,例子见例 5.1。

(4) CONSTRUCT。根据模板返回一个 RDF 图。

最常用的是 SELECT 查询模式。例如,在通用的查询处理器 SPARQLer (http://sparql.org/sparql.html)上执行如例 5.3 所示的查询,查询结果见图 5.8。其中,被查询的 RDF 数据位于 Web 中的文件中,其 URL 在 FROM 子句中;

```
| s                                 | o     | name                     |
| <http://3roundstones.com/dave/#me>| _:b0  | "Danny Weitzner"         |
| <http://3roundstones.com/dave/#me>| _:b1  | "Ralph Swick"            |
| <http://3roundstones.com/dave/#me>| _:b2  | "Bernadette Hyland"      |
| <http://3roundstones.com/dave/#me>| _:b3  | "Dan Connolly"           |
| <http://3roundstones.com/dave/#me>| _:b4  | "Eric Miller"            |
| <http://3roundstones.com/dave/#me>| _:b5  | "Paul Gearon"            |
| <http://3roundstones.com/dave/#me>| _:b6  | "Ian Davis"              |
| <http://3roundstones.com/dave/#me>| _:b7  | "Dan Brickley"           |
| <http://3roundstones.com/dave/#me>| _:b8  | "David Jericho"          |
| <http://3roundstones.com/dave/#me>| _:b9  | "Andrae Muys"            |
| <http://3roundstones.com/dave/#me>| _:b10 | "Tom Heath"              |
| <http://3roundstones.com/dave/#me>| _:b11 | "Chris Sukornyk"         |
| <http://3roundstones.com/dave/#me>| _:b12 | "Dave Carrington"        |
| <http://3roundstones.com/dave/#me>| _:b13 | "Simon Kaplan"           |
| <http://3roundstones.com/dave/#me>| _:b14 | "Darren Govoni"          |
| <http://3roundstones.com/dave/#me>| _:b15 | "Libby Miller"           |
| <http://3roundstones.com/dave/#me>| _:b16 | "Tim Berners-Lee"        |
| <http://3roundstones.com/dave/#me>| _:b17 | "Jim Hendler"            |
| <http://3roundstones.com/dave/#me>| _:b18 | "Brian Sletten"          |
| <http://3roundstones.com/dave/#me>| _:b19 | "Jason Parker-Burlingham"|
| <http://3roundstones.com/dave/#me>| _:b20 | "Michael Hausenblas"     |
```

图 5.8 SPARQL 查询结果

SELECT 子句是返回结果变量的列表,?s、?o 和?name 是变量,要用实际数据匹配它们;WHERE 子句的内容是图模式,指明查询条件;LIMIT 子句限制返回的行数(100 行)。被查询的 RDF 数据见例 5.4 和图 5.9。

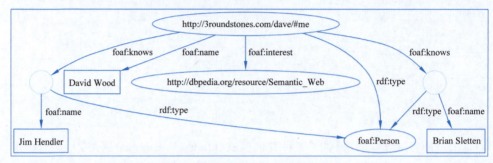

图 5.9　被查询数据的 RDF 图(部分)

例 5.3　基本图模式的 SPARQL 查询。

```
PREFIX  foaf: <http://xmlns.com/foaf/0.1/>
SELECT  ?s ?o ?name
FROM    <http://3roundstones.com/dave/me.rdf>
WHERE   { ?s foaf: knows ?o .
          ?o foaf: name ?name. }
LIMIT 100
```

例 5.4　被查询的 RDF 数据(部分)。

```
@prefix foaf: <http://xmlns.com/foaf/0.1/>.
<http://3roundstones.com/dave/#me>  a    foaf: Person ;
            foaf: name  "David Wood" ;
            foaf: workplaceHomepage  <http://3roundstones.com/>;
            foaf: interest <http://dbpedia.org/resource/Linked_Data>,
<http://dbpedia.org/page/Metadata>, <http://dbpedia.org/resource/Semantic_
Web>;
            foaf: knows    [    a foaf: Person ;
                                foaf: name "Jim Hendler"   ],
                           [    a foaf: Person ;
                                foaf: name "Brian Sletten" ].
```

(来源：http://3roundstones.com/dave/me.rdf)

下面的查询(例 5.5)增加了 FILTER 子句,通过正则表达式(regular expression)寻找?name 属性值以 J 或 I 开头,且以 r 结尾的个体。查询结果见图 5.10。

图 5.10　带 FILTER 的 SPARQL 查询结果

例 5.5　增加 FILTER 子句的查询。

```
PREFIX foaf: <http://xmlns.com/foaf/0.1/>
SELECT   ?s ?o ?name
FROM     <http://3roundstones.com/dave/me.rdf>
WHERE    {  ?s foaf: knows ?o .
            ?o foaf: name ?name.
FILTER (REGEX(?name, "^[JI].* r$" ))}
LIMIT 100
```

5.2.3　SPARQL 服务和查询端点

相关概念的定义如下。

定义 5.5　SPARQL 客户端(SPARQL client)：一个 HTTP 客户端,向服务器发送"SPARQL 协议操作"(SPARQL protocol operations)的请求。

定义 5.6　SPARQL 服务(SPARQL service)：一个 HTTP 服务,接收"SPARQL 协议操作"的请求并返回响应结果。

定义 5.7　SPARQL 查询端点(SPARQL endpoints)：一个 URI,SPARQL 服务器通过它侦听来自客户端的请求。

定义 5.8　SPARQL 协议操作(SPARQL protocol operation)：符合规范的 HTTP 请求和响应。

许多知识图谱系统都提供了 SPARQL 服务,并向外暴露 SPARQL 查询端点,一些例子见表 5.4。

表 5.4　知识图谱的 SPARQL 查询端点举例

序号	知识图谱的名称	SPARQL 查询端点
1	DBpedia	http://dbpedia.org/sparql
2	Wikidata	https://query.wikidata.org
3	Open Research Knowledge Graph(ORKG)	https://orkg.org/sparql/https://orkg.org/triplestore/

续表

序号	知识图谱的名称	SPARQL 查询端点
4	Scholarlydata	http://www.scholarlydata.org/sparql/
5	Computer Science Knowledge Graph(CS-KG)	https://scholkg.kmi.open.ac.uk/sparql/
6	AIDA KG	https://aida.kmi.open.ac.uk/sparql/
7	SemOpenAlex	https://semopenalex.org/sparql
8	KBpedia	http://sparql.kbpedia.org/

(来源：http://prod-dekalog.inria.fr/)

"SPARQL 1.1 服务描述"(service description)规范定义了描述"SPARQL 服务"的词汇表，通过它分别描述 DBpedia SPARQL 服务和 MAKG SPARQL 服务的例子见例 5.6 和例 5.7。

例 5.6 描述 DBpedia SPARQL 服务的三元组。

```
@prefix sd: <http://www.w3.org/ns/sparql-service-description#>.
<https://dbpedia.org/sparql#service>  a  sd:Service;
sd:endpoint    <https://dbpedia.org/sparql>;
sd:url         <https://dbpedia.org/sparql>;
sd:resultFormat <http://www.w3.org/ns/formats/SPARQL_Results_XML>,
<http://www.w3.org/ns/formats/Turtle>,
<http://www.w3.org/ns/formats/SPARQL_Results_CSV>;
sd:feature    sd:UnionDefaultGraph, sd:DereferencesURIs.
```

例 5.7 描述 MAKG SPARQL 服务的三元组。

```
@prefix sd: <http://www.w3.org/ns/sparql-service-description#>.
<http://localhost:8890/sparql>  a  sd:Service;
sd:endpoint    <http://localhost:8890/sparql>;
sd:url         <http://localhost:8890/sparql>;
sd:resultFormat <http://www.w3.org/ns/formats/SPARQL_Results_XML>,
<http://www.w3.org/ns/formats/Turtle>,
<http://www.w3.org/ns/formats/SPARQL_Results_CSV>;
sd:feature    sd:UnionDefaultGraph, sd:DereferencesURIs.
```

SPARQL 客户端既可以是浏览器，也可以是用户自己开发的程序。例如，对于 MAKG 的 SPARQL 服务，发送"DESCRIBE < https://makg.org/entity/100363>"查询请求的 Java 程序见例 5.8。

例 5.8 发送 SPARQL 查询请求及接收查询结果的 Java 程序。

```
import java.net.*;
import java.io.*;
public class RemoteQuery {
final static String sql ="GET " +
"/sparql?default-graph-uri="+
"&query=DESCRIBE+%3Chttps%3A%2F%2Fmakg.org%"+
"2Fentity%2F100363%3E&format=application%2Fx-nice-"+
"turtle&timeout=0&debug=on&run=+Run+Query+"+" HTTP/1.1";
public static void main(String args[]) {
    try {//建立到服务器的连接
Socket s =new Socket("ma-graph.org",8890);
        OutputStream os =s.getOutputStream();
        OutputStreamWriter osw =new OutputStreamWriter(os);
        PrintWriter pw =new PrintWriter(osw, true);
        //发送请求报文
        pw.println(sql);
        pw.println("Host: ma-graph.org");
        pw.println("Connection: Keep-Alive");
        pw.println("");
        //接收响应报文
        InputStream is =s.getInputStream() ;
        InputStreamReader isr =new InputStreamReader(is) ;
        BufferedReader br =new BufferedReader(isr) ;
        //输出响应报文
        do{System.out.println(br.readLine()) ;
            }while(br.ready());
    } catch (Exception e) {}
}} .
```

该语句查询描述论文"Lymphoepithelial Cyst of the Mediastinum"的所有三元组,服务器的返回结果见例 5.9。

例 5.9 服务器的返回结果。

```
@prefix rdf: <http://www.w3.org/1999/02/22-rdf-syntax-ns#>.
@prefix ns1: <https://makg.org/class/>.
@prefix xsd: <http://www.w3.org/2001/XMLSchema#>.
@prefix ns3: <http://purl.org/dc/terms/>.
@prefix ns4: <https://makg.org/property/>.
@prefix ns5: <http://purl.org/spar/fabio/>.
```

```
@prefix ns6: <https://www.ncbi.nlm.nih.gov/pmc/articles/>.
@prefix ns7: <http://prismstandard.org/namespaces/basic/2.0/>.
@prefix ns8: <http://purl.org/spar/cito/>.
<https://makg.org/entity/100363>
    rdf: type      ns1: JournalArticle , ns1: Paper ;
    ns3: created    "2016-06-24"^^xsd: date ;
    ns4: citationCount1 ;
    ns4: rank23454 ;
    ns3: publisher"Texas Heart Institute"^^xsd: string ;
    ns5: hasPubMedCentralId ns6: PMC1336730 ;
    ns5: hasPubMedId     <https://pubmed.ncbi.nlm.nih.gov/16392239>;
       ns5: hasURL
          "https://www.ncbi.nlm.nih.gov/pmc/articles/PMC1336730"^^xsd:
          anyURI ,
          "http://europepmc.org/articles/PMC1336730"^^xsd: anyURI ;
    ns7: startingPage    440 ;
    ns7: endingPage      441 ;
    ns7: issueIdentifier     "3"^^xsd: string ;
    ns7: publicationDate    "2005-01-01"^^xsd: date ;
    ns7: volume    32 ;
    ns3: title    "Lymphoepithelial cyst of the mediastinum."^^xsd: string ;
    ns4: appearsInJournal    <https://makg.org/entity/162735806>;
    ns4: estimatedCitationCount    1 ;
    ns4: referenceCount    0 ;
    ns5: hasDiscipline    <https://makg.org/entity/71924100>;
    ns3: creator    <https://makg.org/entity/2691438691>,
                    <https://makg.org/entity/2344597223>.
                    <https://makg.org/entity/2736632509>
    ns8: cites    <https://makg.org/entity/100363>.
```

5.3 基于 SPARQL 查询的学术画像

5.3.1 学术画像的定义和分类

学术画像(scholarly profiles)是用数字化的方式对学术对象进行形象化的描述所形成的具体化的表达,可以利用这一表达为特定用户提供有针对性的服务。学术画像源于用户画像(user profiles)。用户画像是将用户的属性、行为与期望联结起来的实际用户的虚拟代表,属于计算社会科学的范畴,最早应用于电子商务领域,它使产品的服务对象更加聚焦和专注。

学术画像包括学科画像、学者画像、期刊画像、基金画像、科研机构画像、学术团体画像、学术会议画像和个人用户画像等,见图 5.11。

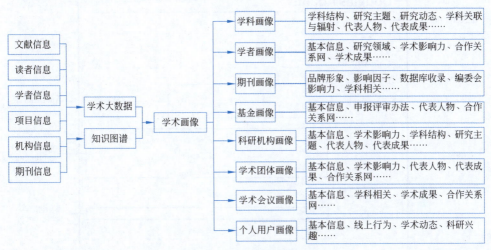

图 5.11　学术画像的分类

随着开放科学运动的兴起,多源异构的科学大数据为学术画像的构建提供了丰富的数据基础,同时也给相关研究带来了更大的挑战,包括多源数据获取与融合难度大、动态更新困难等。

5.3.2　Scholia 和 Wikidata

Scholia 是一个在线的学术画像服务,其网址是 https://scholia.toolforge.org/。

Scholia 利用 Wikidata(维基数据)提供的 SPARQL 查询服务构建各种类型的学术画像,包括主题(topic)、机构(organization)、作者(author)和作品(work)等。

Wikidata 是一个开放的、协作编辑的知识图谱,由维基媒体(Wikimedia)德国分会负责建设,其目标是开发"世界知识的一个协作编辑的数据库",为 280 多种语言版本的维基百科(Wikipedia)提供支持。

Wikidata 是一个面向文档的数据库(document-oriented database),用来描述各类实体。实体在 Wikidata 中被称为条目(item),每个条目都被分配一个唯一的持久标识符,称为 QID(Q+数字)。例如,英国作家道格拉斯·亚当斯(Douglas Adams)的 QID 是 Q42,主页和实体的 URL/IRI 分别是:

```
https://www.wikidata.org/wiki/Q42
http://www.wikidata.org/entity/Q42
```

通过它们都可以定位到该条目的网页,其结构见图 5.12。

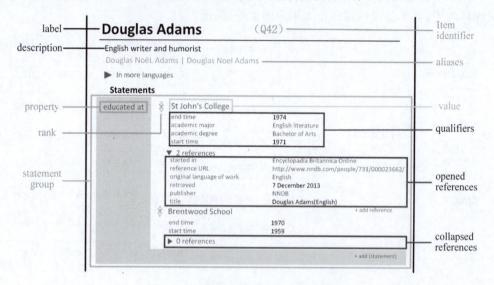

图 5.12　Wikidata 中条目(item)的结构

(来源:https://www.wikidata.org/wiki/Wikidata:Introduction)

对条目的描述称为陈述(statement),采用 RDF 三元组形式。其中的属性(property)被分配了唯一的编号,形式是 P+数字,例如属性 educated at 的编号是P69,它的主页和实体的 URL/IRI 分别是:

```
https://www.wikidata.org/wiki/Property:P69
http://www.wikidata.org/entity/P69
```

描述 Q42 的部分三元组见例 5.10。

例 5.10　描述 Q42 的三元组(部分)。

```
@prefix rdf: <http://www.w3.org/1999/02/22-rdf-syntax-ns#>.
@prefix xsd: <http://www.w3.org/2001/XMLSchema#>.
@prefix rdfs: <http://www.w3.org/2000/01/rdf-schema#>.
@prefix wikibase: <http://wikiba.se/ontology#>.
@prefix schema: <http://schema.org/>.
@prefix wd: <http://www.wikidata.org/entity/>.
@prefix wdt: <http://www.wikidata.org/prop/direct/>.
@prefix wdtn: <http://www.wikidata.org/prop/direct-normalized/>.
wd:Q42    a    wikibase:Item ;
```

```
wdt: P69      wd: Q4961791,
              wd: Q691283 ;
wdt: P569    "1952-03-11T00: 00: 00Z"^^xsd: dateTime ;
wdt: P570    "2001-05-11T00: 00: 00Z"^^xsd: dateTime ;
wdtn: P1015  <https://livedata.bibsys.no/authority/90196888>.
<https://en.wikipedia.org/wiki/Douglas_Adams< a schema: Article ;
    schema: about         wd: Q42 ;
    schema: inLanguage    "en" ;
    schema: isPartOf      <https://en.wikipedia.org/>;
    schema: name          "Douglas Adams"@en .
```

（来源：https://www.wikidata.org/wiki/Special：EntityData/Q42.ttl）

Wikidata 描述了条目之间的关联信息。例如，图 5.13 是旧金山（San Francisco）条目及其关联信息。

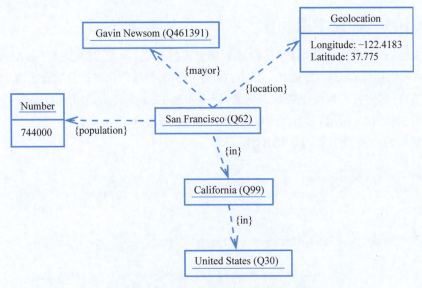

图 5.13　旧金山条目及其关联信息

（来源：https://www.wikidata.org/wiki/Wikidata：Introduction）

截至 2024 年 5 月初，Wikidata 已含有超过 1.097 亿个条目（即实体），其中包括大量的学术数据。例如，图 5.14 查询了 scholarly article（学术论文，Q13442814）的实例（instance of，P31）数量，返回结果是 41680911。

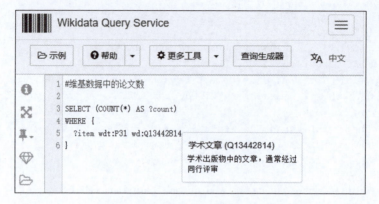

图 5.14 查询学术论文的条目数量
（来源：https://query.wikidata.org/）

5.3.3 研究主题画像

Scholia 的"研究主题画像"包括该主题发表的论文、作者、共现主题（co-occurring topics）和引用（citations）等信息。其中，对"年度出版数量""作者评分""合著者""共现主题"等内容进行了可视化展示。例如，研究主题 Google Knowledge Graph 的共现主题图如图 5.15 所示，其 SPARQL 查询代码见例 5.11。

例 5.11 共现主题的 SPARQL 查询。

```
#defaultView: Graph
PREFIX target: <http://www.wikidata.org/entity/Q648625>
SELECT  ?topic1 ?topic1Label ?topic2 ?topic2Label
WITH {
    SELECT  (COUNT(DISTINCT ?work) AS ?count) ?topic1 ?topic2
    WHERE {
      #Find works that are marked with main subject of the topic.
      ?work wdt: P921 / ( wdt: P31 * /wdt: P279 *  | wdt: P361+ | wdt: P1269+)
      target: .
      #Identify co-occuring topics.
      ?work wdt: P921 ?topic1, ?topic2 .
      #Exclude the topic it self
      FILTER (target: != ?topic1 && target: != ?topic2 && ?topic1 != ?
      topic2) }
    GROUP BY ?topic1 ?topic2
    ORDER BY DESC(?count)
```

```
    LIMIT 400
} AS %results
WHERE {
    INCLUDE %results
    #Label the results
    SERVICE wikibase: label {
        bd: serviceParam wikibase: language "en,da,de,es,fr,jp,nl,no,ru,
        sv,zh".
    }
}
```

(来源：https://github.com/WDscholia/scholia/blob/master/scholia/app/templates/topic_co-occurring.sparql)

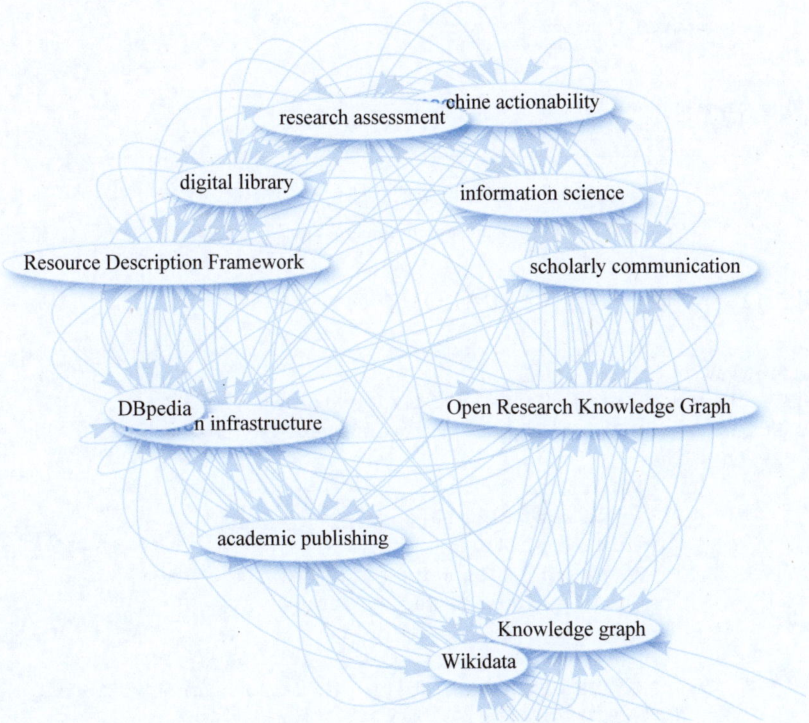

图 5.15　共现主题图

(来源：https://scholia.toolforge.org/topic/Q648625)

5.3.4 出版机构画像

Scholia 的"出版机构画像"包括期刊列表、编辑人员和论文引用情况等内容。其中,对"期刊创刊年份"进行了图表展示。例如,PLOS(Public Library of Science)出版的各个期刊的创刊年份见图 5.16,其 SPARQL 查询代码见例 5.12,查询界面见图 5.17。

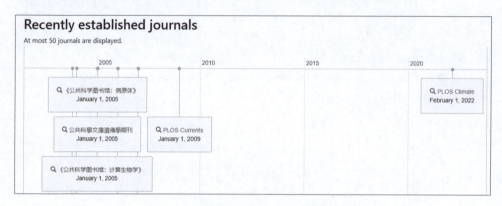

图 5.16　PLOS 出版期刊的创刊年份(部分)

(来源：https://scholia.toolforge.org/publisher/Q233358)

例 5.12　期刊创刊年份的 SPARQL 查询。

```
#defaultView: Timeline
PREFIX target: <http://www.wikidata.org/entity/Q233358>
SELECT DISTINCT ?datetime ?venue ?venueLabel
WHERE {
          # Publisher
          ?venue wdt: P123 target: .
          # Periodic literature
          ?venue wdt: P31 / wdt: P279* wd: Q1002697 .
          # When the journal was started
          ?venue wdt: P571 ?datetime.
          # Label the journal
          SERVICE wikibase: label { bd: serviceParam wikibase: language
          "[AUTO_LANGUAGE],en". } }
ORDER BY DESC(?datetime)
LIMIT 50
```

(来源：https://github.com/WDscholia/scholia/blob/master/scholia/app/templates/publisher_timeline.sparql)

图 5.17　期刊创刊年份的 SPARQL 查询及结果

（来源：https://query.wikidata.org/）

5.3.5　作者画像

Scholia 的作者画像包括作品、研究主题、合著者和引用情况等内容。其中，对"年度出版数量""论文的主题分布""合著者""年度引用次数"等进行了可视化展示。例如，知识图谱领域的著名学者 Aidan Hogan（Q51366847）的合著者（co-authors）的 SPARQL 查询代码见例 5.13，查询结果的可视化展示见图 5.18。

例 5.13　合著者的 SPARQL 查询。

```
#defaultView: Graph
PREFIX target: <http://www.wikidata.org/entity/Q51366847>
#Egocentric co-author graph for an author
SELECT ?author1 ?author1Label ?rgb ?author2 ?author2Label
WITH {
    SELECT (COUNT(?work) AS ?count) ?author1 ?author2
WHERE {   #Find co-authors
        ?work wdt: P50 target: , ?author1, ?author2 .   }
    GROUP BY ?author1 ?author2
    ORDER BY DESC(?count)
    LIMIT 1000
```

```
} AS %authors
WITH {
    SELECT ?author1 ?author2 ?rgb
WHERE { INCLUDE %authors
        #Exclude self-links
        FILTER (?author1 !=?author2)
        #Color according to gender
        OPTIONAL {   ?author1 wdt: P21 ?gender1 .
     BIND( IF(?gender1 =wd: Q6581097, "3182BD", "E6550D") AS ?rgb) } }
} AS %result
WHERE { INCLUDE %result
        #Label the results
        SERVICE wikibase: label { bd: serviceParam wikibase: language
        "en,fr,de,ru,es,zh,jp". }}
```

（来源：https://github.com/WDscholia/scholia/blob/master/scholia/app/templates/author_coauthors.sparql）

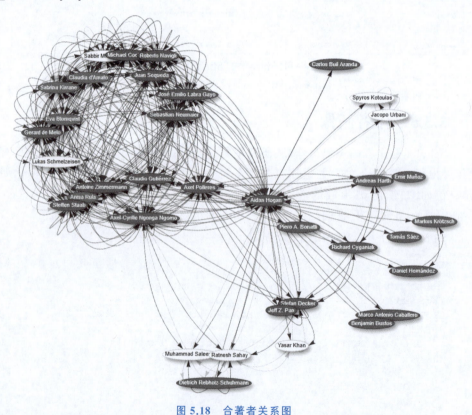

图 5.18　合著者关系图

（来源：https://scholia.toolforge.org/author/Q51366847）

参 考 文 献

[1] MARIA-EVANGELIA P, TZITZIKAS Y, MOUNTANTONAKIS M. A brief survey of methods for analytics over RDF knowledge graphs[J]. Analytics, 2023(2): 55-74.

[2] MICHAEL F, LAMPRECHT D, KRAUSE J T, et al. SemOpenAlex: The scientific landscape in 26 billion RDF triples[J]. ArXiv abs/2308.03671, 2023.

[3] 杜方,陈跃国,杜小勇.RDF 数据查询处理技术综述[J].软件学报,2013,24(6):1222-1242.

[4] Twinkle: A SPARQL query tool[EB/OL]. [2024-05-15]. http://www.ldodds.com/projects/twinkle/.

[5] SPARQL 1.1 query language[EB/OL]. [2024-05-15]. https://www.w3.org/TR/sparql11-query/.

[6] SPARQL 1.1 protocol[EB/OL]. [2024-05-15]. https://www.w3.org/TR/sparql11-protocol/.

[7] SPARQL 1.1 service description[EB/OL]. [2024-05-15]. https://www.w3.org/TR/sparql11-service-description/.

[8] 翟军.关联政府数据原理与应用[M].北京:电子工业出版社,2016.

[9] 王雅娇,路佳,柯晓静.学术画像在科技期刊中的应用研究[J].中国编辑,2021(4):45-49.

[10] 王世奇,刘智锋,王继民.学者画像研究综述[J].图书情报工作,2022,66(20):73-81.

[11] NIELSEN F Å, MIETCHEN D, WILLIGHAGEN E. Scholia and scientometrics with Wikidata. ArXiv abs/1703.04222, 2017.

[12] Wikidata[EB/OL]. [2024-05-15]. https://en.wikipedia.org/wiki/Wikidata.

[13] 贾君枝,崔西燕.Wikidata 属性特征及关系分析[J].情报科学,2019,37(6):80-86,118.

[14] 贾君枝,薛秋红.Wikidata 的特点、数据获取与应用[J].图书情报工作,2016,60(17):136-141,148.

[15] 王瑞云,贾君枝.基于外部 ID 的中文实体对齐分析——以中国科学院院士 Wikidata 数据子集为例[J].国家图书馆学刊,2020,29(2):102-113.

第6章 知识图谱的元数据

6.1 元数据的作用

元数据（metadata）是描述数据的数据（data about data）。一个知识图谱的元数据指它的"名称""创作者""版本""发布者"等数据，图 6.1 展示了 SemOpenAlex 知识图谱的部分元数据记录。

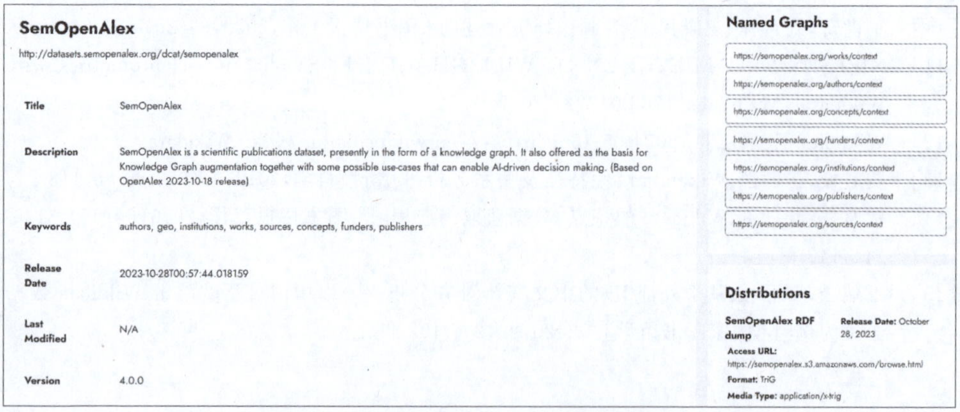

图 6.1 SemOpenAlex 的元数据记录（部分）

（来源：https://semopenalex.org/）

元数据在知识图谱的开发、管护和开放共享中发挥着关键作用。德国莱比锡大学科研团队提出的增量构建知识图谱的流水线（pipeline）如图 6.2 所示，其中包含"元数据管理"（Metadata Management）环节，利用"元数据仓储库"（metadata repository，MDR）存储和组织各类元数据，包括描述型元数据（descriptive metadata)、结构型元数据(structural metadata)和管理型元数据(administrative metadata)。

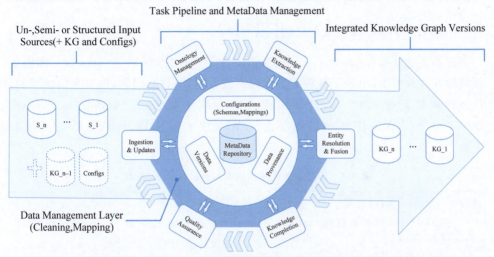

图 6.2　增量构建知识图谱的流水线

法国蔚蓝海岸大学科研团队开发了知识图谱目录和索引系统——IndeGx,已建立 300 多个 RDF 知识图谱的索引。IndeGx 系统利用和生成的知识图谱元数据包括断言元数据(asserted metadata)、可计算的描述型元数据(computable descriptive metadata)和可计算的质量元数据(computable quality metadata)等,见图 6.3。

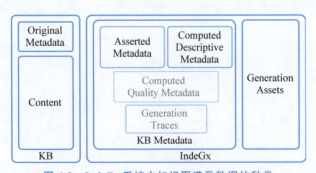

图 6.3　IndeGx 系统中知识图谱元数据的种类

根据 FAIR 原则,知识图谱的元数据应是可发现(findable)、可获取(accessible)、互操作(interoperable)和可重用的(re-usable),这要求元数据标准采用本体模型和机器可读的(machine-readable)编码方式。

6.2 数据目录词汇表 DCAT

6.2.1 W3C DCAT 的开发历程

在各类仓储库(repositories)中,知识图谱是一种"数据集"(dataset)。面向各领域的开放数据集,出现了各种元数据标准或方案,既有通用的,也有专门领域的,代表性成果见表 6.1。其中,W3C 数据目录词汇表(data catalog vocabulary,DCAT)由于具有通用性和采用了语义 Web 技术等优势,得到了广泛关注和采纳。

表 6.1 面向开放数据集的主要元数据标准/方案

序号	元数据标准/方案	网址	使用范围
1	W3C 开放数据元数据标准 DCAT	https://www.w3.org/TR/vocab-dcat/	通用,不依赖于软件平台
2	CKAN 软件平台元数据	https://ckan.org/	软件平台
3	Schema.org 数据集描述词汇表	http://schema.org/Dataset	通用,各大搜索引擎支持
4	W3C VoID Vocabulary	https://www.w3.org/TR/void/	关联开放数据集
5	统计元数据 SDMX	https://sdmx.org/	描述统计数据
6	欧盟 CERIF	https://www.eurocris.org/services/main-features-cerif	描述科研实体及其关系
7	欧盟地理信息基础设施元数据	https://inspire.ec.europa.eu/metadata/6541	描述地理信息
8	ISO19115:2003	https://www.iso.org/standard/26020.html	描述地理信息
9	DDI 元数据标准	http://www.ddialliance.org/explore-documentation	描述社会科学数据
10	W3C Dataset Descriptions:HCLS	https://www.w3.org/TR/hcls-dataset/	科学数据:卫生保健和生命科学
11	DatA Tag Suite (DATs)	https://github.com/biocaddie/WG3-MetadataSpecifications	描述生物医学领域的数据集
12	Core Scientific MetaData model(CSMD)	https://icatproject-contrib.github.io/CSMD/csmd-4.0.html	描述科学活动、设施和数据
13	DataID	http://dataid.dbpedia.org/ns/core.html	DBpedia 数据集
14	DataCite	https://datacite.org/	描述数据引用

随着开放数据目录(open data catalogs)的增多,目录间的异构问题日益突出。分布式目录系统的聚合和数据集的跨目录统一搜索,迫切需要在数据目录间交换元数据,实现目录的互操作。为此,在 2010 年,爱尔兰国立大学数字企业研究所启动了 DCAT 的研制工作,2012 年转由 W3C 政府关联数据工作组(Government Linked Data Working Group)开展标准化工作,2014 年发布正式推荐标准,即 DCAT v1.0 版。

在推广应用的过程中,DCAT v1.0 的不足与缺陷也逐步暴露出来。2016 年 11 月 30 日至 12 月 1 日期间,由 W3C 与欧盟项目 VRE4EIC 共同发起,在荷兰阿姆斯特丹举行了"智能描述与智能词汇表研讨会"(Smart Descriptions & Smarter Vocabularies Workshop,SDSVoc),探讨了 DCAT 在科学数据共享和开放等领域的应用前景,指出当前的 DCAT 对 API、数据溯源、引用和质量等的描述不足,在扩展时更缺乏操作指南、约束描述语言和验证工具的支持;并在"应修订 DCAT 使其适应于更广泛的社区"方面达成共识。SDSVOC 促成 W3C 于 2017 年 5 月 4 日成立"数据集交换工作组"(DXWG),联合欧盟 ISA(Interoperability Solutions for Administrations,行政部门的互操作性解决方案)计划(ec.europa.eu/isa2)与研究数据联盟(Research Data Alliance,www.rd-alliance.org)等社区,致力于 DCAT 的修订及相关工作,于 2020 年 2 月 4 日发布了 DCAT v2.0 版,其开发历程见图 6.4。

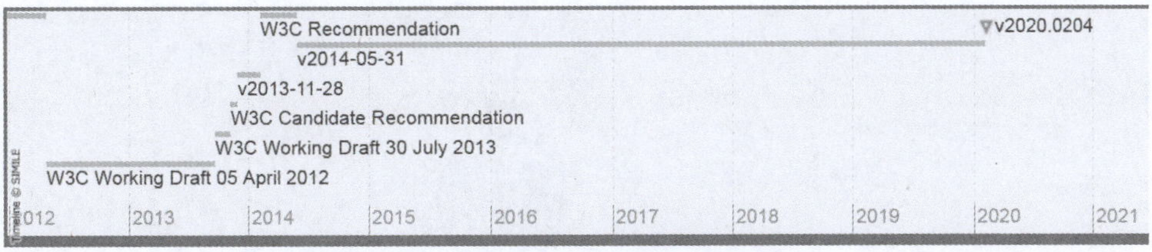

图 6.4　DCAT 的开发历程

(来源:https://lov.linkeddata.es/dataset/lov/vocabs/dcat)

2020 年 2 月以后,DXWG 的主要任务是开发 DCAT v3.0 版,以使其支持"版本控制"和"数据集序列"。

6.2.2　DCAT 元数据模型

DCAT 模型是 RDF 词汇表(即本体),该词汇表的命名空间是 http://www.w3.org/ns/dcat#,前缀是 dcat,主要类、关系和属性见图 6.5 和表 6.2。

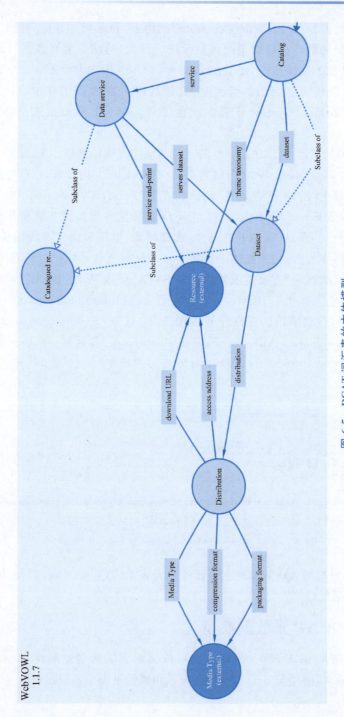

图 6.5 DCAT 词汇表的本体模型

(来源：https://service.tib.eu/webvowl/#iri=https://www.w3.org/ns/dcat.ttl)

表 6.2　DCAT 词汇表的主要类

类	说明	属性和关系
dcat：Catalog	数据目录	dc：title,dc：description,dc：issued,dc：modified, dc：language,dc：license,dc：rights,dc：spatial, dcat：dataset,foaf：homepage,dcat：themeTaxonomy
dcat：Dataset	数据集,数据的逻辑组织单元	dc：title,dc：description,dc：issued,dc：modified, dc：identifier,dcat：keyword,dc：language, dcat：contactPoint,dcat：distribution, dcat：landingPage,dcat：theme
dcat：Distribution	数据集包含数据的物理存在,包括数据文件和 API 等	dc：title,dc：description,dc：issued,dc：modified, dc：license,dc：rights,dc：format,dcat：accessURL, dcat：mediaType,dcat：byteSize,dcat：downloadURL

6.2.3　元数据实例

科学仓储库 Zenodo 上的知识图谱数据集 Wikipedia Knowledge Graph Dataset 的 DCAT 元数据记录如例 6.1 所示,它是机器可读的 Turtle 格式,对应的 RDF 图见图 6.6。

例 6.1　Wikipedia Knowledge Graph Dataset 的元数据(部分)如下所示。

```
@prefix dcat: <http://www.w3.org/ns/dcat#>.
@prefix dc: <http://purl.org/dc/terms/>.
@prefix xsd: <http://www.w3.org/2001/XMLSchema#>.
@prefix foaf: <http://xmlns.com/foaf/0.1/>.
@prefix owl: <http://www.w3.org/2002/07/owl#>.
@prefix ns0: <http://www.w3.org/ns/adms#>.
@prefix skos: <http://www.w3.org/2004/02/skos/core#>.
@prefix wdrs: <http://www.w3.org/2007/05/powder-s#>.
@prefix schema: <http://schema.org/>.
@prefix org: <http://www.w3.org/ns/org#>.
@prefix rdfs: <http://www.w3.org/2000/01/rdf-schema#>.
<https://doi.org/10.5281/zenodo.6346900>
    a  dcat: Dataset ;
    dc: type     <http://purl.org/dc/dcmitype/Dataset>;
    dc: identifier   "https://doi.org/10.5281/zenodo.6346900"^^xsd: anyURI ;
    foaf: page    <https://doi.org/10.5281/zenodo.6346900>;
    dc: creator   <http://orcid.org/0000-0001-9437-8757>,
<http://orcid.org/0000-0001-8790-3314>,
```

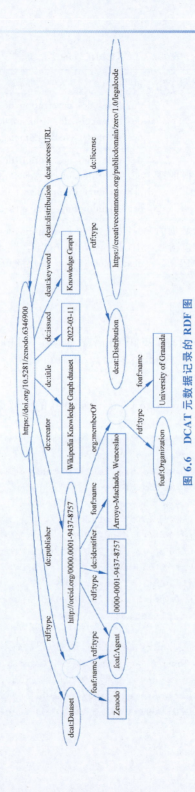

图 6.6 DCAT 元数据记录的 RDF 图

```
<http://orcid.org/0000-0002-7465-6462>;
    dc: title      "Wikipedia Knowledge Graph dataset";
    dc: publisher  [   a   foaf: Agent;
                      foaf: name "Zenodo"];
    dc: issued    "2022"^^xsd: gYear, "2022-03-11"^^xsd: date;
    dcat: keyword "Wikipedia", "dataset", "Knowledge Graph", "informetrics";
    dc: language
<http://publications.europa.eu/resource/authority/language/ENG>;
    owl: sameAs    <https://zenodo.org/record/6346900>;
    dcat: distribution [
           a    dcat: Distribution;
           dc: license
<https://creativecommons.org/publicdomain/zero/1.0/legalcode>;
           dcat: accessURL  <https://doi.org/10.5281/zenodo.6346900<].
<http://orcid.org/0000-0001-9437-8757>
    a   foaf: Agent;
    dc: identifier    "0000-0001-9437-8757"^^xsd: string;
    foaf: name        "Arroyo-Machado, Wenceslao";
    foaf: givenName   "Wenceslao";
    foaf: familyName  "Arroyo-Machado";
    org: memberOf    [   a   foaf: Organization;
                        foaf: name  "University of Granada"].
```

（来源：https://www.zenodo.org/record/6346900）

6.3 关联数据集元数据 VoID

6.3.1 VoID 元数据模型

关联数据集词汇表 VoID（vocabulary of interlinked datasets）专门用来描述 RDF 数据集，建立 RDF 数据的发布者和使用者之间的桥梁。VoID 含有 4 个类、27 个属性（见图 6.7），主要涵盖四方面的元数据：

（1）通用元数据（general metadata）。使用都柏林核心元数据（Dublin core metadata，DC）的术语 dcterms：title、dcterms：description、dcterms：creator、dcterms：publisher 等描述一个 void：Dataset 或 void：Linkset 的实例。

（2）访问元数据（access metadata）。描述获取一个 void：Dataset 中的 RDF

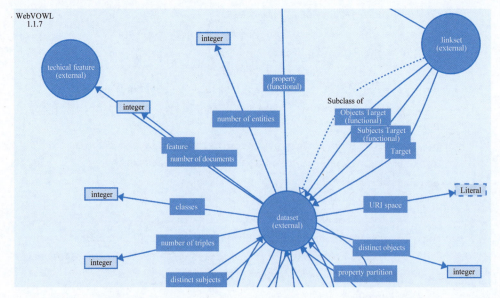

图 6.7　VoID 词汇表的本体模型

（来源：https://service.tib.eu/webvowl/#file=void_2011-03-06.n3）

三元组的途径和方式。例如 void：dataDump 属性指出 RDF 文档的下载路径，void：sparqlEndpoint 属性指出 SPARQL 查询端点的 URL。

（3）结构元数据（structural metadata）。提供一个 void：Dataset 数据集的模式和内部结构的信息。例如 void：uriSpace 属性指出数据集中资源 URI 的模式，void：vocabulary 属性指出数据集使用的词汇表，void：subset 属性指出数据集的子集等。结构元数据还提供数据集的统计信息，如三元组的个数（void：triples）、实体的个数（void：entities）等。

（4）描述链接（descriptions of links）的元数据。void：Linkset 类用来描述两个数据集之间的链接的集合，它的属性有 void：target、void：linkPredicate、void：triples 等。

6.3.2　元数据实例

SemOpenAlex 知识图谱的 Turtle 格式的 VoID 元数据见例 6.2，对应的 RDF 图见图 6.8。

例 6.2　SemOpenAlex 的 VoID 元数据如下所示。

图 6.8 VoID 元数据记录的 RDF 图

```
@prefix rdf: <http://www.w3.org/1999/02/22-rdf-syntax-ns#>.
@prefix rdfs: <http://www.w3.org/2000/01/rdf-schema#>.
@prefix foaf: <http://xmlns.com/foaf/0.1/>.
@prefix dcterms: <http://purl.org/dc/terms/>.
@prefix void: <http://rdfs.org/ns/void#>.
@prefix xsd: <http://www.w3.org/2001/XMLSchema#>.
@prefix owl: <http://www.w3.org/2002/07/owl#>.
@prefix : <#>.
: SemOpenAlex
    rdf: type            void: Dataset ;
    foaf: homepage       <https://semopenalex.org/>;
    dcterms: title       "SemOpenAlex" ;
    void: sparqlEndpoint  <https://semopenalex.org/sparql>;
    dcterms: contributor  < http://dbpedia. org/resource/Karlsruhe_
    Institute_of_Technology>;
    dcterms: contributor  <https://www.wikidata.org/wiki/Q22132500>;
    dcterms: source      <https://github.com/metaphacts/semopenalex>;
    dcterms: modified    "2023-04-24"^^xsd: date ;
    dcterms: license     < https://creativecommons.org/share-your-work/
    public-domain/cc0/>;
    dcterms: subject     <http://dbpedia.org/resource/Computer_science>;
    dcterms: subject     <http://dbpedia.org/resource/Knowledge_graph>;
    void: feature        <http://www.w3.org/ns/formats/TriG>;
    void: triples        26401183867 ;
    void: vocabulary     <http://xmlns.com/foaf/0.1/>;
    void: vocabulary     <http://purl.org/dc/terms/>;
    void: vocabulary     <http://purl.org/spar/cito/>;
    void: vocabulary     <http://purl.org/spar/fabio/>;
    void: vocabulary     <http://purl.org/spar/bido/>;
    void: vocabulary     <https://semopenalex.org/vocab#>;
    void: vocabulary     <http://prismstandard.org/namespaces/basic/2.0/>;
    void: vocabulary     <http://dbpedia.org/ontology/>;
    void: vocabulary     <http://dbpedia.org/property/>;
    void: vocabulary     <http://www.w3.org/ns/org/#>;
    void: vocabulary     <https://www.geonames.org/ontology/#>;
    void: linkPredicate  owl: sameAs ;
    void: linkPredicate  rdfs: seeAlso .
```

(来源：https://github.com/metaphacts/semopenalex/blob/main/linked-dataset-descrip-tion/semopenalex-description-void.ttl)

在上面的元数据记录中含有 VoID 词汇表定义的元数据项 void：sparqlEndpoint、

void：triples、void：vocabulary 和 void：linkPredicate，其值分别为数据集的 SPARQL 查询端点的 URI、三元组个数、使用的词汇表和链接谓词。

其中，链接谓词有两个，分别是 owl：sameAs（表示两个不同的 IRI 指向同一个实体）和 rdfs：seeAlso，通过它们建立了到 MAKG（Microsoft Academic Knowledge Graph）、Wikidata 和 Wikipedia 的联系。

在 SemOpenAlex 数据集中，含有这两个谓词的三元组实例见例 6.3。

例 6.3 SemOpenAlex 中链接到外部数据集的三元组实例。

```
<https://semopenalex.org/work/W3038003025>
    <http://www.w3.org/2002/07/owl#sameAs>
                    <https://makg.org/entity/3038003025>.
<https://semopenalex.org/publisher/P4310311002>
    <http://www.w3.org/2002/07/owl#sameAs>
                    <https://www.wikidata.org/entity/Q52637117>.
<https://semopenalex.org/concept/C2987255567>
    rdfs: seeAlso
                    <https://en.wikipedia.org/wiki/Knowledge_graph>.
```

在例 6.3 中，第一个三元组的主体是论文"Building a PubMed Knowledge Graph"，它同时出现在 MAKG 中；第二个三元组的主体是期刊 *Mediterranean BioMedical Journals*，它同时出现在 Wikidata 中；第三个三元组的主体是概念 knowledge graph，它也是 Wikipedia 的一个条目。

MAKG 的元数据也采用了 VoID 词汇表，见例 6.4。例 6.5 给出 MAKG 数据集中三元组的例子，表明它关联了 DBpedia 知识图谱。

例 6.4 MAKG 的元数据。

```
@prefix rdf: <http://www.w3.org/1999/02/22-rdf-syntax-ns#>.
@prefix rdfs: <http://www.w3.org/2000/01/rdf-schema#>.
@prefix foaf: <http://xmlns.com/foaf/0.1/>.
@prefix dcterms: <http://purl.org/dc/terms/>.
@prefix void: <http://rdfs.org/ns/void#>.
@prefix xsd: <http://www.w3.org/2001/XMLSchema#>.
@prefix : <#>.
: MicrosoftAcademicGraph
    rdf: type           void: Dataset ;
    foaf: homepage      <http://ma-graph.org/>;
    dcterms: title      "Microsoft Academic Knowledge Graph" ;
```

```
        void: sparqlEndpoint    <http://ma-graph.org/sparql>;
        void: feature           <http://www.w3.org/ns/formats/N-Triples>;
        void: triples           8272187245 ;
        void: vocabulary        <http://purl.org/vocab/frbr/core>;
        void: vocabulary        <http://purl.org/spar/fabio/>;
        void: vocabulary        <http://url.org/spar/cito/>;
        void: vocabulary        <http://purl.org/spar/datacite>;
        void: vocabulary        <http://prismstandard.org/namespaces/1.2/basic/>;
        void: vocabulary        <http://purl.org/spar/c4o/>;
        void: linkPredicate     owl: sameAs .
```

（来源：https://makg.org/void.ttl）

例 6.5 MAKG 中链接到外部数据集的三元组实例。

```
<https://makg.org/entity/41125697>
<http://www.w3.org/2002/07/owl#sameAs>
<http://dbpedia.org/resource/AgResearch>.
<https://makg.org/entity/79941097>
<http://www.w3.org/2002/07/owl#sameAs>
<http://dbpedia.org/resource/American_Civic_Association>.
```

（来源：https://makg.org/sparql）

6.4 DBpedia Databus 元数据

6.4.1 DataID 本体模型

DBpedia Databus（数据总线）是数据目录和版本控制平台（databus.dbpedia.org），面向数据开发者和消费者，提供数据的发布、存储、版本控制和查询服务，具有可信、遵循 FAIR 原则和自动化程度高等特点。DBpedia Databus 也是分散数据集的元数据注册中心，元数据模型采用 DataID 本体，见图 6.9。

DataID 本体复用了 DCAT、VoID、Prov-O 和 FOAF 等本体，对 Dataset 类的定义见例 6.6。

例 6.6 Dataset 类的定义。

```
@prefix dataid: <http://dataid.dbpedia.org/ns/core#>.
@prefix dcat: <http://www.w3.org/ns/dcat#>.
@prefix prov: <http://www.w3.org/ns/prov#>.
```

第6章 知识图谱的元数据

```
@prefix void: <http://rdfs.org/ns/void#>.
@prefix rdf: <http://www.w3.org/1999/02/22-rdf-syntax-ns#>.
@prefix rdfs: <http://www.w3.org/2000/01/rdf-schema#>.
@prefix owl: <http://www.w3.org/2002/07/owl#>.
dataid: Dataset    a   owl: Class ;
        rdfs: isDefinedBy      <http://dataid.dbpedia.org/ns/core#>;
        rdfs: label            "Dataset"@en ;
        rdfs: subClassOf       void: Dataset, dcat: Dataset, prov: Entity,
                               [ a owl: Restriction ;
                               owl: allValuesFrom dataid: DataId ;
                               owl: onProperty foaf: isPrimaryTopicOf ],
                               [ a owl: Restriction ;
                               owl: allValuesFrom dataid: Dataset ;
                               owl: onProperty dataid: nextVersion ],
                               [ a owl: Restriction ;
                               owl: allValuesFrom dataid: SimpleStatement;
                               owl: onProperty dct: rights ].
```

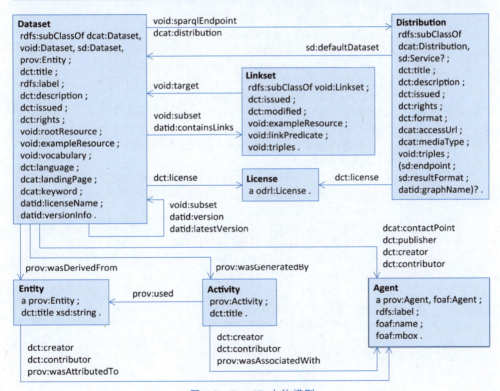

图 6.9　DataID 本体模型

6.4.2 元数据实例

DBpedia Databus 采用 JSON-LD 格式给出数据集的机器可读的元数据记录文件,例 6.7 给出一个实例,环境定义文件见例 6.8。

例 6.7 Databus 元数据实例。

```
{ "@context": "https://databus.dbpedia.org/res/context.jsonld",
    "@graph": [
        { "@id": "https://databus.dbpedia.org/dbpedia/wikidata",
          "@type": "Group",
          "account": "https://databus.dbpedia.org/dbpedia"   },
{ "@id":
"https://databus.dbpedia.org/dbpedia/wikidata/labels/2018.10.20",
          "@type": [ "Version",
                     "http://dataid.dbpedia.org/ns/core#Dataset" ],
          "abstract": " Contains the name in all the languages in
wikidata.",
          "hasVersion": "2018.10.20",
          "issued": "2018-10-20T00: 00: 00Z",
          "license": "http://purl.oclc.org/NET/rdflicense/cc-by3.0",
          "modified": "2023-06-26T12: 45: 31.820Z",
          "publisher": "https://databus.dbpedia.org/dbpedia#this",
          "title": "Wikidata Labels",
          "distribution": [ " https://databus. dbpedia. org/dbpedia/
wikidata/labels/2018.10.20#labels.ttl.bzip2",
"https://databus.dbpedia.org/dbpedia/wikidata/labels/2018.10.20
#labels_tag=nmw.ttl.bzip2" ],
          "account": "https://databus.dbpedia.org/dbpedia",
          "artifact": " https://databus. dbpedia. org/dbpedia/wikidata/
labels",
          "group": "https://databus.dbpedia.org/dbpedia/wikidata",
          "proof": "b5621529c668084b4e87313a7dd34a8c"    },
        { " @ id": " https://databus. dbpedia. org/dbpedia/wikidata/
labels/2018.10.20#labels_tag=nmw.ttl.bzip2",
          "@type": "Part",
          "hasVersion": "2018.10.20",
          "issued": "2018-10-20T00: 00: 00Z",
          "modified": "2023-06-26T12: 45: 31.820Z",
          "dcat: byteSize": 375880752,
```

第6章 知识图谱的元数据

```
            "downloadURL": "https://downloads.dbpedia.org/repo/lts/
wikidata/labels/2018.10.20/labels_nmw.ttl.bz2",
            "compression": "bzip2",
             "file": "https://databus.dbpedia.org/dbpedia/wikidata/
labels/2018.10.20/labels_tag=nmw.ttl.bzip2",
            "formatExtension": "ttl",
            "sha256sum":
"cde1a154e70741929c9ecec6e81cd4df002a4b708e271203f7239fd8b64a2ea0",
            "dcv: tag": "nmw"    } ]
}
```

（来源：https://databus.dbpedia.org/dbpedia/wikidata/labels/2018.10.20）

例 6.8 环境定义文件（部分）。

```
{   "@context": {
         "databus": "https://dataid.dbpedia.org/databus#",
         "dcv": "https://dataid.dbpedia.org/databus-cv#",
         "rdfs": "http://www.w3.org/2000/01/rdf-schema#",
         "dct": "http://purl.org/dc/terms/",
         "dcat": "http://www.w3.org/ns/dcat#",
         "xsd": "http://www.w3.org/2001/XMLSchema#",
         "cert": "http://www.w3.org/ns/auth/cert#",
         "dbo": "http://dbpedia.org/ontology/",
         "foaf": "http://xmlns.com/foaf/0.1/",
         "prov": "http://www.w3.org/ns/prov-o#",
         "sec": "https://w3id.org/security#",
         "Group": "databus: Group",
         "group": {   "@id": "databus: group",
                      "@type": "@id"   },
         "title": {   "@id": "dct: title"   },
         "abstract": { "@id": "dct: abstract"   },
         "description": {   "@id": "dct: description"   },
         "issued": {   "@id": "dct: issued",
                           "@type": "xsd: dateTime"   },
     "modified": { "@id": "dct: modified",
                  "@type": "xsd: dateTime"   },
            "wasDerivedFrom": {   "@id": "prov: wasDerivedFrom",
                            "@type": "@id" } }
}
```

（来源：https://databus.dbpedia.org/res/context.jsonld）

6.5 本体的元数据

6.5.1 DCAT 元数据

LiveSchema 本体库采用 DCAT 词汇表描述本体资源。图 6.10 展示了 DBpedia 本体的元数据，此外还给出了 N3、Turtle、XML 和 JSON-LD 格式的元数据，其中 Turtle 格式的元数据见例 6.9。

Field	Value
Source	https://lov.linkeddata.es/dataset/lov/vocabs/dbpedia-owl/versions/2016-05-21.n3
Version	v4-2-SNAPSHOT
Last Updated	8 November 2021, 11:55 (UTC+08:00)
Created	3 February 2020, 23:06 (UTC+08:00)
Contact URI	http://wiki.dbpedia.org/Ontology
Issued	2016-05-21
Language	ar, be, bg, bn, ca, cs, de, el, en, es, eu, fr, ga, gl, hy, it, ja, ko, kr, lv, nl, pl, pt, ro, ru, sl, sr, tr, zh
Reference Catalog URL	https://lov.linkeddata.es/dataset/lov/vocabs/dbpedia-owl
URI	http://dbpedia.org/ontology/

图 6.10 DBpedia Ontology 的元数据

（来源：http://liveschema.eu/dataset/lov_dbpedia-owl）

例 6.9 DBpedia Ontology 的元数据。

```
@prefix dcat: <http://www.w3.org/ns/dcat#>.
@prefix dct: <http://purl.org/dc/terms/>.
@prefix owl: <http://www.w3.org/2002/07/owl#>.
@prefix rdf: <http://www.w3.org/1999/02/22-rdf-syntax-ns#>.
@prefix rdfs: <http://www.w3.org/2000/01/rdf-schema#>.
@prefix xml: <http://www.w3.org/XML/1998/namespace>.
@prefix xsd: <http://www.w3.org/2001/XMLSchema#>.
<http://dbpedia.org/ontology/> a dcat: Dataset ;
    dct: description    "The DBpedia ontology provides the classes and properties used in the DBpedia data set. @en" ;
    dct: issued     "2016-05-21T00: 00: 00"^^xsd: dateTime ;
    dct: modified    "2021-11-08T03: 55: 46.012252"^^xsd: dateTime ;
    dct: title      "The DBpedia Ontology" ;
```

```
        dcat: contactPoint    <http://wiki.dbpedia.org/Ontology>;
        dcat: distribution
<http://liveschema.eu/dataset/5b5927ad-097c-4394-81c6-4939bf36bdd0/
resource/1139caf7-4ffa-4eb8-82e8-2a2ec844a72d>,
<http://liveschema.eu/dataset/5b5927ad-097c-4394-81c6-4939bf36bdd0/
resource/d4090f9f-93b8-4a1a-a2ef-06a7c4c43351>;
        dcat: keyword    "general upper";
        dcat: landingPage <https://lov.linkeddata.es/dataset/lov/vocabs/
dbpedia-owl/versions/2016-05-21.n3>.
```

（来源：http://liveschema.eu/dataset/5b5927ad-097c-4394-81c6-4939bf36bdd0.ttl）

6.5.2 VOAF 元数据

Linked Open Vocabularies（LOV）目录系统采用 VOAF（Vocabulary of a Friend）词汇表描述本体资源。VOAF 词汇表的核心类是 voaf：Vocabulary，如图 6.11 所示。DBpedia 本体的 VOAF 元数据见例 6.10。

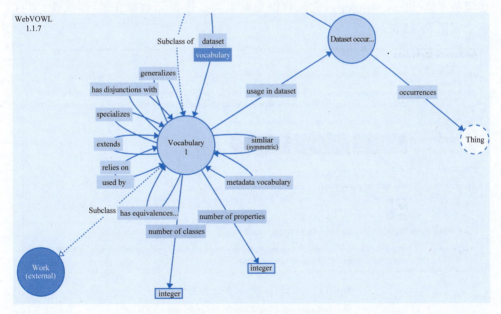

图 6.11　VOAF 词汇表的本体模型

（来源：https://service.tib.eu/webvowl/#file=voaf_2013-05-24.n3）

例 6.10　DBpedia Ontology 的 VOAF 元数据。

```
@prefix dct: <http://purl.org/dc/terms/>.
@prefix xsd: <http://www.w3.org/2001/XMLSchema#>.
@prefix vann: <http://purl.org/vocab/vann/>.
@prefix voaf: <http://purl.org/vocommons/voaf#>.
<http://dbpedia.org/ontology/>a voaf: Vocabulary ;
dct: title       "The DBpedia Ontology"@en;
vann: preferredNamespacePrefix    "dbpedia-owl";
vann: preferredNamespaceUri       <http://dbpedia.org/ontology/>;
voaf: classNumber                 "775"^^xsd: integer;
voaf: propertyNumber              "2861"^^xsd: integer;
voaf: occurrencesInDatasets       "348009"^^xsd: integer;
voaf: reusedByDatasets            "15"^^xsd: integer.
```

（来源：https://lov.linkeddata.es/dataset/lov/sparql）

6.5.3 AgroPortal 元数据

农学本体库 AgroPortal 采用丰富的元数据元素描述每个本体资源。例如，描述植物本体（plant ontology）的元数据见图 6.12。这些元数据元素（即属性）来自多个词汇表，见表 6.3。

Additional Metadata	
URI	http://purl.obolibrary.org/obo/po.owl
Abstract	A non extensive collection of terms that describe structure and developmental stages of a plant. Arranged in a structured order/network based on the biological concept describing the term's relationship in an ontology tree.
Bug Database	https://github.com/Planteome/plant-ontology/issues
From The Same Domain Than	EO , TO , TAXREF-LD , C3POPLANT
Deprecated	false
Endorsed By	RDA WDI (http://ist.blogs.inra.fr/wdi/)
Endpoint	SPARQL
Example Identifier	http://purl.obolibrary.org/obo/NCBITaxon_33090
Has Domain	https://data.agroportal.lirmm.fr/categories/PLANTDEV, https://data.agroportal.lirmm.fr/categories/BIODIV, https://data.agroportal.lirmm.fr/categories/PLANT

图 6.12　Plant Ontology 的元数据（部分）

（来源：https://agroportal.lirmm.fr/ontologies/PO）

网站提供四种机器可读的元数据文件，分别是 CSV、N-Triple、JSON-LD 和 RDF/XML，其中 JSON-LD 格式的元数据见例 6.11。

第6章 知识图谱的元数据

表 6.3　AgroPortal 元数据复用的主要词汇表

序号	词汇表	URI	代 表 属 性
1	dc	http://purl.org/dc/elements/1.1/	creator，publisher，title
2	dcterms	http://purl.org/dc/terms/	Abstract，identifier，modified
3	omv	http://omv.ontoware.org/2005/05/ontology#	URI，usedOntologyEngineeringTool，usedOntologyEngineeringMethodology
4	mod	http://www.isibang.ac.in/ns/mod#	ontologyDesignLanguage，toolUsed
5	door	http://kannel.open.ac.uk/ontology#	similarTo，imports，priorVersion
6	voaf	http://purl.org/vocommons/voaf#	classNumber，usedBy，reliesOn
7	void	http://rdfs.org/ns/void#	sparqlEndpoint，triples，uriSpace
8	vann	http://purl.org/vocab/vann/	usageNote，example，changes
9	dcat	http://www.w3.org/ns/dcat#	keyword，theme，contactPoint
10	schema	http://schema.org/	citation，isPartOf，dateCreated
11	cito	http://purl.org/spar/cito/	citesAsAuthority

（来源：https://github.com/agroportal/project-management/tree/master/metadata）

例 6.11　Plant Ontology 的元数据。

```
{ "@id": "http://purl.obolibrary.org/obo/po.owl",
"@type": "http://www.w3.org/2002/07/owl#Ontology",
"pullLocation": "http://purl.obolibrary.org/obo/po.owl",
"exampleIdentifier": " http://purl.obolibrary.org/obo/NCBITaxon_33090",
"comesFromTheSameDomain": [
        "https://data.agroportal.lirmm.fr/ontologies/EO",
        "https://data.agroportal.lirmm.fr/ontologies/TO",
        "https://data.agroportal.lirmm.fr/ontologies/C3POPLANT" ],
"ontologyRelatedTo": [
        "https://data.agroportal.lirmm.fr/ontologies/CL",
        "http://bioportal.bioontology.org/ontologies/CHEBI",
        "https://data.agroportal.lirmm.fr/ontologies/TO" ],
"URI": "http://purl.obolibrary.org/obo/po.owl",
"creationDate": "2023-07-14T18: 02: 46+02: 00",
"hasDomain": [
        "https://data.agroportal.lirmm.fr/categories/PLANTDEV",
        "https://data.agroportal.lirmm.fr/categories/BIODIV",
```

```
            "https://data.agroportal.lirmm.fr/categories/PLANT",
            "https://data.agroportal.lirmm.fr/categories/GENPLANT" ],
    "hasLicense": "http://creativecommons.org/licenses/by/4.0/",
    "hasOntologyLanguage": "OWL",
    "hasOntologySyntax": "http://www.w3.org/ns/formats/RDF_XML",
    "naturalLanguage": "http://lexvo.org/id/iso639-3/eng",
    "numberOfClasses": 2025,
    "numberOfIndividuals": 9,
    "numberOfProperties": 129,
    "status": "production",
    "useImports": [
        "http://purl.obolibrary.org/obo/po/imports/ncbitaxon_import.owl",
        "http://purl.obolibrary.org/obo/po/imports/ro_import.owl" ],
    "usedOntologyEngineeringTool": "OWL API",
    "version": "July 2023",
    " dataDump ":  " http://data. agroportal. lirmm. fr/ontologies/PO/
download",
    "includedInDataCatalog": [
            "http://bioportal.bioontology.org/ontologies/PO",
            "http://www.ontobee.org/ontology/PO",
            "https://agroportal.lirmm.fr/" ],
    "repository": "https://github.com/Planteome/plant-ontology",
    "deprecated": false,
    "endpoint": "http://sparql.agroportal.lirmm.fr/test",
    "homepage": "http://www.planteome.org",
    "logo": "http://wiki.plantontology.org/images/2/2f/PO_logo_wiki.png"
}
```

（来源：https://agroportal.lirmm.fr/ontologies/PO）

6.5.4 MOD 元数据

MOD(metadata for ontology description and publication)是本体描述和出版的新一代元数据方案。在复用 OMV(ontology metadata vocabulary)、DC、DCAT 和 VoID 等词汇表的基础上，印度统计研究所（Indian Statistical Institute）联合法国蒙彼利埃大学（University of Montpellier）于 2015 年 8 月推出 MOD v1.0，到 2021 年 12 月已更新到 v2.0。MOD v2.0 含有 95 个类、149 个关系和 111 个属性，其中核心类是 SemanticArtefact，见图 6.13，它的定义见例 6.12。

例 6.12 SemanticArtefact 类的定义。

第6章 知识图谱的元数据

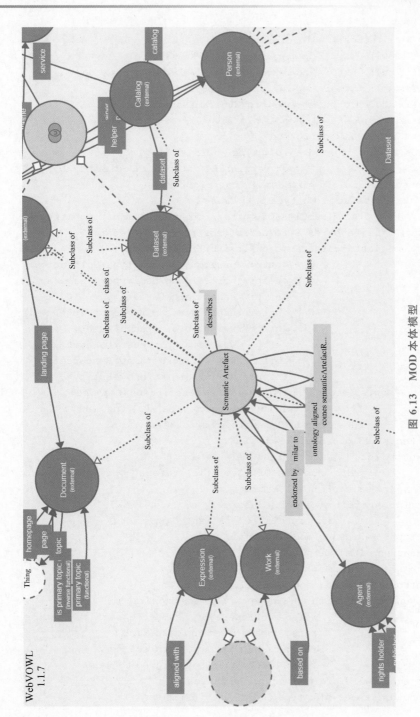

图 6.13 MOD 本体模型

（来源：https://service.tib.eu/webvowl/#iri=https://www.isibang.ac.in/ns/mod/ontology.ttl）

```
@prefix : <https://w3id.org/mod#> .
@prefix owl: <http://www.w3.org/2002/07/owl#> .
@prefix rdf: <http://www.w3.org/1999/02/22-rdf-syntax-ns#> .
@prefix xml: <http://www.w3.org/XML/1998/namespace> .
@prefix xsd: <http://www.w3.org/2001/XMLSchema#> .
@prefix rdfs: <http://www.w3.org/2000/01/rdf-schema#> .
@base <https://w3id.org/mod> .
<https://w3id.org/mod>   rdf: type   owl: Ontology ;
                         owl: versionIRI <https://w3id.org/mod/2.0> .
###https://w3id.org/mod#SemanticArtefact
: SemanticArtefact rdf: type owl: Class ;
             rdfs: subClassOf <http://creativecommons.org/ns#work>,
<http://iflastandards.info/ns/fr/frbr/frbrer/Expression>,
<http://iflastandards.info/ns/fr/frbr/frbrer/Work>,
                        <http://purl.org/dc/dcmitype/Collection>,
                        <http://purl.org/dc/dcmitype/Dataset>,
                        <http://schema.org/Dataset>,
                        <http://usefulinc.com/ns/doap#Project>,
                        <http://www.w3.org/ns/adms#Asset>,
                        <http://www.w3.org/ns/dcat#Dataset>,
                        <http://www.w3.org/ns/dcat#Resource>,
                        <http://www.w3.org/ns/prov#Entity>,
<http://www.w3.org/ns/sparql-service-description#Service>,
                        <http://xmlns.com/foaf/0.1/Document> ;
             rdfs: label "Semantic Artefact"@en .
###https://w3id.org/mod#Taxonomy
: Taxonomy rdf: type owl: Class ;
             rdfs: subClassOf : SemanticArtefact .
###https://w3id.org/mod#Terminology
: Terminology rdf: type owl: Class ;
             rdfs: subClassOf : SemanticArtefact .
###https://w3id.org/mod#Thesaurus
: Thesaurus rdf: type owl: Class ;
             rdfs: subClassOf : SemanticArtefact .
###https://w3id.org/mod#hasEquivalencesWith
: hasEquivalencesWith rdf: type owl: ObjectProperty ;
                     rdfs: subPropertyOf : semanticArtefactRelation ;
                     rdfs: domain : SemanticArtefact ;
                     rdfs: range : SemanticArtefact ;
                     rdfs: label "ontology aligned to"@en .
###https://w3id.org/mod#numberOfClasses
: numberOfClasses rdf: type owl: DatatypeProperty ;
```

```
rdfs: subPropertyOf : metrics ;
rdfs: range xsd: nonNegativeInteger ;
rdfs: label "number of classes"@en .
```

（来源：https://www.isibang.ac.in/ns/mod/ontology.ttl）

BioPortal 平台为 MOD v2.0 定义了一些新属性，见表 6.4。应用这些属性描述 Schema.org 词汇表的例子见图 6.14。

表 6.4 MOD 元数据项举例

序号	元数据项	说明
1	https://w3id.org/mod#averageChildCount	每个类的子类的平均数量
2	https://w3id.org/mod#maxDepth	层次结构树的最大深度
3	https://w3id.org/mod#classesWithOneChild	只有一个子类的类的个数
4	https://w3id.org/mod#numberOfIndividuals	本体中实例的数量
5	https://w3id.org/mod#numberOfDataProperties	本体中属性的数量
6	https://w3id.org/mod#numberOfObjectProperties	本体中关系的数量

Metrics

Classes	822
Individuals	989
Properties	1,319
Maximum depth	5
Maximum number of children	61
Average number of children	5
Classes with a single child	45
Classes with more than 25 children	6
Classes with no definition	19

图 6.14 Schema.org 词汇表的部分属性

（来源：https://bioportal.bioontology.org/ontologies/SCHEMA/?p=summary）

参考文献

[1] MARVIN H，OBRACZKA D，SAEEDI A，et al. Construction of knowledge graphs：State and challenges[J]. ArXiv abs/2302.11509 ，2023.

[2] MAILLOT P, CORBY O, FARON C, et al. IndeGx: a model and a framework for indexing RDF knowledge graphs with SPARQL-based test suits [J]. Web Semantics: Science, Services and Agents on the World Wide Web, 2023(76): 100775.

[3] W3C. W3C Data activity building the web of data [EB/OL]. [2023-09-29]. https://www.w3.org/2013/data/.

[4] 谢真强,翟军,李红芹,等. W3C开放数据的元数据标准DCAT建设进展及对我国的启示[J]. 情报杂志, 2019, 38(11): 167-174.

[5] W3C. Data catalog vocabulary (DCAT)-version 2 [EB/OL]. [2023-09-29]. https://www.w3.org/TR/vocab-dcat/.

[6] W3C. Data catalog vocabulary (DCAT)-version 3 [EB/OL]. [2023-09-29]. https://www.w3.org/TR/vocab-dcat-3/.

[7] W3C. Describing linked datasets with the VoID vocabulary [EB/OL]. [2023-09-29]. https://www.w3.org/TR/void/.

[8] FREUDENBERG M, BRÜMMER M, RÜCKNAGEL J, et al. The metadata ecosystem of DataID[C]. International Conference on Metadata and Semantics Research, 2016.

[9] DUTTA B, TOULET A, EMONET V, et al. New generation metadata vocabulary for ontology description and publication [C]. International Conference on Metadata and Semantics Research, 2017.

第7章 知识图谱验证技术

7.1 知识图谱验证

知识图谱验证(knowledge graph validation)就是判断知识图谱中的断言在语义上的正确性及与实际的符合情况,是保障知识图谱提供正确和可靠知识的重要手段。

在知识图谱的生命周期中,初始创建的知识图谱通常是不完整的,还会含有重复(冗余)、矛盾(不一致),甚至错误的陈述,特别是源自多个数据源的大规模知识图谱。例如,DBpedia 中的一些乐队(bands)实体曾经被错误地赋予 dbo:City 类型。

因此,知识图谱管护(knowledge graph curation)的一个关键环节是质量评价(quality assessment)。这里的质量指"客体的一组固有特性满足要求的程度"(fitness for purpose)。其中,"一致性"(coherency)是一个重要的质量维度(quality dimension),用以衡量知识图谱符合模式级别(schema-level)定义的语义(semantics)和约束(constraints)的程度。

知识图谱验证涉及各种数据验证(data validation)技术,见表 7.1。随着 RDF 知识图谱的普及,RDF 数据验证技术得到了日益广泛的应用。例如,DBpedia 和 YAGO 都用到了 RDF 数据验证的 SHACL(shapes constraint language)技术。

表 7.1 主要的数据验证技术

序号	数据格式	验证技术
1	关系数据库	DDL(Data Definition Language)
2	XML	DTD,XML Schema,RelaxNG,Schematron

续表

序号	数据格式	验证技术
3	JSON	JSON Schema
4	RDF	SHACL，ShEx

7.2 知识图谱的验证模式

定义一组约束的数据模式称之为验证模式（validating schema）。例如，图 7.1 所示的 UML 类图定义了两个类（User 和 Course）的属性约束、关系约束及它们的基数约束。

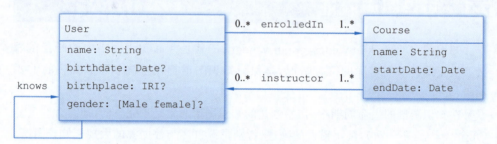

图 7.1 UML 类图的例子

RDF 数据的验证模式称为"模板"(shape)，一个例子见图 7.2。

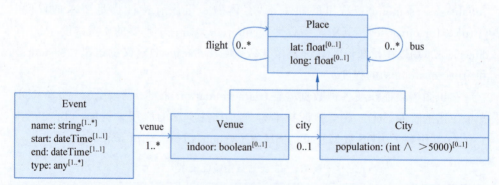

图 7.2 模板的例子

7.3　W3C SHACL 的基本概念

模板约束语言（shapes constraint language，SHACL）以结构化的方式定义 RDF 数据的约束，由 W3C RDF Data Shapes 工作组负责开发。该工作组成立于 2014 年 9 月，于 2015 年 10 月发布 SHACL 草案，于 2017 年 7 月发布 SHACL 正式版。

W3C SHACL 标准规范分成两部分：SHACL Core 和 SHACL SPARQL。SHACL Core 定义了两类模板——结点模板（node shape）和属性模板（property shape），分别建立结点和属性的约束，见图 7.3。

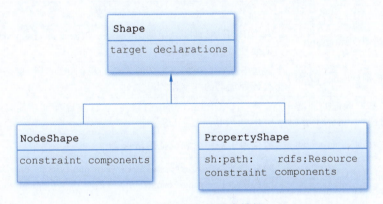

图 7.3　SHACL 的两类模板

SHACL 采用 RDF 语法描述各种约束，相应的 RDF 图称为"模板图"（shapes graph），相对照的，被验证的 RDF 数据称为"数据图"（data graph），它们的例子分别见图 7.4 和图 7.5。SHACL 定义的其他概念收录在表 7.2 中。

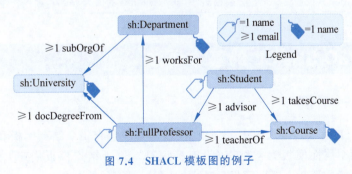

图 7.4　SHACL 模板图的例子

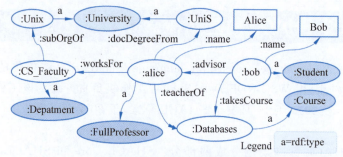

图 7.5 SHACL 数据图的例子

表 7.2 SHACL 定义的基本概念

序号	概 念	定 义
1	数据图(data graph)	一个 RDF 图(即三元组的集合)——被验证的对象,SHACL 验证处理器的一个输入
2	模板图(shapes graph)	通过 SHACL 词汇表定义的表达约束的 RDF 图,也是 SHACL 验证处理器的一个输入
3	SHACL 验证处理器(SHACL processor)	支持 SHACL Core 语法的软件模块,实现验证功能,如 Zazuko SHACL Playground 等
4	焦点结点(focus node)	数据图中被约束和验证的结点
5	约束组件(constraint components)	约束的基本单元,分为基数约束(cardinality constraint)、值的范围约束(value range constraint)和逻辑约束(logical constraint)等各种类型
6	参数(parameters)	约束组件中定义具体约束的属性,如 sh:minCount、sh:not 和 sh:minExclusive 等,分为强制的(mandatory)和可选的(optional)两类
7	验证报告(validation report)	SHACL 验证处理器以三元组的形式给出验证结果,如果数据图符合模板图,则 sh:conforms 的值为 true,否则报告违规情况

7.4 W3C SHACL 的基本语法

7.4.1 引例

例 7.1 以 Turtle 格式描述了一组"模板",其中含有 1 个结点模板和 3 个属性模板。前两个属性模板为空结点(没有标识符),位于结点模板内(通过谓词 sh:property 连接);第 3 个属性模板是独立的(有标识符),见图 7.6。

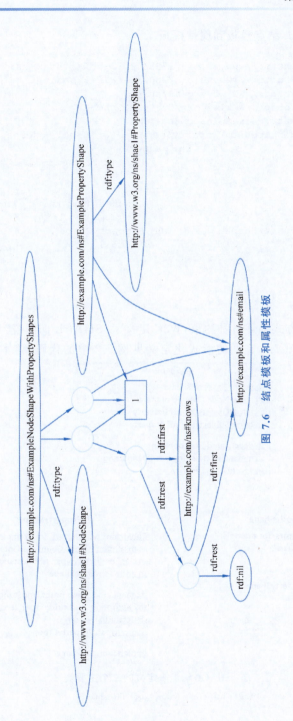

图 7.6 结点模板和属性模板

例 7.1　SHACL 结点模板和属性模板。

```
@prefix rdf: <http://www.w3.org/1999/02/22-rdf-syntax-ns#>.
@prefix rdfs: <http://www.w3.org/2000/01/rdf-schema#>.
@prefix sh: <http://www.w3.org/ns/shacl#>.
@prefix xsd: <http://www.w3.org/2001/XMLSchema#>.
@prefix ex: <http://example.com/ns#>.
ex: ExampleNodeShapeWithPropertyShapes    a    sh: NodeShape ;
                        sh: property [
                                sh: path ex: email ;
                                sh: minCount 1; ] ;
                        sh: property [
                                sh: path (ex: knows ex: email) ;
                                sh: minCount 1; ] .
ex: ExamplePropertyShape    a    sh: PropertyShape ;
                sh: path    ex: email ;
                sh: minCount 1 .
```

7.4.2　SHACL 词汇表

为以结构化的方式描述各种约束，W3C 定义了"SHACL 词汇表"（即本体），其中的 3 个主要类见图 7.7，它们的形式化定义见例 7.2 中的代码，该本体可视化的

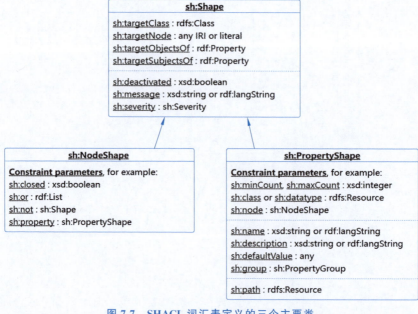

图 7.7　SHACL 词汇表定义的三个主要类

（来源：https://www.w3.org/TR/shacl/）

部分结果见图 7.8。

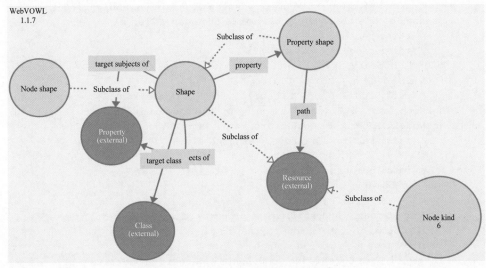

图 7.8　SHACL 词汇表的可视化（部分）

例 7.2　SHACL 词汇表的定义（部分）。

```
#W3C Shapes Constraint Language (SHACL) Vocabulary
#Version from 2017-07-20
@prefix owl:  <http://www.w3.org/2002/07/owl#>.
@prefix rdf:  <http://www.w3.org/1999/02/22-rdf-syntax-ns#>.
@prefix rdfs: <http://www.w3.org/2000/01/rdf-schema#>.
@prefix xsd:  <http://www.w3.org/2001/XMLSchema#>.
@prefix sh:   <http://www.w3.org/ns/shacl#>.
#Shapes vocabulary
sh: Shape      a    rdfs: Class ;
      rdfs: comment   "A shape is a collection of constraints that may be
      targeted for certain nodes."@en ;
      rdfs: subClassOf  rdfs: Resource.
sh: NodeShape    a    rdfs: Class ;
          rdfs: comment    " A node shape is a shape that specifies
      constraint that need to be met with respect to focus nodes."@en;
          rdfs: subClassOf    sh: Shape.
sh: PropertyShape    a    rdfs: Class ;
          rdfs: comment    "A property shape is a shape that specifies
constraints on the values of a focus node for a given property or path."@en ;
          rdfs: subClassOf    sh: Shape.
```

```
sh: targetClass    a    rdf: Property ;
      rdfs: comment     "Links a shape to a class, indicating that all
instances of the class must conform to the shape."@en ;
      rdfs: domain     sh: Shape ;
      rdfs: range      rdfs: Class .
#Node kind vocabulary
sh: NodeKind    a    rdfs: Class ;
      rdfs: comment     " The class of all node kinds, including sh:
BlankNode, sh: IRI, sh: Literal or the combinations of these: sh:
BlankNodeOrIRI, sh: BlankNodeOrLiteral, sh: IRIOrLiteral."@en ;
      rdfs: subClassOf    rdfs: Resource .
sh: IRI    a    sh: NodeKind ;
      rdfs: comment    "The node kind of all IRIs."@en .
#Path vocabulary
sh: path    a    rdf: Property ;
      rdfs: comment     "Specifies the property path of a property shape."@en ;
      rdfs: domain    sh: PropertyShape ;
      rdfs: range     rdfs: Resource .
#Library of Core Constraint Components and their properties
sh: property    a    rdf: Property ;
      rdfs: comment     "Links a shape to its property shapes."@en ;
      rdfs: domain    sh: Shape ;
      rdfs: range     sh: PropertyShape .
sh: maxCount    a    rdf: Property ;
      rdfs: comment    "Specifies the maximum number of values in the set
of value nodes."@en ;
      rdfs: range     xsd: integer .
sh: nodeKind    a    rdf: Property ;
      rdfs: comment    "Specifies the node kind (e.g. IRI or literal)
each value node."@en ;
      rdfs: range     sh: NodeKind .
```

7.4.3 目标声明

SHACL通过"目标声明"(target declarations)明确约束指向的结点集,采用多种声明方式,用到的属性见表7.3。

表 7.3 SHACL 用于目标声明的属性

序号	属 性	说 明
1	sh：targetNode	指明特定结点
2	sh：targetClass	类的实例对应的所有结点

续表

序号	属性	说明
3	sh：targetSubjectsOf	谓词的主体对应的所有结点
4	sh：targetObjectsOf	谓词的客体对应的所有结点

例 7.3 声明的目标结点有：alice、：bob 和：carol，要求它们具有一个 schema：name 属性，值的类型为 xsd：string。该例的数据部分含有 4 个结点，第 1 个结点的陈述通过验证，第 2、第 3 个结点的陈述没有通过验证，第 4 个结点被验证器忽略（不是目标结点）。

例 7.3 sh：targetNode 的例子。

```
#模板部分
:UserShape    a       sh:NodeShape ;
sh:targetNode :alice , :bob , :carol;
sh:property   [
sh:path    schema:name ;
sh:minCount  1;   sh:maxCount  1;
sh:datatype  xsd:string  ].
#数据部分
:alice   schema:name  "Alice Cooper" .  # ✓ Passes as :UserShape
:bob     foaf:name    "Bob" .           # ✗ Fails as :UserShape
:carol   schema:name  23.               # ✗ Fails as :UserShape
:dave    schema:name  45.               # Ignored
```

例 7.4 声明的目标结点为类：User 的任意实例，也包括它的子类的实体，例子中的子类为：Student。

例 7.4 sh：targetClass 的例子。

```
#模板部分
:UserShape     a      sh:NodeShape ;
sh:targetClass :User ;
sh:property    [
sh:path    schema:name ;
sh:minCount  1;   sh:maxCount  1;
sh:datatype  xsd:string  ].
#数据部分
:alice    a       :User;        # ✓ Passes as :UserShape
```

```
schema:name     "Alice Cooper".
:bob       a          :User;       # ✗ Fails as :UserShape
foaf:name    "Bob".
:carol      a          :User;       # ✗ Fails as :UserShape
schema:name    23.
:dave       a          :Student;    # ✗ Fails as :UserShape
schema:name    45.
:emily      a          :Student;    # ✓ Passes as :UserShape
schema:name    "Emily".
:Student    rdfs:subClassOf    :User.
```

例 7.5 声明的目标结点是谓词：teaches 的主体（subject），包括：alice 和：bob，而：carol 不是目标结点，被验证器忽略。

例 7.5 sh：targetClass 的例子。

```
#模板部分
:UserShape             a       sh:NodeShape;
sh:targetSubjectsOf    :teaches;
sh:property            [
    sh:path         schema:name;
    sh:minCount     1; sh:maxCount 1;
    sh:datatype     xsd:string    ].
#数据部分
:alice      :teaches    :Algebra;    # ✓ Passes as :UserShape
schema:name    "Alice".
:bob       :teaches    :Logic;       # ✗ Fails as :UserShape
foaf:name    "Robert".
:carol      foaf:name   23.                  #Ignored
```

上面的例子中用到了基数约束，涉及的两个属性见表 7.4，例子见例 7.6。

表 7.4 SHACL 的基数约束

序号	属性（参数）	说明
1	sh：minCount	结点属性值个数的最小值，若没有声明，则最小值约束为 0
2	sh：maxCount	结点属性值个数的最大值，若没有声明，则没有最大值约束

例 7.6 基数约束的例子。

```
#模板部分
: User        a         sh: NodeShape , rdfs: Class ;
sh: property  [
sh: path      schema: follows ;
sh: minCount  2 ;    sh: maxCount 3 ] .
#数据部分
: alice       a         : User ;          # ✓ Passes as : User
schema: follows : bob, : carol .
: bob         a         : User ;          # ✗ Fails as : User
schema: follows : alice .
: carol       a         : User ;          # ✗ Fails as : User
schema: follows : alice, : bob, : carol, : dave .
```

7.4.4　约束组件

每一个模板都包含一个或多个约束组件（constraint components）。每个约束组件带有两类参数，分别是强制的（mandatory）和可选的（optional）。参数及其值用以声明一个具体的约束。

例 7.7 给出了两个约束的例子。

例 7.7　带有两个约束的"模板"如下所示。

```
#模板部分
: UserShape     a         sh: NodeShape ;
sh: nodeKind    sh: IRI ;
sh: class       schema: Person .
#数据部分
: alice         a         schema: Person.     # ✓ Passes as : UserShape
<http://other.uri.com/bob>
   a     schema: Person.                      # ✓ Passes as : UserShape
_: 1            a         schema: Person.     # ✗ Fails as : UserShape
```

该例子中的两个约束分别关联两个约束组件：

（1）第一个约束指出，符合该模板的结点必须是 IRI。关联的约束组件是 sh：NodeKindConstraintComponent，参数为 sh：nodeKind，值是 sh：IRI。

（2）第二个约束指出，符合该模板的结点必须是 schema：Person 类的实例。关联的约束组件是 sh：ClassConstraintComponent，参数为 sh：class，值是 schema：Person。

常用的约束组件及其参数见表 7.5。

表 7.5　SHACL Core 的约束组件

序号	约束组件	参　　数
1	基数约束	sh：minCount，sh：maxCount
2	值的类型	sh：class，sh：datatype，sh：nodeKind，sh：in，sh：hasValue
3	值的范围约束	sh：minInclusive，sh：maxInclusive sh：minExclusive，sh：maxExclusive
4	字符串约束	sh：minLength，sh：maxLength，sh：length，sh：pattern
5	语言约束	sh：uniqueLang，sh：languageIn
6	逻辑约束	sh：and，sh：or，sh：xone，sh：not
7	模板约束	sh：node，sh：property，sh：qualifiedValueShape， sh：qualifiedValueShapesDisjoint， sh：qualifiedMinCount，sh：qualifiedMaxCoun
8	封闭约束	sh：closed，sh：ignoredProperties
9	属性对约束	sh：equals，sh：disjoint sh：lessThan，sh：lessThanOrEquals
10	非验证属性	sh：name，sh：description，sh：order，sh：group

7.4.5　路径表达

在属性模板中，属性 sh：path 的值为 SHACL 路径（paths），它可以是一个简单的谓词（如 schema：name），也可以是多个谓词的组合，用以说明对哪些属性或属性组合定义了约束，应用的例子见例 7.8。

例 7.8　SHACL 路径的例子。

```
#模板部分
:UserShape     a    sh:NodeShape;
sh:targetClass :User ;
sh:property    [
sh:path    [sh:alternativePath (schema:knows schema:follows)];
sh:nodeKind  sh:IRI ;
sh:minCount  1  ];
sh:property       [
```

```
sh:path        ([sh:oneOrMorePath schema:knows] schema:email) ;
sh:nodeKind    sh:IRI ] .
#数据部分
:alice              a               :User ;         #✓ Passes as :UserShape
schema:follows     <mailto:alice@mail.org>;
schema:knows       :bob, :carol .
:bob    schema:email     <mailto:bob@mail.org>;
schema:knows       :carol .
:carol    schema:email     <mailto:carol@mail.org>.
:dave              a               :User ;         #✗ Fails as :UserShape
schema:knows     <mailto:dave@mail.org>;
schema:knows       :carol, :emily .
:Emily    schema:email     "Unknown" .
```

这个例子定义：User 类的实例的 schema:knows 或 schema:follows 属性的值必须为 IRI，且从 :User 类的实例出发，沿着一个或多个 schema:knows 组成的属性路径，到达的结点必须有 schema:email 属性，且其值为 IRI。

更多的 SHACL 路径的例子见表 7.6，表中同时给出了等价的 SPARQL 路径。

表 7.6 SHACL 和 SPARQL 路径的例子

序号	SHACL 路径	SPARQL 路径	说明
1	schema:name	schema:name	1 个属性
2	[sh:inversePath schema:knows]	^schema:knows	逆属性
3	(schema:knows schema:name)	schema:knows/schema:name	属性的复合
4	[sh:alternativePath (schema:knows schema:follows)]	schema:knows|schema:follows	多个属性选一
5	[sh:zeroOrOnePath schema:knows]	schema:knows?	0 个或 1 个属性
6	[sh:oneOrMorePath schema:knows]	schema:knows+	1 个或多个属性复合形成传递闭包
7	[sh:zeroOrMorePath schema:knows]	schema:knows*	0 个或多个属性
8	([sh:zeroOrMorePath schema:knows] schema:name)	schema:knows*/schema:name	属性复合（带基数约束）

7.4.6 值约束

SHACL 以多种方式定义结点的取值约束,常用的参数见表 7.7。

表 7.7 定义 SHACL 的值约束的参数

序号	属性(参数)	说　　明
1	sh：datatype	取值为某个数据类型,如 xsd：string 等
2	sh：class	取值为类的实例
3	sh：nodeKind	结点类型,包括 sh：BlankNode、sh：IRI 等
4	sh：in	取值为枚举值
5	sh：hasValue	取值为给定值

例 7.9 通过简单数据类型 xsd：string 和 xsd：date,定义了两个属性 schema：name 和 schema：birthDate 的取值类型。

例 7.9　简单数据类型的例子。

```
#模板部分
:UserShape      a         sh:NodeShape ;
sh:targetClass   :User ;
sh:property      [
sh:path        schema:name ;
sh:datatype    xsd:string   ] ;
sh:property      [
sh:path        schema:birthDate ;
sh:datatype    xsd:date     ] .
#数据部分
:alice          a          :User ;     #✓ Passes as :UserShape
    schema:name      "Alice";
    schema:birthDate "1981-07-10"^^xsd:date .
:bob            a          :User ;     #✗ Fails as :UserShape
    schema:name      "Robert" ;
    schema:birthDate 1981 .
:carol          a          :User ;     #✗ Fails as :UserShape
    schema:name      :Carol ;
    schema:birthDate "2003-06-10"^^xsd:date .
:dave           a          :User ;     #✗ Fails as :UserShape
    schema:name      "Dave" ;
    schema:birthDate "Unknown"^^xsd:date .
```

例 7.10 声明：User 类的实例的 schema：worksFor 属性的值为：Organization

类的实例。

例 7.10　取值为类的实例。

```
#模板部分
:UserShape         a         sh:NodeShape ;
    sh:targetClass :User ;
sh:property      [
                sh:path schema:worksFor ;
                sh:class :Organization ] .
#数据部分
:alice       a            :User ;     #✓ Passes as :UserShape
schema:worksFor :aCompany .
:bob         a            :User ;     #✗ Passes as :UserShape
schema:worksFor :aUniversity .
:carol       a            :User ;     #✗ Fails as :UserShape
schema:worksFor :Unknown .
:aCompany       a       :Organization .
:aUniversity    a       :University .
:University     rdfs:subClassOf :Organization .
```

例 7.11 是定义结点类型约束的例子,结点类型的可能取值见表 7.8。

例 7.11　结点类型的例子。

```
#模板部分
:UserShape         a         sh:NodeShape ;
    sh:targetClass   :User ;
sh:property           [
sh:path     schema:name ;
sh:nodeKind   sh:Literal   ];
sh:property           [
sh:path    schema:follows ;
sh:nodeKind   sh:BlankNodeOrIRI   ];
sh:nodeKind   sh:IRI .
#数据部分
:alice       a            :User ;       #✓ Passes as :UserShape
schema:name       "Alice" ;
schema:follows    [ schema:name "Dave" ] .
```

```
: bob          a           : User ;       # Fails as : UserShape
schema: name    _ : 1 ;
schema: follows     : alice .
: carol        a           : User ;       # Passes as : UserShape
```

表 7.8 结点类型的取值

序号	类型	说明
1	sh：IRI	结点为 IRI
2	sh：BlankNode	结点为空结点
3	sh：Literal	结点为文本
4	sh：BlankNodeOrLiteral	结点为空结点或文本
5	sh：BlankNodeOrIRI	结点为空结点或 IRI
6	sh：IRIOrLiteral	结点为 IRI 或文本

例 7.12 是枚举值的例子，定义 schema：gender 属性值的集合为｛schema：Male，schema：Female｝。

例 7.12 枚举值的例子。

```
#模板部分
: UserShape      a       sh: NodeShape ;
sh: targetClass    : User ;
sh: property      [
 sh: path      schema: gender ;
 sh: in        (schema: Male  schema: Female) ] .
#数据部分
: alice         a           : User;        # Passes as : UserShape
schema: gender     schema: Female .
: bob           a           : User;        # Fails as : UserShape
schema: gender     schema: male .
```

7.4.7 字符串约束

参数 sh：minLength、sh：maxLength、sh：pattern 和 sh：flags 用于对字符串进行约束。例如，例 7.13 要求 schema：name 的值的字符串长度在 4 和 20 之间。

例 7.13 字符串约束。

```
#模板部分
:User         a      sh:NodeShape , rdfs:Class ;
sh:property   [
sh:path     schema:name ;
sh:minLength  4 ;
sh:maxLength  20 ; ] .
#数据部分
:alice        a       :User;       #✓ Passes as :User
schema:name   "Alice".
:bob          a       :User;       #✗ Fails as :User
schema:name   "Bob".
```

例 7.14 利用正则表达式 ^P\\d{3,4} 定义 :Product 类的实例的 schema:productID 属性值的约束,sh:flags 为 i 表示"不区分大小写"。

例 7.14 正则表达式约束。

```
#模板部分
:ProductShape     a       sh:NodeShape ;
sh:targetClass   :Product ;
sh:property      [
sh:path         schema:productID ;
sh:pattern      "^P\\d{3,4}" ;
sh:flags        "i" ; ] .
#数据部分
:car            a        :Product ;      #✓ Passes as :ProductShape
schema:productID   "P2345" .
:bus            a        :Product ;      #✓ Passes as :ProductShape
schema:productID   "p567" .
:truck          a        :Product ;      #✗ Fails as :ProductShape
schema:productID   "p12" .
:bike           a        :Product ;      #✗ Fails as :ProductShape
schema:productID   "B123" .
```

7.4.8 属性对约束

SHACL 还可以定义两个属性值之间的关系,用到的参数及其说明见表 7.9。

表 7.9 定义属性对约束的参数及其说明

序号	参数	说明
1	sh：equals	两个属性的值相等
2	sh：disjoint	两个属性的值不同
3	sh：lessThan	一个属性值小于另一个属性值
4	sh：lessThanOrEquals	一个属性值不大于另一个属性值

例 7.15 定义了 schema：givenName 属性取值与 foaf：firstName 属性一样，且不同于 schema：lastName 属性的值。

例 7.15 两个属性的值相等或不等。

```
#模板部分
: UserShape         a         sh: NodeShape ;
sh: targetClass     : User ;
sh: property        [
sh: path       schema: givenName ;
sh: equals     foaf: firstName   ];
sh: property        [
sh: path       schema: givenName ;
               sh: disjoint schema: lastName    ].
#数据部分
: alice            a            : User ;     #✓ Passes as : UserShape
schema: givenName      "Alice";
schema: lastName       "Cooper";
foaf: firstName        "Alice" .
: bob              a            : User ;     #✗ Fails as : UserShape
schema: givenName      "Bob";
schema: lastName       "Smith" ;
foaf: firstName        "Robert" .
```

例 7.16 定义了时间属性取值之间的先后关系。

例 7.16 属性值比较。

```
#模板部分
: ConcertShape        a       sh: NodeShape ;
sh: targetClass     : Concert ;
sh: property        [
sh: path       schema: doorTime ;
```

```
sh: datatype  xsd: dateTime ;
sh: lessThanOrEquals  schema: startDate ; ];
sh: property    [
sh: path    schema: startDate ;
sh: datatype  xsd: dateTime ;
sh: lessThan  schema: endDate   ];
sh: property    [
sh: path    schema: endDate ;
sh: datatype  xsd: dateTime ;    ] .
#数据部分
: concert1       a       : Concert ;      # ✓ Passes as : ConcertShape
schema: doorTime "2019-06-20T20: 00: 00"^^xsd: dateTime ;
schema: startDate "2019-06-20T21: 30: 00"^^xsd: dateTime ;
schema: endDate "2019-06-20T23: 00: 00"^^xsd: dateTime .
: concert2       a       : Concert ;      # ✗ Fails as : ConcertShape
schema: doorTime "2019-06-20T20: 00: 00"^^xsd: dateTime ;
schema: startDate "2018-06-20T21: 30: 00"^^xsd: dateTime ;
schema: endDate "2018-06-20T21: 00: 00"^^xsd: dateTime .
```

7.4.9 逻辑约束

SHACL 通过逻辑运算将多个约束组件组合在一起,形成复杂的约束,用到的参数及其说明见表 7.10。

表 7.10 定义逻辑约束的参数及其说明

序 号	参 数	说 明
1	sh: and	必须满足所有约束
2	sh: or	只要满足一个约束就通过验证
3	sh: not	不能满足约束

例 7.17 给出使用参数 sh：or 实现逻辑或的例子。

例 7.17 sh：or 的例子。

```
#模板部分
: UserShape      a      sh: NodeShape ;
sh: targetClass    : User ;
sh: or         ( [ sh: path    foaf: name ;
sh: minCount  1; ]
```

```
    [ sh:path       schema:name;
sh:minCount  1; ]) .
#数据部分
:alice       a        :User;      #✓ Passes as :UserShape
schema:name "Alice".
:bob         a        :User;      #✓ Passes as :UserShape
foaf:name    "Robert" .
:carol       a        :User;      #✓ Passes as :UserShape
foaf:name    "Carol";
schema:name  "Carol" .
:Dave        a        :User;      #✗ Fails as :UserShape
rdfs:label   "Dave" .
```

7.4.10 封闭模板

一般情况下,SHACL遵从"开放世界假设"(Open World Assumption,OWA),即结点可以具有任意属性。但在有些情况下,需要"封闭世界假设"(Closed World Assumption,CWA),即结点只能具有指定的属性。当sh:closed参数的值为true时,定义的模板为"封闭模板"(Closed Shapes),意味着结点的属性只能是sh:property引导的属性模板定义的属性。这时,可以通过参数sh:ignoredProperties声明例外的属性。

例7.18定义的模板要求只能有一个属性schema:name,除了rdf:type属性。

例7.18 封闭模板的例子。

```
#模板部分
:UserShape         a         sh:NodeShape ;
sh:targetClass    :User ;
sh:closed         true ;
sh:ignoredProperties  ( rdf:type );
sh:property [
sh:path    schema:name ;
sh:minCount  1;   sh:maxCount 1;
sh:datatype  xsd:string  ].
#数据部分
:alice        a         :User;      #✓ Passes as :UserShape
      schema:name    "Alice".
```

```
:bob          a           :User ;      # ✓ Passes as :UserShape
                          :Person ;
schema:name   "Robert" .
:Dave         a           :User ;      # ✗ Fails as :UserShape
rdfs:label    "Dave" .
```

7.5　W3C SHACL 的支持工具

目前，已出现各种 W3C SHACL 的支持工具，详见表 7.11。很多工具都是开源的，一些工具提供了在线服务，如 Zazuko SHACL Playground 和 RDFShape API 等。

表 7.11　W3C SHACL 的支持工具

序号	工具名称	主页
1	Zazuko SHACL Playground	https://shacl-playground.zazuko.com/
2	RDFShape API	https://rdfshape.weso.es/
3	SHaclEX	https://github.com/weso/shaclex
4	TopBraid SHACL API	https://github.com/TopQuadrant/shacl
5	pySHACL	https://github.com/RDFLib/pySHACL
6	SHACL processor	https://github.com/dotnetrdf/dotnetrdf/pull/236
7	Shacl check	https://github.com/linkeddata/shacl-check

SHACL 支持工具的核心是 SHACL 验证处理器，它接收模板（shape）和 RDF 数据，输出验证报告（validation report），见图 7.9。

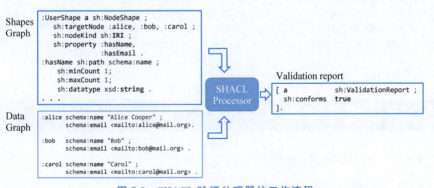

图 7.9　SHACL 验证处理器的工作流程

例 7.19 给出例 7.6（基数约束的例子）的验证报告，其格式也是 RDF 三元组，用到的属性见表 7.12。

表 7.12　SHACL 验证报告的常用属性

序号	属　　性	说　　明
1	sh：focusNode	被验证的结点
2	sh：resultPath	被验证的属性或属性组合，属于被验证的结点
3	sh：sourceShape	sh：focusNode 所在的模板
4	sh：sourceConstraintComponent	产生冲突的约束组件
5	sh：resultMessage	报告冲突的详细情况
6	sh：resultSeverity	错误等级，默认值为 sh：Violation（冲突）

例 7.19　存在冲突的验证报告的例子。

```
[
    a                              sh: ValidationResult ;
    sh: resultSeverity             sh: Violation ;
    sh: sourceConstraintComponent  sh: MinCountConstraintComponent ;
    sh: sourceShape                _: n112 ;
    sh: focusNode                  ex: bob ;
    sh: resultPath                 schema: follows ;
    sh: resultMessage              "Less than 2 values" ; ] .
[
    a                              sh: ValidationResult ;
    sh: resultSeverity             sh: Violation ;
    sh: sourceConstraintComponent  sh: MaxCountConstraintComponent ;
    sh: sourceShape                _: n112 ;
    sh: focusNode                  ex: carol ;
    sh: resultPath                 schema: follows ;
    sh: resultMessage              "More than 3 values" ; ] .
```

（来源：https://shacl.org/playground/）

7.6　验证模板实例

7.6.1　SN SciGraph SHACL

SciGraph 知识图谱使用了 SHACL 技术，主要用于：

① 面向各种数据源，在 ETL（extract-transform-load）过程中进行"数据验证"；

② 面向用户，限制查询的类型和属性；
③ 支持模式转换，将 SciGraph 本体映射为 Schema.org 词汇表。
SciGraph 定义的模板都是封闭模板，例 7.20 给出 Article(论文)的模板。
例 7.20   Article 模板(部分)。

```
@prefix owl:    <http://www.w3.org/2002/07/owl#>.
@prefix rdf:    <http://www.w3.org/1999/02/22-rdf-syntax-ns#>.
@prefix rdfs:   <http://www.w3.org/2000/01/rdf-schema#>.
@prefix sg:     <http://www.springernature.com/scigraph/ontologies/core/>.
@prefix sgg:    <http://www.springernature.com/scigraph/graphs/>.
@prefix sgo:    <http://www.springernature.com/scigraph/ontologies/>.
@prefix sh:     <http://www.w3.org/ns/shacl#>.
@prefix xsd:    <http://www.w3.org/2001/XMLSchema#>.
@prefix shapes: <http://www.springernature.com/scigraph/shapes/>.
#shape-Article
shapes:Article       a              sh:NodeShape ;
                     sh:targetClass sg:Article ;
                     sh:closed      true ;
                     #Type
                     sh:property [
                                    sh:path     rdf:type ;
                                    sh:hasValue sg:Article ;
                                    sh:minCount 1 ;
                                    sh:maxCount 1 ;     ] ;
                     #Identity
                     sh:property [
                                    sh:path     sg:scigraphId ;
                                    sh:datatype xsd:string ;
                                    sh:minCount 1 ;
                                    sh:maxCount 1 ;     ] ;
                     sh:property [
                                    sh:path     sg:doi ;
                                    sh:datatype xsd:string ;
                                    sh:pattern "^10\\.\\d{4,5}\\/\\S+$" ;
                                    sh:maxCount 1 ;     ] ;
                     #Label
                     sh:property [
                                    sh:path     sg:language ;
                                    sh:datatype xsd:string ;     ] ;
                     sh:property [
                                    sh:path     sg:title ;
                                    sh:datatype xsd:string ;     ] ;
                     sh:property [
```

```
                              sh: path      sg: abstract ;
                              sh: datatype  xsd: string ;    ];
              #Publisher
              sh: property [
                              sh: path   sg: publicationYear ;
                              sh: datatype  xsd: gYear ;
                              sh: pattern    "^\\d{4}$" ;
                              sh: maxCount   1 ;
                              sh: minInclusive "2012"^^xsd: gYear ;
                              sh: maxInclusive "2016"^^xsd: gYear ;];
              sh: property [
                              sh: path sg: publicationYearMonth ;
                              sh: datatype xsd: gYearMonth ;
                              sh: pattern "^\\d{4}-\\d{2}$" ;
                              sh: maxCount 1 ; ] ;
              sh: property [
                              sh: path     sg: publicationDate ;
                              sh: datatype xsd: date ;
                              sh: pattern "^\\d{4}-\\d{2}-\\d{2}$" ;
                              sh: maxCount   1 ;    ] ;
              sh: property [
                              sh: path      sg: webpage ;
                              sh: nodeKind   sh: IRI ;
                              sh: maxCount   1 ;    ] .
```

(来源：https://github.com/springernature/scigraph/blob/master/2017Q1/shapes/articles.ttl)

7.6.2 LUBM SHACL

丹麦奥尔堡大学计算机系的科研团队在丹麦独立研究基金会（DFF）的资助下，开发了从 RDF 数据自动抽取 SHACL 模板的方法，步骤包括：

① 实体抽取；

② 实体约束抽取；

③ 信任度计算；

④ 模板抽取，见图 7.10（参见图 7.4 和图 7.5）。

该团队抽取了 WikiData、DBpedia、YAGO-4 和 LUBM 等知识图谱或 RDF 数据的 SHACL 模板，发布在 Zenodo 上。对于图 7.4 和图 7.10 所示的模板，其 Turtle 表达见例 7.21 中的代码。

例 7.21 LUBM SHACL 模板（部分）。

第7章 知识图谱验证技术

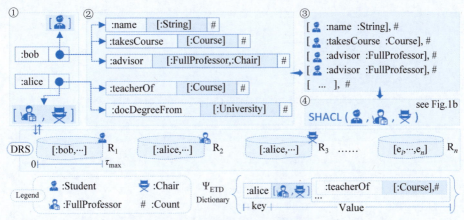

图 7.10 SHACL 模板的自动抽取方法

```
@prefix owl: <http://www.w3.org/2002/07/owl#>.
@prefix rdf: <http://www.w3.org/1999/02/22-rdf-syntax-ns#>.
@prefix rdfs: <http://www.w3.org/2000/01/rdf-schema#>.
@prefix sh: <http://www.w3.org/ns/shacl#>.
@prefix xsd: <http://www.w3.org/2001/XMLSchema#>.
#shape -FullProfessor
<http://shaclshapes.org/FullProfessorShape>
rdf: type                      sh: NodeShape ;
     <http://rdfs.org/ns/void#entities>   "85006"^^xsd: int ;
sh: targetClass
<http://swat.cse.lehigh.edu/onto/univ-bench.owl#FullProfessor>;
sh: property
<http://shaclshapes.org/nameFullProfessorShapeProperty>;
sh: property
<http://shaclshapes.org/researchInterestFullProfessorShapeProperty>;
sh: property
<http://shaclshapes.org/teacherOfFullProfessorShapeProperty>.
<http://shaclshapes.org/teacherOfFullProfessorShapeProperty>
                    rdf: type      sh: PropertyShape;
                    sh: path
         <http://swat.cse.lehigh.edu/onto/univ-bench.owl#teacherOf>;
                    sh: minCount    1;
            sh: or            ([
```

```
                                    sh: NodeKind    sh: IRI;
                                    sh: class
            <http://swat.cse.lehigh.edu/onto/univ-bench.owl#Course<;]
[
sh: NodeKind    sh: IRI;
sh: class
        <http://swat.cse.lehigh.edu/onto/univ-bench.owl#Work<;]
[
sh: NodeKind sh: IRI;
sh: class
<http://swat.cse.lehigh.edu/onto/univ-bench.owl#GraduateCourse<;]).
#shape -Student
<http://shaclshapes.org/StudentShape>
rdf: type         sh: NodeShape ;
        <http://rdfs.org/ns/void#entities>    "5220814"^^xsd: int ;
sh: targetClass
<http://swat.cse.lehigh.edu/onto/univ-bench.owl#Student>;
sh: property
                                        < http://shaclshapes. org/
advisorStudentShapeProperty>;
sh: property
                                        < http://shaclshapes. org/
nameStudentShapeProperty>;
sh: property
                                        < http://shaclshapes. org/
takesCourseStudentShapeProperty>.
<http://shaclshapes.org/advisorStudentShapeProperty>
            rdf: type     sh: PropertyShape;
            sh: path
            <http://swat.cse.lehigh.edu/onto/univ-bench.owl#advisor>;
                sh: or      ([
                                sh: NodeKind    sh: IRI;
                                sh: class
 <http://swat.cse.lehigh.edu/onto/univ-bench.owl#Professor>; ]
[
sh: NodeKind    sh: IRI;
                                sh: class
<http://swat.cse.lehigh.edu/onto/univ-bench.owl#FullProfessor>; ]
    [
    sh: NodeKind    sh: IRI;
    sh: class
    <http://swat.cse.lehigh.edu/onto/univ-bench.owl#Chair>;]).
```

(来源：https://www.zenodo.org/record/7598613)

7.6.3　DBpedia SHACL

例 7.22 是 DBpedia SHACL 中 University（大学）的模板。

例 7.22　University 模板（部分）。

```
@prefix owl: <http://www.w3.org/2002/07/owl#>.
@prefix rdf: <http://www.w3.org/1999/02/22-rdf-syntax-ns#>.
@prefix rdfs: <http://www.w3.org/2000/01/rdf-schema#>.
@prefix sh: <http://www.w3.org/ns/shacl#>.
@prefix xsd: <http://www.w3.org/2001/XMLSchema#>.
#shape - University
<http://shaclshapes.org/UniversityShape>
rdf: type             sh: NodeShape ;
    <http://rdfs.org/ns/void#entities>      "22693"^^xsd: int ;
sh: targetClass    <http://dbpedia.org/ontology/University>;
sh: property
        <http://shaclshapes.org/nameUniversityShapeProperty>;
sh: property
     <http://shaclshapes.org/homepageUniversityShapeProperty>;
sh: property
       <http://shaclshapes.org/countryUniversityShapeProperty>;
sh: property
         <http://shaclshapes.org/cityUniversityShapeProperty>;
sh: property
        <http://shaclshapes.org/sameAsUniversityShapeProperty>.
<http://shaclshapes.org/nameUniversityShapeProperty>
rdf: type            sh: PropertyShape;
    <http://rdfs.org/ns/void#entities>      "22452"^^xsd: int ;
                sh: path        <http://xmlns.com/foaf/0.1/name>;
                sh: NodeKind    sh: Literal;
                sh: datatype    rdf: langString .
<http://shaclshapes.org/homepageUniversityShapeProperty>
rdf: type           sh: PropertyShape;
      <http://rdfs.org/ns/void#entities>      "16236"^^xsd: int ;
                sh: path        < http://xmlns.com/foaf/0.1/homepage>;
                sh: NodeKind    sh: IRI;
                sh: minCount    1.
<http://shaclshapes.org/countryUniversityShapeProperty>
rdf: type              sh: PropertyShape;
                sh: path        <http://dbpedia.org/ontology/country>;
```

```
sh: or           ([
                                       sh: NodeKind    sh: IRI;
                              sh: class <http://dbpedia.org/ontology/
Country>;]
[
sh: NodeKind       sh: IRI;
                       sh: class < http://dbpedia.org/ontology/
AdministrativeRegion>;]
[
sh: NodeKind       sh: IRI;
sh: class    <http://dbpedia.org/ontology/Settlement<;]).
<http://shaclshapes.org/cityUniversityShapeProperty>
rdf: type         sh: PropertyShape;
                  sh: path       <http://dbpedia.org/ontology/
city>;
sh: or          ([
                                         sh: NodeKind   sh: IRI;
                       sh: class    <http://dbpedia.org/ontology/City>;]
[
sh: NodeKind       sh: IRI;
                       sh: class <http://dbpedia.org/ontology/Venue>;]
[
sh: NodeKind       sh: IRI;
sh: class   <http://dbpedia.org/ontology/Town>;]).
<http://shaclshapes.org/sameAsUniversityShapeProperty>
rdf: type           sh: PropertyShape;
                    sh: path       owl: sameAs;
sh: NodeKind        sh: IRI;
                    sh: minCount        1.
```

(来源: https://www.zenodo.org/record/7598613)

7.6.4　Science On Schema.Org SHACL

由美国地质勘探局和 NASA 等支持的学术社区"地球科学信息合作伙伴"（Earth Science Information Partners，ESIP）开发了 Science On Schema.Org（SOSO）词汇表，将 Schema.org 词汇表应用于科学数据领域，目的是提高科学数据集的 Web 可发现性。

图 7.11 是 SOSO 给出的数据集的属性定义，进而给出了这些属性的 SHACL

约束,见例 7.23 的模板文档。例 7.24 给出一个数据集描述的 JSON-LD 文档,它通过了该 SHACL 模板的验证,见图 7.12。

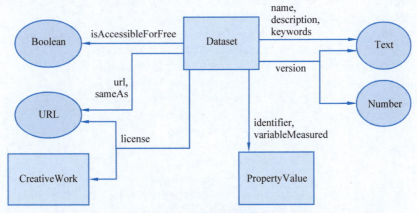

图 7.11　数据集的属性定义

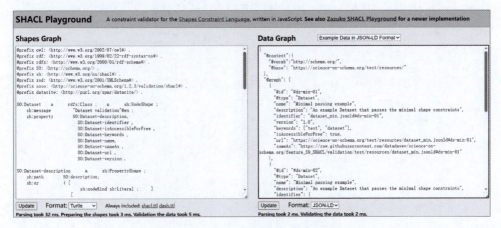

图 7.12　数据集文档的验证

(来源:https://shacl.org/playground/)

例 7.23　Dataset 的模板文档。

```
@prefix owl: <http://www.w3.org/2002/07/owl#>.
@prefix rdf: <http://www.w3.org/1999/02/22-rdf-syntax-ns#>.
@prefix rdfs: <http://www.w3.org/2000/01/rdf-schema#>.
@prefix SO: <http://schema.org/>.
```

```
@prefix sh: <http://www.w3.org/ns/shacl#>.
@prefix xsd: <http://www.w3.org/2001/XMLSchema#>.
@prefix soso: <http://science-on-schema.org/1.2.3/validation/shacl#>.
@prefix datacite: <http://purl.org/spar/datacite/>.
SO: Dataset        a       rdfs: Class ;    a    sh: NodeShape ;
      sh: message       "Dataset validation"@en ;
      sh: property      SO: Dataset-description,
                        SO: Dataset-identifier,
                        SO: Dataset-isAccessibleForFree,
                        SO: Dataset-keywords,
                        SO: Dataset-name,
                        SO: Dataset-sameAs,
                        SO: Dataset-url,
                        SO: Dataset-version.
SO: Dataset-description     a    sh: PropertyShape ;
      sh: path     SO: description;
      sh: or       ( [
                          sh: nodeKind sh: Literal ;  ]
                      [
                          sh: class SO: Text ;        ] );
      sh: minCount 1 ;
      sh: message  "Dataset must have a description"@en .
SO: Dataset-identifier    a    sh: PropertyShape ;
      sh: path     SO: identifier;
      sh: minCount  1 ;
      sh: or       ( [
                          sh: nodeKind sh: Literal ; ]
                     [
                          sh: class  SO: URL ;       ]
                     [
                          sh: class SO: PropertyValue ; ] );
      sh: message " Dataset identifiers must be a URL, Text or PropertyValue"@en.
SO: Dataset-isAccessibleForFree    a    sh: PropertyShape ;
      sh: path        SO: isAccessibleForFree ;
      sh: minCount    1 ;   sh: maxCount    1 ;
      sh: dataType    xsd: boolean ;
      sh: severity    sh: Warning ;
      sh: message     " It is recommended that a Dataset indicates accessibility for free or otherwise"@en .
SO: Dataset-keywords    a    sh: PropertyShape ;
      sh: path        SO: keywords ;
```

```
        sh: minCount      1 ;
        sh: or            ( [
                            sh: nodeKind sh: Literal ; ]
                          [
                            sh: class SO: DefinedTerm ; ] ) ;
        sh: message       "A Dataset should include descriptive keywords as
literals or DefinedTerm"@en .

SO: Dataset-name     a    sh: PropertyShape ;
     sh: path        SO: name ;
     sh: nodeKind    sh: Literal ;
     sh: minCount    1 ;
     sh: message     "Name is required for a Dataset"@en .

SO: Dataset-sameAs   a   sh: PropertyShape ;
     sh: path        SO: sameAs ;
     sh: minCount    1 ;
     sh: nodeKind    sh: IRIOrLiteral ;
     sh: severity    sh: Warning ;
     sh: message "It is recommended that a Dataset includes a sameAs URL"
@en .

SO: Dataset-url      a   sh: PropertyShape ;
     sh: path        SO: url ;
     sh: maxCount    1 ;  sh: minCount 1 ;
     sh: nodeKind    sh: IRIOrLiteral ;
     sh: message     "Dataset requires a URL for the location of a page
describing the dataset"@en .

SO: Dataset-version   a   sh: PropertyShape ;
     sh: path        SO: version ;
     sh: maxCount    1 ; sh: minCount 1 ;
     sh: or          [ (
                          sh: nodeKind sh: Literal ; ]
                        [
                          sh: class SO: Number ; ] ) ;
     sh: message     "Dataset must have a version as Literal or Number"@en .
```

（来源：https://github.com/ESIPFed/science-on-schema.org/blob/1.3.0/validation/shapegraphs/soso_common_v1.2.3.ttl）

例 7.24　Dataset 的数据文档（JSON-LD）。

```
{
    "@context": {
                "@vocab": "http://schema.org/",
                "@base":    " https://science-on-schema.org/test/
                resources/"},
    "@graph":    [
                {
                "@id": "#ds-min-01",
                "@type":  "Dataset",
                "name":   "Minimal passing example",
                "description":      "An example Dataset that
                passes the minimal shape constraints",
                "identifier":    "dataset_min.jsonld#ds-min-
                01",
                "version": "1.0",
                "keywords":  ["test", "dataset"],
                "isAccessibleForFree": true,
                "url":
"https://science-on-schema.org/test/resources/dataset_min.jsonld#ds
-min-01",
                "sameAs": " https://raw.githubusercontent.com/
datadavev/science-on-schema.org/feature_59_SHACL/validation/test/
resources/dataset_min.jsonld#ds-min-01"    }]
    }
```

7.7 SHACL 与 OWL 的关系

7.7.1 SHACL 与 OWL 的对比分析

SHACL 用来进行数据验证，OWL 用来定义词汇表（本体）。这两个词汇表的语法功能有重叠部分，见表 7.13。但 OWL 中的限制不是数据约束，而是为推理而设计的。

表 7.13 SHACL 词汇表与 OWL 词汇表的对比（部分）

序 号	SHACL 词汇	OWL 词汇
1	sh：maxCount	owl：maxCardinality
2	sh：minCount	owl：minCardinality

续表

序号	SHACL 词汇	OWL 词汇
3	sh：minLength	owl：onDatatype/owl：withRestrictions/xsd：minLength
4	sh：equals	owl：equivalentProperty
5	sh：path	owl：onProperty，owl：propertyChainAxiom
6	sh：lessThan	无
7	sh：in	owl：oneOf
8	sh：or	owl：unionOf
9	sh：and	owl：intersectionOf
10	sh：not	owl：complementOf

SHACL 主要用于封闭世界，OWL 用于开放世界。因此，这两种技术具有互补性，可以一起使用，也可以单独使用。例如，图 7.13 显示了 RDFS、OWL 和 SHACL 三种语言的协作，用于定义 Customer 的模式，相应的文档见例 7.25。

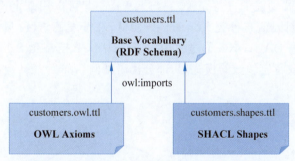

图 7.13　SHACL 与 RDFS 和 OWL 的协作关系

例 7.25　关于 Customer 的本体、公理和模板。

```
#File: customers.ttl,本体定义文档,采用 RDFS 语言
ex: Customer    a    rdfs: Class ;
        rdfs: label    "Customer"@en ;
        rdfs: subClassOf    schema: Person .
ex: moneySpent    a    rdf: Property ;
    rdfs: domain    ex: Customer ;
    rdfs: range    xsd: float .
#File: customers.owl.ttl,本体公理,采用 OWL 语言
<http://example.org/customers.owl>    a    owl: Ontology ;
```

```
                    owl: imports <http://example.org/customers>.
ex: Customer    a    owl: Class ;
        rdfs: subClassOf [
                        a           owl: Restriction ;
                owl: onProperty     ex: moneySpent ;
                owl: maxCardinality 1 ;                    ].
ex: moneySpent    a    owl: DatatypeProperty.
#File: customers.shapes.ttl,模板文档,采用 SHACL 语言
<http://example.org/customers.shapes>    a    owl: Ontology ;
                owl: imports    <http://example.org/customers>.
ex: Customer    a    sh: NodeShape ;
        sh: property [
                sh: path    ex: moneySpent ;
                sh: datatype xsd: float ;
                sh: maxCount 1 ;            ].
```

(来源:https://spinrdf.org/shacl-and-owl.html)

7.7.2 Schema.org SHACL

随着 SHACL 功能的日益完善,它与 OWL 一起可以用来定义知识图谱的模式。例如,奥地利因斯布鲁克大学的科研团队,在开发德语区(奥地利、德国和瑞士)旅游知识图谱 DACH-KG 的过程中,采用 SHACL 定制化 Schema.org 词汇表(见图 7.14),形成特定领域的模式层,部分代码见例 7.26。

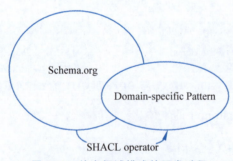

图 7.14 特定领域模式的开发过程

例 7.26 Hotel 的定义(部分)。

```
@prefix sh: <http://www.w3.org/ns/shacl#>.
@prefix schema: <http://schema.org/>.
@prefix ds-tourism: <https://ds.sti2.org/tourism/>.
```

```
@prefix xsd: <http://www.w3.org/2001/XMLSchema#>.
ds-tourism: Hotel      a      sh: NodeShape;
sh: targetClass schema: Hotel ;
sh: property      [
sh: path schema: name;
sh: minCount 1;        ];
sh: property      [
sh: path schema: checkInTime;
sh: minCount 1;        ];
sh: property      [
sh: path schema: checkOutTime;
sh: minCount 1;        ].
```

TopQuadrant 公司的开发团队则开发了 Schema.org 词汇表的 SHACL 版,有 Turtle、JSON-LD 和 RDF/XML 三种格式,部分代码见例 7.27。

例 7.27 Schema.org SHACL(部分)。

```
#baseURI: http://datashapes.org/schema
#imports: http://datashapes.org/dash
@prefix owl: <http://www.w3.org/2002/07/owl#>.
@prefix rdf: <http://www.w3.org/1999/02/22-rdf-syntax-ns#>.
@prefix rdfs: <http://www.w3.org/2000/01/rdf-schema#>.
@prefix schema: <http://schema.org/>.
@prefix sh: <http://www.w3.org/ns/shacl#>.
@prefix xsd: <http://www.w3.org/2001/XMLSchema#>.
<http://datashapes.org/schema>     a     owl: Ontology ;
                  rdfs: label "Schema.org SHACL shapes" ;
                  owl: imports <http://datashapes.org/dash>;
              owl: versionInfo "2021-04-21T09: 18: 09.748+10: 00"^^
xsd: dateTime .
schema: Person     a     rdfs: Class ;      a     sh: NodeShape ;
                  rdfs: subClassOf  schema: Thing ;
                  owl: equivalentClass  <http://xmlns.com/foaf/0.1/Person>;
                       sh: property     schema: Person-address ;
                       sh: property     schema: Person-birthDate ;
                       sh: property     schema: Person-knows ;
                       sh: property     schema: Person-worksFor .
schema: Person-address    a  sh: PropertyShape ;
                  sh: path    schema: address ;
```

```
                    sh: or ( [
                             sh: class  schema: PostalAddress ; ]
                           [
                             sh: datatype xsd: string ;    ] ) .
schema: Person-knows    a    sh: PropertyShape ;
            sh: path   schema: knows ;
            sh: class  schema: Person .
schema: Article   a    rdfs: Class ;   a   sh: NodeShape ;
          rdfs: subClassOf     schema: CreativeWork ;
          sh: property       schema: Article-articleBody ;
          sh: property       schema: Article-articleSection ;
          sh: property       schema: Article-backstory ;
          sh: property       schema: Article-pageEnd ;
          sh: property       schema: Article-pageStart ;
          sh: property       schema: Article-pagination ;
          sh: property       schema: Article-speakable ;
          sh: property       schema: Article-wordCount .
schema: Article-backstory    a    sh: PropertyShape ;
              sh: path   schema: backstory ;
              sh: or     ( [
                           sh: class schema: CreativeWork ; ]
                         [
                           sh: datatype xsd: string ; ] ) .
schema: Article-pageEnd    a    sh: PropertyShape ;
              sh: path    schema: pageEnd ;
              sh: or    ( [
                          sh: datatype   xsd: integer ; ]
                        [
                          sh: datatype   xsd: string ; ] ) .
schema: NewsArticle   a   rdfs: Class ;   a   sh: NodeShape ;
          rdfs: subClassOf    schema: Article ;
          sh: property       schema: NewsArticle-dateline ;
          sh: property       schema: NewsArticle-printColumn ;
          sh: property       schema: NewsArticle-printEdition ;
          sh: property       schema: NewsArticle-printPage ;
          sh: property       schema: NewsArticle-printSection .
schema: ScholarlyArticle   a   rdfs: Class ;   a   sh: NodeShape ;
              rdfs: label    "Scholarly article" ;
              rdfs: subClassOf   schema: Article .
```

(来源：https://www.datashapes.org/schema.ttl)

参 考 文 献

[1] ELWIN H, KÄRLE E, FENSEL D A. Knowledge graph validation[J]. ArXivabs/2005.01389, 2020.

[2] HOGAN A, BLOMQVIST E, COCHEZ M. Knowledge graphs[M]. Cham：Springer Nature Switzerland AG, 2021.

[3] MARVIN H, OBRACZKA D, SAEEDI A, et al. Construction of knowledge graphs：state and challenges[J]. ArXiv abs/2302.11509, 2023.

[4] GAYO J E L, PRUD'HOMMEAUX E, BONEVA I, et al. Validating RDF data[M]. Cham：Springer Nature Switzerland AG, 2017.

[5] 王鑫, 邹磊, 王朝坤, 等. 知识图谱数据管理研究综述[J]. 软件学报, 2019, 30(7)：2139-2174.

[6] W3C.Shapes Constraint Language（SHACL）[EB/OL].[2024-05-11]. https://www.w3.org/TR/shacl/.

[7] RABBANI K, LISSANDRINI M, HOSE K, et al. SHACTOR：Improving the quality of large-scale knowledge graphs with validating shapes[C]. Companion of the 2023 International Conference on Management of Data, 2023.

[8] W3C. SHACL test suite and implementation report[EB/OL]. [2024-05-11]. https://w3c.github.io/data-shapes/data-shapes-test-suite/.

[9] HAMMOND T, PASIN M, THEODORIDIS E, et al. Data integration and disintegration：managing springer nature SciGraph with SHACL and OWL[C]. International Workshop on the Semantic Web, 2017.

[10] LUTHFI M J, DARARI F, ASHRARDIAN A C, et al. SoCK：SHACL on Completeness Knowledge[C]. WOP@ISWC, 2022.

[11] Science On Schema.Org (SOSO) Guidance Documents[EB/OL]. [2024-05-11]. https://github.com/ESIPFed/science-on-schema.org/.

[12] SHACL and OWL compared[EB/OL]. [2024-05-11]. https://spinrdf.org/shacl-and-owl.html.

[13] UMUTCAN S, ANGELE K, KÄRLE E, et al. Domain-specific customization of schema.org based on SHACL[C]. International Workshop on the Semantic Web, 2020.

[14] UMUTCAN S, ANGELE K, KÄRLE E, et al. A formal approach for customization of schema.org based on SHACL[J]. ArXiv abs/1906.06492, 2019.

[15] Schema.org (converted to SHACL by TopQuadrant)[EB/OL]. [2024-05-11]. https://www.datashapes.org/schema.html.

[16] ZHU R, SHIMIZU C, STEPHEN S, et al. SOSA-SHACL：Shapes constraint for the sensor, observation, sample, and actuator ontology[C]. In The 10th International Joint Conference on Knowledge Graphs (IJCKG'21), 2021.

第8章 学术知识图谱

8.1 学术知识图谱概述

知识图谱分为通用知识图谱(general-purpose knowledge graph)与领域知识图谱(domain-specific knowledge graph)两类。领域知识图谱又称行业知识图谱或垂直知识图谱,是特定领域知识的概念化明确表达,及该领域实体和关系的语义描述。相对于通用知识图谱,领域知识图谱对知识表示的深度和精度有更高的要求,其应用的复杂性也更大。

领域知识图谱已涉及教育、科技、医疗、社会、交通和旅游等领域。其中,学术知识图谱(scholarly knowledge graphs,SKG)是近年来研究和应用的热点之一。学术知识图谱也称科学知识图谱(scientific knowledge graphs),专注于学术领域,描述该领域的参与者(作者和机构等)、成果(出版物、数据、软件和专利等)和知识(研究主题、任务、方法和技术等)等实体以及它们之间的相互关系,其概念模型见图8.1。

在2020年8月召开的第24届数字图书馆理论与实践(Theory and Practice of Digital Libraries,TPDL)国际会议上,召开了第一届科学知识图谱研讨会(Workshop on Scientific Knowledge Graphs),指出科学知识图谱研究所面临的三个挑战:

① 设计概念化学术知识的本体;

② 自动或半自动提取实体和概念,整合异构数据源,识别重复实体和发现实体之间的联系;

③ 利用科学知识图谱开发新的学术服务,衡量研究的影响力并加速科学发展。

2017年7月,"微软学术"(Microsoft Academic,MA)正式上线,成为仅次于

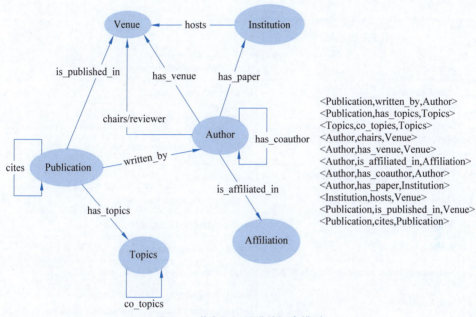

图 8.1　学术知识图谱的概念模型

"谷歌学术"(Google Scholar)的第二大学术搜索引擎。MA 建立在"微软学术图谱"(Microsoft Academic Graph，MAG)和语义推理基础上。在 MAG 的带动下，出现了众多的学术知识图谱，其代表性成果见表 8.1，这些知识图谱大多是开放的。

表 8.1　代表性的学术知识图谱

序号	知识图谱名称	网　　址
1	Microsoft Academic Graph（MAG）（已关闭服务）	https://www.microsoft.com/en-us/research/project/microsoft-academic-graph/
2	Microsoft Academic Knowledge Graph（MAKG）	https://makg.org/
3	Springer Nature SciGraph(SciGraph)（已关闭服务）	https://www.springernature.com/gp/researchers/scigraph
4	Open Research Knowledge Graph（ORKG）	https://orkg.org/
5	Research Graph	https://researchgraph.org/
6	OpenAIRE Graph	https://graph.openaire.eu/
7	PID Graph	https://www.researchobject.org/

续表

序号	知识图谱名称	网址
8	Scholarlydata	http://www.scholarlydata.org/
9	OpenCitations	https://opencitations.net/
10	AIDA KG	https://aida.kmi.open.ac.uk/
11	Computer Science Knowledge Graph (CS-KG)	https://scholkg.kmi.open.ac.uk/
12	Data Set Knowledge Graph (DSKG)	http://dskg.org/
13	Open Academic Graph (OAG)	https://www.aminer.cn/oag-2-1
14	SoftwareKG	https://data.gesis.org/softwarekg/
15	Aminer	https://www.aminer.cn/
16	Semantic Scholar Academic Graph(S2AG)	https://www.semanticscholar.org/
17	unarXive	https://github.com/IllDepence/unarXive https://paperswithcode.com/dataset/unarxive
18	OpenAlex	https://openalex.org/
19	SemOpenAlex	https://semopenalex.org/resource/semopenalex:UniversalSearch
20	Acemap Knowledge Graph	https://archive.acemap.info/acekg/index
21	PubGraph	https://pubgraph.isi.edu/
22	Linked Papers With Code	https://linkedpaperswithcode.com/

运行五年后,"微软学术"于2021年12月31日关闭服务,MAG的数据移植到OpenAlex和OpenAIRE Graph等新的知识图谱中。2022年1月3日,OpenAlex测试版上线,宣称将替代MAG提供免费的学术搜索服务。除了MAG和Web中的资源,OpenAlex的数据源还包括一些开放科学资源,如arXiv、Zenodo和Pubmed等平台中的资源。利用各种开放科学资源的学术知识图谱也称为开放科学图谱(open science graph,OSG),如ORKG、PID Graph和OpenAIRE Graph等。各种OSG之间互操作性的增加,使得它们成为一种新型的学术交流和开放科学基础设施,见图8.2。其中,欧盟的OpenAIRE图谱(OpenAIRE Graph)是最大的开放学术知识库之一。截至2024年5月初,OpenAIRE图谱已收录超过1.76亿个出版物、0.60亿个研究数据集和36.9万个研究软件。

2019 年 6 月,"研究数据联盟"(Research Data Alliance,RDA)成立"开放科学图谱兴趣组"(Open Science Graphs Interest Group,OSG IG),联合 DBPedia/Wikipedia、ORKG、PID Graph 和 OpenAIRE Graph 等领域的专家,研究开放科学图谱互操作的解决方案,以提高开放科学的 FAIR 化水平。目前,代表性的开放科学图谱对 FAIR 原则的支持情况见表 8.2。

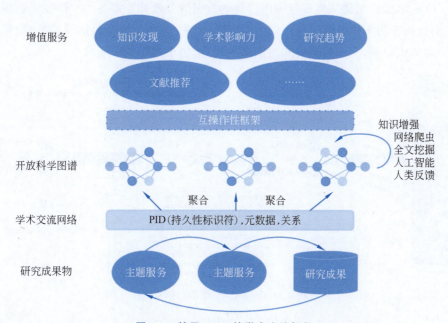

图 8.2　基于 OSGs 的学术交流框架

表 8.2　代表性的开放科学图谱对 FAIR 原则的支持情况

序号	名称	可发现性	可获取性	互操作	可重用
1	OpenAIRE Graph	通过 DOI 搜索	HTTP API、批量下载	XML、JSON	CC-BY 许可
2	ORKG	ORKG 搜索	通过 URL 获取	基于图的数据模型	CC BY-SA 许可
3	PID Graph	通过 PID 和元数据 API 搜索	通过 PID 访问实体	XML、JSON、GraphQL 等	整个图可重用
4	Research Graph	元数据可访问	受控访问	RDF、XML、JSON 等	部分子图在 CC-BY 许可下可复用

8.2 OpenAIRE 图谱的构建过程

8.2.1 知识图谱的供应链

OpenAIRE 图谱从世界范围内广泛的数据源抽取和汇聚各类实体的元数据记录,形成初步的实体及其关系图,通过去重、合并、全文本挖掘和推理等过程,精炼和丰富知识记录,完成最终的知识图谱的构建,整个过程见图 8.3。

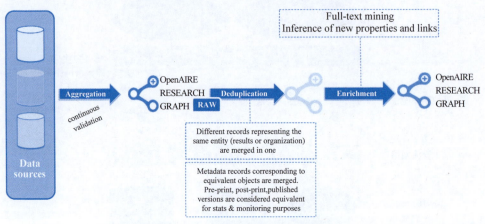

图 8.3 OpenAIRE 图谱的供应链

8.2.2 数据源

截至 2024 年 5 月初,OpenAIRE 图谱收录的数据源(data sources)已超过 13.1 万个,主要的类别见表 8.3,包括期刊、仓储库、科研信息管理系统(current research information system,CRIS)和注册中心等。其中,可信数据源(trusted sources)的数量在逐步提高,一些例子见表 8.4。来自中国的数据源已达数百个,例子见表 8.5。

表 8.3 OpenAIRE 图谱数据源的分类

序号	大 类	子 类	个 数
1	Journal Archive	Journal	118119
2		Journal Aggregator/Publisher	273

续表

序号	大类	子类	个数
3	Repository	Institutional Repository	10595
4		Institutional Repository Aggregator	
5		Data Repository	
6		Data Repository Aggregator	
7		Publication Repository	
8		Software Repository	
9		Software Repository Aggregator	
10		Thematic Repository	
11	CRIS System	National Multidisciplinary CRIS	1315
12		Funder CRIS	
13		Institutional CRIS	
14		Regional CRIS	
15		CRIS Aggregator	
16	Registry	Registry of organizations	3
17		Registry of repositories	5
18		Registry of research products	3

（来源：https://api.openaire.eu/vocabularies/dnet：datasource_typologies）

表 8.4 可信数据源举例

序号	名称	网址	实体个数
1	Microsoft Academic Graph	https://www.microsoft.com/en-us/research/project/microsoft-academic-graph/	出版物：93519530 其他：3
2	Zenodo	https://www.zenodo.org/	出版物：2649912 数据：1421060 软件：216799
3	NSF	https://www.nsf.gov/	项目：572318

续表

序号	名称	网址	实体个数
4	Datacite	https://datacite.org/	出版物：11024760 数据：15892034 软件：133940
5	DOE Code	https://www.osti.gov/doecode/	软件：5169
6	Scientific Data	https://www.nature.com/sdata/	出版物：3240
7	FAIRsharing	https://fairsharing.org/	数据源：2056
8	Re3data	https://www.re3data.org/	数据源：3127

（调查日期：2023年9月3日）

表8.5 来自中国的数据源

序号	名称	网址
1	国家重要野生植物种质资源库	https://seed.iflora.cn/Home/Index
2	中国科学数据	http://csdata.org/
3	中国生态农业学报	http://www.ecoagri.ac.cn/
4	电力工程技术	https://www.epet-info.com/dlgcjs/home
5	环境与职业医学	https://www.jeom.org/
6	大数据	https://www.infocomm-journal.com/bdr/CN/2096-0271/home.shtml
7	国家基因库生命大数据平台	https://db.cngb.org/
8	国家气象科学数据中心	http://data.cma.cn/
9	网络与信息安全学报	https://www.infocomm-journal.com/cjnis/CN/2096-109X/home.shtml
10	国家海洋水产种质资源库	http://marine.fishinfo.cn/

8.2.3 内容聚合

上述数据源收集了各类研究成果及其元数据，见图8.4。OpenAIRE聚合器（aggregator）负责采集数据源中的元数据记录和文章全文，聚合来自不同数据源的各类实体及其关系，形成初步的知识图谱，见图8.5。

OpenAIRE聚合器采集的信息主要有：

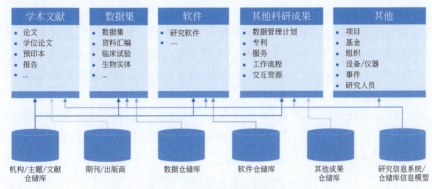

图 8.4　科学仓储库与研究成果

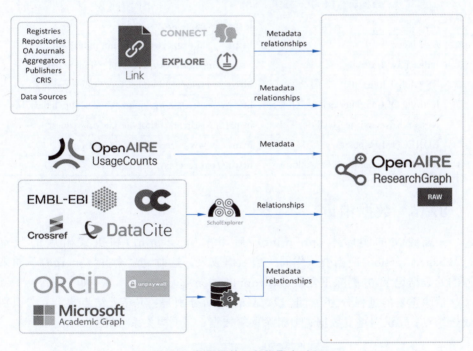

图 8.5　数据源的元数据聚合过程

① 学术文献的全文及其元数据；
② 数据集和科学软件的元数据；
③ 数据源、机构、项目和资助等实体的元数据；
④ 工作流程、实验方案和研究方法等实体的元数据；
⑤ 描述各类实体间链接和关系的元数据。

为保障和提升系统间的互操作性（interoperability），OpenAIRE 出台专门的"聚合政策"（Aggregation Policy），规范各类数据源的元数据模式、格式和 API。例如，对于数据仓储库，OpenAIRE 要求使用 DataCite 元数据，并通过 OAI-PMH（Open Archives Initiative Protocol for Metadata Harvesting，元数据收集的开放档案计划协议）v2.0 采集元数据记录。

符合 OpenAIRE 政策和指南的数据源，被称为"兼容的数据源"（compatible sources），一些例子见表 8.6；否则是"不兼容的数据源"（non-compatible sources），如 PubMed、Crossref 和 MAG 等。

表 8.6 兼容数据源举例

序号	数据源名称	OAI-PMH URL
1	Zenodo	https://zenodo.org/oai2d
2	AI Magazine	http://aaai.org/ojs/index.php/index/oai
3	Index Law Journals	http://indexlaw.org/index.php/index/oai
4	RS Global Journals	https://rsglobal.pl/index.php/index/oai
5	Institute Of Computer Science (IOCS)	https://iocscience.org/ejournal/index.php/index/oai
6	Research Repository UCD	https://researchrepository.ucd.ie/oai/request
7	EURECOM Repository	http://www.eurecom.fr/oai/oai2.php
8	Research Repository of Catalonia	http://oai.recercat.cat/request

8.2.4 数据消重

一篇论文的预印本（pre-print）、后印本（post-print）和正式出版的版本（published version）应当被认作同一项工作成果。这时，要"合并"（merge）不同来源的元数据记录，并删除重复数据（deduplication）。

消除重复的过程分为 5 个阶段（见图 8.6），分别是：①导入结点集合；②识别候选结点；③识别重复数据；④删除重复数据；⑤重构关系（见图 8.7）。

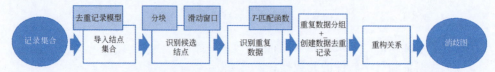

图 8.6 删除重复数据的流程

对于论文等出版物，识别相似实体的策略是（见图 8.8）：
① 可信 PID(persistent identifier)检查：如果至少有 1 个可信 PID 等效，则二

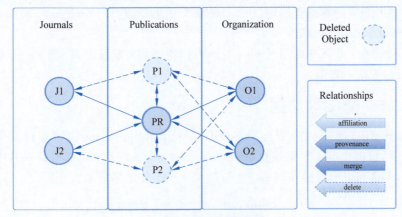

图 8.7 重构实体关系

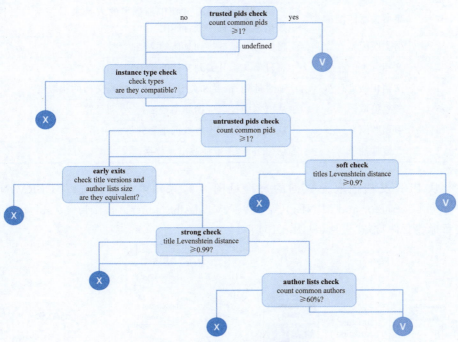

图 8.8 相似出版物的识别策略

者相似；

② 类型检查：如果出版物的类型不兼容，则它们不相似；

③ 不可信 PID 检查：如果至少有 1 个不可信 PID 等效，则进入"软检查"，否则进入"强检查"；

④ 软检查：计算两者标题（titles）的莱文斯坦距离（Levenshtein distance），如果不小于 0.9，则它们相似；

⑤ 强检查：共同作者超过 60% 且两者标题的莱文斯坦距离大于 0.99，则认为两者相似，否则不相似。

8.2.5 全文本挖掘

OpenAIRE 通过 PDF 聚合服务（PDF Aggregation Service）采集科学文献的 PDF 全文，借助文本和数据挖掘（text and data mining，TDM）算法提取其中的有用信息，丰富知识图谱的知识库。主要的文本挖掘算法见表 8.7。

表 8.7 OpenAIRE 采用的主要文本挖掘算法

序号	算法名称	说明
1	隶属关系匹配	将从 PDF 和 XML 文档中抽取出的人员隶属关系与机构数据库中的机构进行匹配
2	引文匹配	将参考文献链接到具体的文档
3	文档分类	将科学文献分类到具体的子类
4	文档相似度计算	通过标题、摘要和关键字等计算两篇文档的相似度
5	概念提取	从文本中提取资助和项目信息、专利号等
6	引用匹配	从文本中识别出对数据集和软件的引用
7	元数据抽取	从 PDF 文档中抽取出元数据

从 PDF 文档抽取元数据的过程见图 8.9，采用的软件系统为 CERMINE（content extractor and MINEr），结果以 XML JATS（journal article tag suite，期刊文章标签套件）格式表达（见图 8.10）。

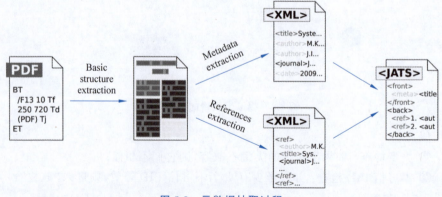

图 8.9 元数据抽取过程

```
▼<article xmlns:xlink="http://www.w3.org/1999/xlink">
  ▼<front>
    ▼<journal-meta>
      ▼<journal-title-group>
        <journal-title>Clinical Science</journal-title>
      </journal-title-group>
    </journal-meta>
    ▼<article-meta>
      <article-id pub-id-type="doi">10.1042/CS20130403</article-id>
      ▼<title-group>
        <article-title>Fragment-based design for the development of N-domain-selective angiotensin-1-converting enzyme inhibitors</article-title>
      </title-group>
      ▼<contrib-group>
        ▼<contrib contrib-type="author">
          <string-name>Ross G. DOUGLAS</string-name>
          <xref ref-type="aff" rid="aff2">2</xref>
        </contrib>
```

图 8.10　XML JATS 格式的元数据

（来源：http://cermine.ceon.pl/index.html）

8.3　OpenAIRE 图谱的数据模型

8.3.1　实体类别

OpenAIRE 图谱的数据模型（data model）如图 8.11 所示。其中，含有五个实体类型，分别是：

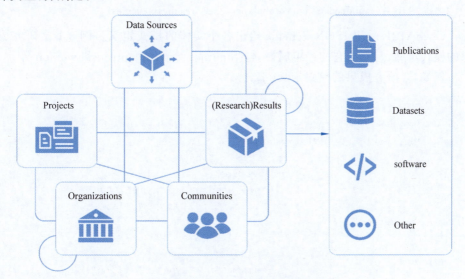

图 8.11　OpenAIRE 图谱的数据模型

（来源：https://graph.openaire.eu/docs/data-model/）

(1) 研究成果(Results)，科研活动产生的数字对象，有四个子类——出版物(Publication)、数据集(Dataset)、软件(Software)和其他研究产品(Other Research Product)，每个子类下还有更细的类别，见表 8.8。

(2) 数据源(Data Sources)，分类见表 8.3。

(3) 机构(Organizations)，负责科研项目、人员管理或数据源管理的科研机构或公司。

(4) 项目(Projects)，主要指获得资助的科研项目。

(5) 社区(Communities)，由具有共同研究意图的人群组成，分为研究计划(Rresearch Initiatives)和研究社区(Research Communities)两类，如大学联盟等。

表 8.8 研究成果的分类(部分)

序号	Publication	Dataset	Software	Other
1	Article	Dataset	Software	Lecture
2	Book	Film	Other software type	Model
3	Doctoral thesis	Image		Physical Object
4	Preprint	Sound		Virtual Appliance
5	Data Paper	Clinical Trial		Research Object
6	Software Paper	Bioentity		Event

(来源：https://api.openaire.eu/vocabularies/dnet：result_typologies)

OpenAIRE 采用 JSON Schema 给出各个实体的模式定义。例 8.1 是研究成果的模式定义，定义了它的一组属性，包括 author、type、maintitle 和 version 等。

例 8.1 研究成果的模式定义(部分)。

```
{
    "$schema":    "http://json-schema.org/draft-07/schema#",
    "definitions":{"Provenance":{
                    "type":    "object",
                    "properties":{
                        "provenance":{"type":"string"},
                        "trust":    {"type":"string"}}},
    "ResultPid":{
                    "type":    "object",
                    "properties":{
                        "scheme":{"type":"string"},
                        "value":{"type":"string"}}},
```

```
"type" :      "object",
    "properties" : {
"author" : {"type" : "array",
                     "items" : {
                      "type" : "object",
                      "properties" : {
                              "fullname" :  {"type" : "string"},
                              "rank" :      {"type" : "integer"},
                              "pid" : {"type" : "object",
                               "properties" : {
                                   "id": {"type" : "object",
                                         "properties" : {
"scheme": {"type": "string"},
                                            "value": {"type": "string"}}},
                                   "provenance" : { "allOf" : [ {
"$ref": "#/definitions/Provenance"}]}}
                     }}},
"type" : { "type" : "string",
                     "description" : "Type of the result: one of
'publication', 'dataset', 'software', 'other' "},
"maintitle" :  { "type" : "string"},
"version" :    { "type" : "string",
               "description" : "Version of the result" },
"programmingLanguage" : {"type" : "string",
                     "description" : "Only for results with type
'software': the programming language" },
        "publicationdate" : { "type" : "string"},
        "publisher" : { "type" : "string" },
        "instance" : { "type" : "array",
                     "items" : { "type" : "object",
                        "properties" : {
                           "pid" : { "type" : "array",
                           "items" : {
                              "$ref" : "#/definitions/ResultPid" } },
                           "publicationdate" : {"type" : "string"},
                           "url" : { "type" : "array",
                              "items" : { "type" : "string" } },
                           "type" : { "type" : "string",
               "description" : "The specific sub-type of this instance" }}}}
         }}
```

（来源：https://www.zenodo.org/record/8238874）

8.3.2 实体关系

2016年3月，RDA（Research Data Alliance）和ICSU-WDS（International Council for Science World Data System）共同支持的"出版数据服务工作组"（RDA/WDS Publishing Data Services WG）提出链接出版物与数据集的互操作框——Scholix（Scholarly Link eXchange），其概念模型和信息模型分别见图8.12和图8.13。

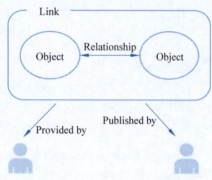

图 8.12 Scholix 的概念模型

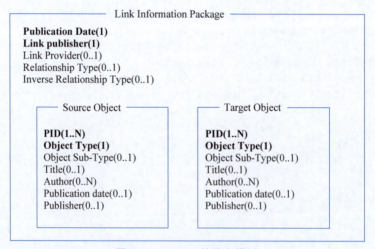

图 8.13 Scholix 的信息模型

OpenAIRE采用Scholix概念模型和信息模型描述实体关系，其定义见例8.2。

例 8.2 实体关系定义。

第8章 学术知识图谱

```
{
    "$schema" : "http://json-schema.org/draft-07/schema#",
    "type" :     "object",
    "properties" : {
        "provenance" : { "type" : "object",
                        "properties" : {
                            "provenance" : {"type" : "string"},
                            "trust" :      {"type" : "string"} } },
        "reltype" :    { "type" : "object",
                        "properties" : {
                            "name" : {"type" : "string" },
                            "type" : {"type" : "string" } } },
        "source" : {"type" : "string" },
        "sourceType" : {"type" : "string" },
        "target" : {"type" : "string" },
        "targetType" : {"type" : "string" },
        "validated" : {"type" : "boolean" },
        "validationDate" : {"type" : "string" } }
}
```

（来源：https://www.zenodo.org/record/8238874）

借鉴 DataCite 元数据模式对关系的定义，OpenAIRE 图谱引入了 29 种实体关系类型，见表 8.9。

表 8.9　实体关系类型

序号	源	目标	关系名称/逆关系	来　　源
1	项目	成果	produces / isProducedBy	自动采集，推理产生，由用户连接
2	项目	机构	hasParticipant / isParticipant	自动采集
3	项目	社区	IsRelatedTo / IsRelatedTo	由用户连接
4	成果	成果	IsAmongTopNSimilarDocuments / HasAmongTopNSimilarDocuments	推理产生
5	成果	成果	IsSupplementTo / IsSupplementedBy	自动采集
6	成果	成果	IsRelatedTo / IsRelatedTo	自动采集，推理产生，由用户连接
7	成果	成果	IsPartOf / HasPart	自动采集
8	成果	成果	IsDocumentedBy / Documents	自动采集
9	成果	成果	IsObsoletedBy / Obsoletes	自动采集

续表

序号	源	目标	关系名称/逆关系	来源
10	成果	成果	IsSourceOf / IsDerivedFrom	自动采集
11	成果	成果	IsCompiledBy / Compiles	自动采集
12	成果	成果	IsRequiredBy / Requires	自动采集
13	成果	成果	IsCitedBy / Cites	自动采集,推理产生
14	成果	成果	IsReferencedBy / References	自动采集
15	成果	成果	IsReviewedBy / Reviews	自动采集
16	成果	成果	IsOriginalFormOf / IsVariantFormOf	自动采集
17	成果	成果	IsVersionOf / HasVersion	自动采集
18	成果	成果	IsIdenticalTo / IsIdenticalTo	自动采集
19	成果	成果	IsPreviousVersionOf / IsNewVersionOf	自动采集
20	成果	成果	IsContinuedBy / Continues	自动采集
21	成果	成果	IsDescribedBy / Describes	自动采集
22	成果	机构	hasAuthorInstitution / isAuthorInstitutionOf	自动采集,推理产生
23	成果	数据源	isHostedBy / hosts	自动采集,推理产生
24	成果	数据源	isProvidedBy / provides	自动采集
25	成果	社区	IsRelatedTo / IsRelatedTo	自动采集,推理产生,由用户连接
26	机构	社区	IsRelatedTo / IsRelatedTo	由用户连接
27	机构	机构	IsChildOf / IsParentOf	由用户连接
28	数据源	社区	IsRelatedTo / IsRelatedTo	由用户连接
29	数据源	机构	isProvidedBy / provides	自动采集

(来源:https://graph.openaire.eu/docs/data-model/relationships/relationship-types)

8.3.3 数据实例

例 8.3 是一篇论文的 JSON 数据,它符合例 8.1 的模式定义,可以通过验证器的验证,见图 8.14。例 8.4 是一个软件的 JSON 数据,例 8.5 为"引用"和"被引用"

关系的 JSON 数据。

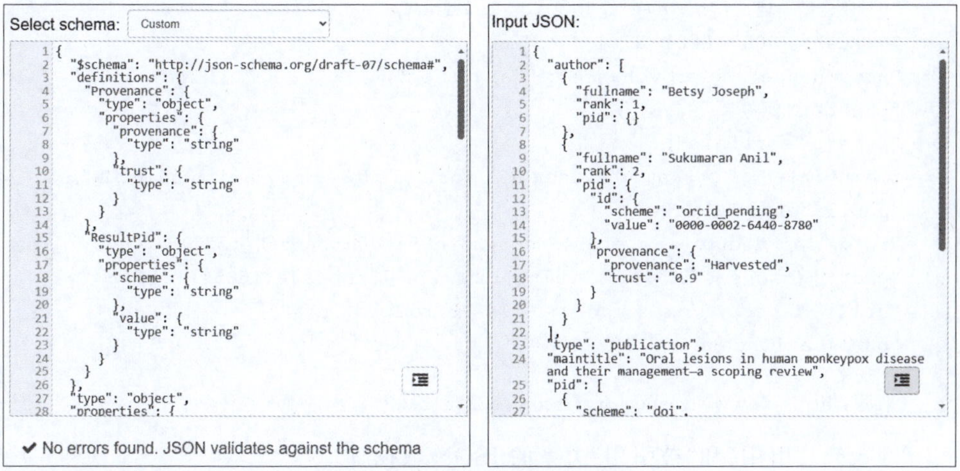

图 8.14　JSON 数据验证

（来源：https://www.jsonschemavalidator.net/）

例 8.3　一篇论文的 JSON 数据。

```
{ "author": [{"fullname": "Betsy Joseph", "rank": 1, "pid": {}},
{"fullname": "Sukumaran Anil", "rank": 2,
"pid": {"id": { "scheme": "orcid_pending",
"value": "0000-0002-6440-8780"},
"provenance": {"provenance": "Harvested",
"trust": "0.9"   }}],
"type": "publication",
"maintitle": " Oral lesions in human monkeypox disease and their management—a scoping review",
"pid": [{"scheme": "doi","value": "10.1016/j.oooo.2022.11.012"}],
"publicationdate": "2023-04-01",
"publisher": "Elsevier BV",
"instance": [ {"pid": [ {"scheme": "doi",
"value": "10.1016/j.oooo.2022.11.012"}],
"type": "Article",
"url": ["https://doi.org/10.1016/j.oooo.2022.11.012"],
"publicationdate": "2023-04-01" }] }
```

（来源：https://www.zenodo.org/record/8223812）

例 8.4　一个软件的 JSON 数据。

```
{ "author": [{"fullname": "Koller, Fabian","rank": 1,
"pid": {"id": {"scheme": "orcid_pending",
"value": "0000-0001-8704-1769"},
"provenance": {"provenance": "Harvested",
"trust": "0.9"      }}}],
"type": "software",
"maintitle": "C++&amp; Python API for Scientific I/O with openPMD",
"publisher": "Rodare",
"id": "doi_dedup___: : afd943ced8455fb95e208cfbe658b463",
"pid": [{"scheme": "doi","value": "10.14278/rodare.1688"}],
"url": ["https://dx.doi.org/10.14278/rodare.1688"],
"publicationdate": "2022-06-07" }
```

(来源: https://www.zenodo.org/record/8223812)

例 8.5 "引用"和"被引用"关系的 JSON 数据。

```
{
"provenance":    {"provenance": "Harvested", "trust": "0.9"},
"reltype":       {"name": "Cites", "type": "citation"},
"source":        "doi_____: : 35dcdce925bd3f79084aa59fa9a0c28e",
"sourceType":    "result",
"target":        "doi_____: 8fd6c97a21c34b436b6a2889c7a83341",
"targetType":    "result",
"validated":     false }
{
"provenance":    {"provenance": "Harvested", "trust": "0.9"},
"reltype":       {"name": "IsCitedBy", "type": "citation"},
"source":        "doi_____: 8a3cc2b7e9e87d4beb6b75e06cd32700",
"sourceType":    "result",
"target":        "doi_____: : ed69cf1f23607938249f890fb2ab2159",
"targetType":    "result",
"validated":     false }
```

(来源: https://www.zenodo.org/record/8223812)

8.4 OpenAIRE 图谱的 API

OpenAIRE 图谱的数据资源已发布到 Zenodo 仓储库,可免费下载。这些数据集每 6 个月发布一个新版本,2019 年 12 月 18 日发布了 1.0-beta 版,2024 年 1 月

16 日发布了 7.0 版,网址如下:

https://www.zenodo.org/record/10488385

同时,OpenAIRE 提供 API(Application Programming Interface,应用程序编程接口),供应用程序获取知识库中的数据。例如,论文"Building a PubMed Knowledge Graph"的 DOI 是"10.1038/s41597-020-0543-2",其查询 API 为:

```
(1) http://api.openaire.eu/search/researchProducts?doi=10.1038/s41597
-020-0543-2
(2) http://api.openaire.eu/search/researchProducts?doi=10.1038/s41597
-020-0543-2&format=json
```

第一个 API 返回的结果是 XML 格式(见图 8.15),第二个 API 返回的结果是 JSON 格式(见例 8.6)。OpenAIRE 定义了 XML 数据的模式,见图 8.16。

```
▼<response>
  ▶<header>
  ...
  </header>
  ▼<results>
    ▼<result xmlns:dri="http://www.driver-repository.eu/namespace/dri">
      ▶<header xmlns:xsi="http://www.w3.org/2001/XMLSchema-instance">
      ...
      </header>
      ▼<metadata>
        ▼<oaf:entity xmlns:oaf="http://namespace.openaire.eu/oaf"
          xmlns:xsi="http://www.w3.org/2001/XMLSchema-instance"
          xsi:schemaLocation="http://namespace.openaire.eu/oaf
          https://www.openaire.eu/schema/1.0/oaf-1.0.xsd">
          ▶<oaf:result>
          ...
          </oaf:result>
          ▶<extraInfo name="result reference list" typology="reference list"
            provenance="iis::document_referencedDocuments" trust="0.9">
          ...
          </extraInfo>
        </oaf:entity>
      </metadata>
    </result>
  </results>
  <browseResults></browseResults>
</response>
```

图 8.15 XML 格式的 API 调用结果

例 8.6 JSON 格式的 API 调用结果(部分)。

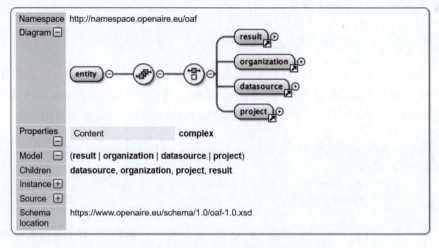

图 8.16　API XML 的模式定义

（来源：https://www.openaire.eu/schema/latest/doc/oaf.html）

```
{"response": {
    "header": { ………… },
    "results": {
        "result": [
            {"header": { ………… },
            "metadata": {
"oaf: entity": {
                "@xsi: schemaLocation": "http://namespace.openaire.eu/oaf
https://www.openaire.eu/schema/1.0/oaf-1.0.xsd",
                "oaf: result": {
                  "collectedfrom": [
                    { "@name": "Scientific Data",
                      "@id":
"openaire____: : c1adf44d00e2895044c5705a8b8ef89e" }],
"pid": [
{ "@classid": "doi",
                        "@classname": "Digital Object Identifier",
                        "@schemeid": "dnet: pid_types",
                        "@schemename": "dnet: pid_types",
                        "$": "10.1038/s41597-020-0543-2" }],
"title": [
                      { "@classid": "main title",
                        "@classname": "main title",
```

```
                        "@schemeid": "dnet: dataCite_title",
                        "@schemename": "dnet: dataCite_title",
                        "@inferred": false,
                        "@trust": "0.9",
                        "$": "Building a PubMed knowledge graph" } ],
"creator": [
                    { "@rank": "1",
                      "@orcid": "0000-0003-4886-4708",
                        "$": "Jian Xu" } ],
"source": [
                    { "$": "Crossref"    },
                { "$": "Scientific Data, Vol 7, Iss 1, Pp 1-15(2020)" } ],
                  "resulttype": {
                    "@classid": "publication",
                    "@classname": "publication",
                    "@schemeid": "dnet: result_typologies",
                    "@schemename": "dnet: result_typologies" },
                  "resourcetype": {
                    "@classid": "0001",
                    "@classname": "Article",
                    "@schemeid": "dnet: publication_resource",
                    "@schemename": "dnet: publication_resource" }},
"extraInfo": {
                    "@name": "result reference list",
                    "@typology": "reference list",
                    "@provenance": "iis: : document_referencedDocuments",
                    "@trust": "0.9",
                    "references": {
                     "reference": [
                       {
                         "@position": "1",
                         "rawText": {
                           "$": "1. Hakala, K., Kaewphan, S., Salakoski, T. & Ginter, F. Syntactic analyses and named entity recognition for PubMed and PubMed Central-up-to-the-minute. In Proceedings of the 15th Workshop on Biomedical Natural Language Processing 102-107, https://doi.org/10.18653/v1/W16-2913 (2016)." }}]}}
     }}}]}}
    }
```

对于例 8.4 所描述的软件,它的查询 API 是:

https://api.openaire.eu/search/software?doi=10.14278/rodare.1688

项目(如 OpenAIRE Nexus)的查询 API 是:

https://api.openaire.eu/search/projects?grantID=101017452

对于一般的研究成果,通用的查询端点如下,常用的参数见表 8.10。

http://api.openaire.eu/search/researchProducts

表 8.10 查询端点的参数

序号	参 数	说 明
1	doi	通过 DOIs 获取研究成果的信息
2	orcid	通过作者的 ORCID iD 获取研究成果
3	title	通过 title 获取研究成果
4	author	通过 author 获取研究成果
5	format	JSON、XML、CSV、TSV,响应格式,默认值为 XML
6	grantID	通过资助号获取项目信息

8.5 基于 OpenAIRE 图谱的 OpenAIRE 服务

8.5.1 主要的服务

OpenAIRE(Open Access Infrastructure for Research in Europe,欧洲开放存取基础架构研究)是欧盟建设的开放学术交流基础设施。OpenAIRE 的许多服务都是基于 OpenAIRE 图谱的,见表 8.11。

表 8.11 主要的 OpenAIRE 服务

序号	名 称	说 明
1	OpenAIRE Graph	聚合各类研究对象的语义图数据库
2	OpenAIRE Explore	人工智能驱动的开放研究搜索引擎

续表

序号	名　称	说　明
3	OpenAIRE Validator	验证各类仓储库的元数据是否符合 OpenAIRE 的要求
4	Open Science Observatory	通过一组指标，观测欧盟开放科学的总体情况
5	OpenAIRE Monitor	通过一组指标监测资助者、研究机构的活动
6	OpenAIRE UsageCounts	观测开放存储仓储库的使用情况
7	OpenAIRE Connect	为特定领域的研究社区、大学、机构和项目定制门户网站，以收集和展示研究成果

（来源：https://catalogue.openaire.eu/search;quantity=10）

8.5.2　开放科学观测服务

开放科学观测服务（open science observatory）是欧盟"地平线 2020"（Horizon 2020）研究计划资助的一个项目，该服务的网址是：

https://osobservatory.openaire.eu/home

该服务的工作流程如图 8.17 所示，从 OpenAIRE 图谱中抽取数据，以可视化的方式展现欧洲及其各国开放科学的总体情况。例如，欧洲部分国家开放获取（OA）数据集的数量见表 8.12。

表 8.12　欧洲部分国家 OA 数据集的数量

序　号	国　家	OA 数据集的数量
1	英国	64645
2	德国	49116
3	西班牙	44335
4	荷兰	28493
5	法国	23705
6	意大利	17740

8.5.3　OpenAIRE 监测器

OpenAIRE 监测器（OpenAIRE monitor）监测的指标分为研究成果、开放科

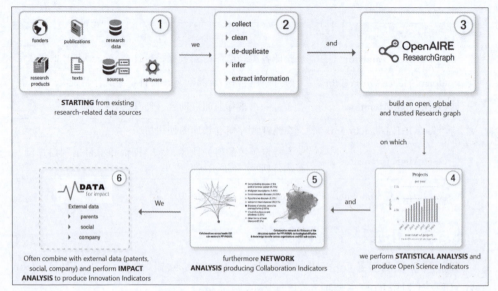

图 8.17　开放科学观测服务的工作流程

学、资助情况、协作情况和影响力五方面。一个国家或研究机构的各项指标显示在"仪表盘"上,图 8.18 给出荷兰的仪表盘。

仪表盘的数据来自 OpenAIRE 图谱。例如,对于"法国国家科研署"(French National Research Agency,ANR),获取相关数据的 API 见表 8.13。

表 8.13　获取 ANR 数据的 API

序号	功　　能	API
1	获取所有研究成果	https://api.openaire.eu/search/researchProducts?funder=ANR
2	获取出版物	https://api.openaire.eu/search/publications?funder=ANR
3	获取 OA 出版物	http://api.openaire.eu/search/publications?funder=ANR&OA=true
4	获取科学数据集	https://api.openaire.eu/search/datasets?funder=ANR
5	获取科学软件	https://api.openaire.eu/search/software?funder=ANR
6	获取其他成果	https://api.openaire.eu/search/other?funder=ANR

(来源:https://monitor.openaire.eu/dashboard/anr/develop)

图 8.18　荷兰的仪表盘

（来源：https://monitor.openaire.eu/dashboard/netherlands）

8.5.4　OpenAIRE Connect

OpenAIRE Connect 服务（connect.openaire.eu）为研究社区（research community）定制网站，支持开放科学实践，一些例子见表 8.14。

表 8.14　研究社区的定制网站举例

序号	名　　称	网站的 URL
1	荷兰研究成果门户网站	https://netherlands.openaire.eu/
2	EUTOPIA 大学联盟	https://eutopia.openaire.eu/
3	交通研究社区	https://beopen.openaire.eu/
4	海洋科学研究社区	https://mes.openaire.eu/
5	遗产科学研究社区	https://heritage-science.openaire.eu/
6	北美研究社区	https://north-american-studies.openaire.eu/
7	可再生能源数据管理平台	https://enermaps.openaire.eu/

例如，北美研究社区（North American Studies，NAS）是为了加强北美与欧洲数字平台之间的整合和自动化互通而建立的，它的网站的构建流程如图 8.19 所

示,API 见表 8.15。

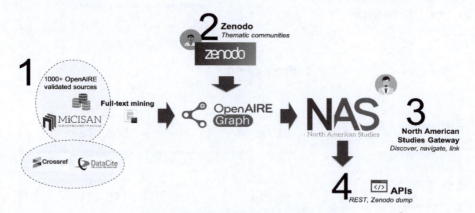

图 8.19　北美研究社区网站的构建流程

(来源：https://north-american-studies.openaire.eu/content)

表 8.15　获取 NAS 数据的 API

序号	功　能	API
1	获取所有研究成果	https://api.openaire.eu/search/researchProducts?community=north-american-studies
2	获取出版物	https://api.openaire.eu/search/publications?community=north-american-studies
3	获取 OA 出版物	http://api.openaire.eu/search/publications?community=north-american-studies&OA=true
4	获取科学数据集	https://api.openaire.eu/search/datasets?community=north-american-studies
5	获取科学软件	https://api.openaire.eu/search/software?community=north-american-studies
6	获取其他成果	https://api.openaire.eu/search/other?community=north-american-studies

(来源：https://north-american-studies.openaire.eu/develop)

参 考 文 献

[1] 刘烨宸,李华昱.领域知识图谱研究综述[J].计算机系统应用,2020,29(6)：1-12.
[2] 肖仰华.领域知识图谱落地实践中的问题与对策[EB/OL].[2024-03-10].https://www.sohu.com/a/280006592_100099320.

[3] ABU-SALIH B. Domain-specific knowledge graphs: a survey[J]. Journal of Network and Computer Applications, 2021, 185(5): 103076.

[4] MANGHI P, MANNOCCI A, OSBORNE F, et al. New trends in scientific knowledge graphs and research impact assessment[J]. Quantitative Science Studies, 2022, 2(4): 1296-1300.

[5] Where does your data come from?[EB/OL].[2024-04-30]. https://docs.openalex.org/additional-help/faq.

[6] Open science graphs for FAIR data IG[EB/OL].[2024-04-30]. https://rd-alliance.org/groups/open-science-graphs-fair-data-ig.

[7] ARYANI A, FENNER M, MANGHI P, et al. Open science graphs must interoperate![C]. ADBIS, TPDL and EDA 2020 Common Workshops and Doctoral Consortium, Springer: 195-206.

[8] SHILPA V, BHATIA R, HARIT S, et al. Scholarly knowledge graphs through structuring scholarly communication: A review[J]. Complex & Intelligent Systems, 2022(9): 1-37.

[9] The OpenAIRE research graph[EB/OL].[2024-04-30]. https://www.openaire.eu/blogs/the-openaire-research-graph.

[10] OpenAIRE graph production workflow[EB/OL].[2024-04-30]. https://graph.openaire.eu/docs/graph-production-workflow/.

[11] CLAUDIO A, BARDI A, MANGHI P, et al. The OpenAIRE workflows for data management[C]. Italian Research Conference on Digital Library Management Systems, 2017.

[12] VICHOS K, BONIS M, KANELLOS I, et al. A preliminary assessment of the article deduplication algorithm used for the OpenAIRE research graph[C]. Italian Research Conference on Digital Library Management Systems, 2022.

[13] MANGHI P, ATZORI C, BONIS M, et al. Entity deduplication in big data graphs for scholarly communication[J]. Data Technologies and Applications, 2020, 54(4): 409-435.

[14] OpenAIRE Graph Data Model[EB/OL].[2024-04-18]. https://graph.openaire.eu/docs/data-model/.

[15] MANGHI P, BARDI A, ATZORI C, et al. The OpenAIRE research graph data model(1.3)[EB/OL].[2024-04-18]. https://doi.org/10.5281/zenodo.2643199.

[16] The OpenAIRE APIs[EB/OL].[2024-04-18]. https://graph.openaire.eu/docs/apis/home.

[17] ORNELLA I, MANNOCCI A, MANGHI P, et al. A novel curated scholarly graph connecting textual and data publications[J]. ACM Journal of Data and Information Quality, 2023, 15(3): 1-24.